ENGLISH HISTORICAL FACTS
1603–1688

ENGLISH HISTORICAL FACTS 1603–1688

Chris Cook and John Wroughton

ROWMAN AND LITTLEFIELD
Totowa, New Jersey

First published in the United States 1980 by Rowman and Littlefield, Totowa, N.J.

Printed in Hong Kong

Library of Congress Cataloging in Publication Data

Cook, Chris, 1945–
 English historical facts, 1603–1688.

 Bibliography: p.
 1. Great Britain—History—Stuarts, 1603–1714—
Dictionaries. I. Wroughton, John, joint author.
II. Title.
DA375.C7 1980   941.06   79–27471
ISBN 0–8476–6295–0

CONTENTS

PREFACE AND ACKNOWLEDGEMENTS

This volume attempts to present, within the space of a single medium-sized book, a reference work on English history from 1603 to 1688 that will be of value to teachers, to students and to research workers. Within this book we have attempted to bring together as many of the important historical facts as can be reasonably assembled here. Inevitably, however, no book of this type can be entirely comprehensive. In some areas the data is unreliable or indeed non-existent. Reasons of space also dictate the amount of information that can be presented.

In any book of this sort, the compilers owe a deep debt both to existing published works and to individual scholars who have offered help and advice. The chapter on the armed forces was compiled by Stephen Brooks, and the chapter on the Church by Anne Lawrence. Throughout this book the modern style of dating has been used.

Finally, we should like to appeal to scholars and others working in this field to point out any omissions or errors in this book, so that the volume may be expanded or enlarged in future editions.

Chris Cook
John Wroughton

June 1979

1 THE MONARCHY

BIOGRAPHICAL DETAILS OF RULERS

James I (1603–25)
Born 19 June 1566, the son of Henry Stewart, Lord Darnley, and Mary Queen of Scots. On 20 August 1589 he married Anne of Denmark. He acceded to the throne on 24 March 1603 and died on 27 March 1625 (he had earlier been James VI, King of Scotland, from 24 July 1567). His marriage to Anne of Denmark produced the following children.

(1) *Henry Frederick:*   Prince Henry Frederick was born on 19 February 1594; he was created Duke of Cornwall in 1603 and Prince of Wales and Earl of Chester in 1610. He died on 6 November 1612.

(2) *Elizabeth:*   Princess Elizabeth was born on 19 August 1596; she married Frederick, Elector Palatine (King of Bohemia after 1619). She died on 13 February 1662.

(3) *Margaret:*   Princess Margaret was born on 24 December 1598; died in infancy.

(4) *Charles:*   Prince Charles (Charles I after 1625) was born on 19 November 1600. He was created Duke of Cornwall in 1603 and Prince of Wales and Earl of Chester in 1616.

(5) *Robert:*   Born on 18 January 1602; died on 27 May 1602.

(6) *Mary:*   Born on 8 April 1605; died on 16 December 1607.

(7) *Sophia:*   Born on 22 June 1606; died the following day.

Charles I (1625–49)
Born on 19 November 1600, the son of James I and Anne of Denmark. Suceeded to the throne 27 March 1625. On 1 May 1625 he married (by proxy) Henrietta Maria, daughter of Henry IV of France. He was executed on 30 January 1649. His marriage produced the following children.

(1) *Charles:*   Born on 29 May 1630; became Charles II (q.v.).

(2) *Mary:*   Born on 4 December 1631; married William II, Prince of Orange, in 1641; died on 24 December 1660.

(3) *James:*   Born on 14 October 1633; became James II (q.v.).

(4) *Elizabeth:*   Born on 28 December 1635; died on 8 September 1650.

(5) *Henry:*   Born on 8 July 1639; died on 13 September 1660.

(6) *Henrietta Maria:* Born on 16 June 1644; married Philip, Duke of Orleans in 1661; died on 30 June 1670.

Note: The Kingship was abolished on 16 March 1649. A Council of State had been established on 14 February 1649, which was dissolved on 20 April 1653. Another Council of State was set up on 29 April 1653, and on 16 December 1653 Oliver Cromwell became Lord Protector.

Oliver Cromwell (1653–8)
Born on 25 April 1599, the son of Robert Cromwell and Elizabeth Steward. He married Elizabeth Bourchier. He became Lord Protector on 16 December 1653 and died on 3 September 1658. His marriage produced the following children.

(1) *Robert:*   Born in 1621; died in May 1639.

(2) *Oliver:*   Born in 1622; died in March 1644.

(3) *Richard:*   Born on 4 October 1626, subsequently Lord Protector (see below).

(4) *Henry:*   Born on 20 January 1628; died on 23 March 1673.

(5) *Bridget:*   Born in August 1624, married Henry Ireton, 1646 and subsequently Charles Fleetwood, 1652; died in 1660.

(6) *Elizabeth:*   Born July 1629; died August 1658.

(7) *Mary:*   Born February 1637.

(8) *Frances:*   Born 1638; died 1721.

Richard Cromwell (1658–9)
Born on 4 October 1626, the son of Oliver Cromwell and Elizabeth Bourchier. Succeeded as Lord Protector on 3 September 1658 and abdicated on 24 May 1659. His marriage to Dorothy Mayor produced one son and three daughters. He died on 12 July 1712.

Charles II (1660–85)
Born on 29 May 1630, the son of Charles I and Henrietta Maria. Succeeded to the throne on 29 May 1660. On 21 May 1662 he married Catherine of Braganza. His illegitimate children included James, created Duke of Monmouth in 1663 and executed 15 July 1685. Charles himself died on 6 February 1685.

James II (1685–8)
Born on 14 October 1633, the son of Charles I and Henrietta Maria. Succeeded to the throne 6 February 1685. He fled the kingdom on 11 December 1688 and died on 6 September 1701. He married twice: Anne Hyde, on 3 September 1660 (she died 31 March 1671), and Mary of Modena, on 30 September 1673. The children of James II were as follows.

(1) *Mary:*   Born 30 April 1662, the daughter of Anne Hyde; married William, Prince of Orange; Proclaimed joint Sovereign with her husband on 13 February 1689; died on 28 December 1694.

(2) *Anne:*   Born on 6 February 1665, the daughter of Anne Hyde; acceded to the throne on 8 March 1702; died on 1 August 1714.

(3) *James:*   The 'Old Pretender'; born on 10 June 1688, the son of Mary of Modena; attainted in 1702, he died on 1 January 1766.

(4) *Louisa Maria Theresa:*   Born on 28 June 1692, the daughter of Mary of Modena; died on 18 August 1712.

Note: The Revolution of 1688
On 11 December 1688, James II fled the country. An interregnum existed until 12 February 1689. On 24 December 1688 the peers in London assumed executive functions. The Convention Parliament offered William and Mary the crown of England and Ireland on 13 February 1689. A Scottish Convention ordered the proclamation of William and Mary the following month.

REGNAL YEARS

The regnal year, as a method of dating, has been in use in England since the eighth century. From the accession of Richard I in 1189, government documents and private charters have expressed the date in this form. Until the death of Henry III in 1272, the regnal year was calculated from the day of coronation. Since 1307, however, it has commenced immediately following the death of the previous monarch. During the Interregnum (1649–60) official documents in England were dated by the year of grace. On the restoration of Charles II in 1660, Parliament declared that his reign had by right commenced immediately after his father's execution. Because his regnal years were, therefore, calculated from January 1649, he was actually crowned in the twelfth year of his reign.

JAMES I

	Regnal year			*Regnal year*	
1	24 Mar 1603 – 23 Mar 1604		13	24 Mar 1615 – 23 Mar 1616	
2	24 Mar 1604 – 23 Mar 1605		14	24 Mar 1616 – 23 Mar 1617	
3	24 Mar 1605 – 23 Mar 1606		15	24 Mar 1617 – 23 Mar 1618	
4	24 Mar 1606 – 23 Mar 1607		16	24 Mar 1618 – 23 Mar 1619	
5	24 Mar 1607 – 23 Mar 1608		17	24 Mar 1619 – 23 Mar 1620	
6	24 Mar 1608 – 23 Mar 1609		18	24 Mar 1620 – 23 Mar 1621	
7	24 Mar 1609 – 23 Mar 1610		19	24 Mar 1621 – 23 Mar 1622	
8	24 Mar 1610 – 23 Mar 1611		20	24 Mar 1622 – 23 Mar 1623	
9	24 Mar 1611 – 23 Mar 1612		21	24 Mar 1623 – 23 Mar 1624	
10	24 Mar 1612 – 23 Mar 1613		22	24 Mar 1624 – 23 Mar 1625	
11	24 Mar 1613 – 23 Mar 1614		23	24 Mar 1625 – 27 Mar 1625	
12	24 Mar 1614 – 23 Mar 1615				

CHARLES I

	Regnal year			*Regnal year*	
1	27 Mar 1625 – 26 Mar 1626		13	27 Mar 1637 – 26 Mar 1638	
2	27 Mar 1626 – 26 Mar 1627		14	27 Mar 1638 – 26 Mar 1639	
3	27 Mar 1627 – 26 Mar 1628		15	27 Mar 1639 – 26 Mar 1640	
4	27 Mar 1628 – 26 Mar 1629		16	27 Mar 1640 – 26 Mar 1641	
5	27 Mar 1629 – 26 Mar 1630		17	27 Mar 1641 – 26 Mar 1642	
6	27 Mar 1630 – 26 Mar 1631		18	27 Mar 1642 – 26 Mar 1643	
7	27 Mar 1631 – 26 Mar 1632		19	27 Mar 1643 – 26 Mar 1644	
8	27 Mar 1632 – 26 Mar 1633		20	27 Mar 1644 – 26 Mar 1645	
9	27 Mar 1633 – 26 Mar 1634		21	27 Mar 1645 – 26 Mar 1646	
10	27 Mar 1634 – 26 Mar 1635		22	27 Mar 1646 – 26 Mar 1647	
11	27 Mar 1635 – 26 Mar 1636		23	27 Mar 1647 – 26 Mar 1648	
12	27 Mar 1636 – 26 Mar 1637		24	27 Mar 1648 – 30 Jan 1649	

CHARLES II

	Regnal year			*Regnal year*	
12	29 May 1660 – 29 Jan 1661		25	30 Jan 1673 – 29 Jan 1674	
13	30 Jan 1661 – 29 Jan 1662		26	30 Jan 1674 – 29 Jan 1675	
14	30 Jan 1662 – 29 Jan 1663		27	30 Jan 1675 – 29 Jan 1676	
15	30 Jan 1663 – 29 Jan 1664		28	30 Jan 1676 – 29 Jan 1677	
16	30 Jan 1664 – 29 Jan 1665		29	30 Jan 1677 – 29 Jan 1678	
17	30 Jan 1665 – 29 Jan 1666		30	30 Jan 1678 – 29 Jan 1679	
18	30 Jan 1666 – 29 Jan 1667		31	30 Jan 1679 – 29 Jan 1680	
19	30 Jan 1667 – 29 Jan 1668		32	30 Jan 1680 – 29 Jan 1681	
20	30 Jan 1668 – 29 Jan 1669		33	30 Jan 1681 – 29 Jan 1682	
21	30 Jan 1669 – 29 Jan 1670		34	30 Jan 1682 – 29 Jan 1683	
22	30 Jan 1670 – 29 Jan 1671		35	30 Jan 1683 – 29 Jan 1684	
23	30 Jan 1671 – 29 Jan 1672		36	30 Jan 1684 – 29 Jan 1685	
24	30 Jan 1672 – 29 Jan 1673		37	30 Jan 1685 – 6 Feb 1685	

JAMES II

Regnal year		*Regnal year*	
1	6 Feb 1685 – 5 Feb 1686	3	6 Feb 1687 – 5 Feb 1688
2	6 Feb 1686 – 5 Feb 1687	4	6 Feb 1688 – 11 Dec 1688

SOURCE: *Handbook of Dates for Students of English History*, ed. C. R. Cheney (Royal Historical Society, 1945).

CONTEMPORARY EUROPEAN RULERS

Denmark and Norway (House of Oldenburg)

Christian IV	1588–1648
Frederick III	1648–70
Christian V	1670–99

France (House of Bourbon)

Henry IV	1589–1610
Louis XIII	1610–43
Louis XIV	1643–1715

Holy Roman Empire (House of Habsburg)

Rudolf II	1576–1612
Matthias	1612–19
Ferdinand II	1619–37
Ferdinand III	1637–58
Leopold I	1658–1705

Ottoman Empire

Mohammed III	1595–1603
Ahmad I	1603–17
Mustafa I	1617–18
Osman II	1618–22
Mustafa I (restored)	1622–3
Murad IV	1623–40
Ibrahim I	1640–8
Mohammed IV	1648–87
Suleiman II	1687–91

The Papacy

Clement VIII	1592–1605
Leo XI	1605
Paul V	1605–21
Gregory XV	1621–3
Urban VIII	1623–44
Innocent X	1644–55
Alexander VII	1655–67
Clement IX	1667–9
Clement X	1670–6
Innocent XI	1676–89

Portugal (under Spanish rule 1580–1640; House of Braganza after 1640)

John IV	1640–56
Alfonso VI	1656–67
Pedro II	1667–1706

Russia

Boris Godunov	1598–1605
Fedor II	1605
Pseudo-Dmitri I	1605–06
Basil IV	1606–10
Pseudo-Dmitri II	1607–10
Ladislaus of Poland	1610–13
Michael Romanov	1613–45
Alexis	1645–76
Fedor III	1676–82
Ivan V	1682–9

Spain (House of Habsburg)

Philip III	1598–1621
Philip IV	1621–65
Charles II	1665–1700

Sweden (House of Vasa)

Sigismund	1592–1604
Charles IX	1604–11
Gustavus II Adolphus	1611–32
Christina	1632–54
Charles X Gustavus	1654–60
Charles XI	1660–97

United Provinces (House of Orange)

Maurice	1584–1625
Frederick Henry	1625–47
William II	1647–50
Stadholdership suspended	1650–72
William III	1672–1702

2 SELECTED HOLDERS OF MAJOR PUBLIC OFFICE*

LORD CHANCELLORS AND LORD KEEPERS OF THE GREAT SEAL

James I
1603 Sir Thomas Egerton (afterwards Lord Ellesmere, 1603, and Viscount Brackley, 1616), *Lord Keeper*, later *Lord Chancellor* (1603)
1617 Sir Francis Bacon (afterwards Lord Verulam, 1618, and Viscount St Albans, 1612), *Lord Keeper*, later *Lord Chancellor* (1618)
1621 The seal was put into commission, May–July (Sir Julius Caesar, Sir John Ley and others)
1621 John Williams, Dean of Westminster (afterwards Bishop of Lincoln, 1621), *Lord Keeper*

Charles I
1625 Sir Thomas Coventry (afterwards Lord Coventry, 1628), *Lord Keeper*
1640 Sir John Finch (afterwards Lord Finch, 1640), *Lord Keeper*
1641 Sir Edward Lyttleton (afterwards Lord Lyttleton, 1641), *Lord Keeper*
1642 The King
1645 Sir Richard Lane, *Lord Keeper*

Civil War and Interregnum
(commissioners entrusted with Parliament's Great Seal)
1643 Henry, Earl of Kent; Oliver, Earl of Bolingbroke; Oliver St John; John Wilde; Samuel Browne; Edmund Prideaux
1646 William, Earl of Salisbury; Edward, Earl of Manchester; William Lenthall
1648 Henry, Earl of Kent; William, Lord Grey of Werke; Sir Thomas Widdrington; Bulstrode Whitelocke
1649 Bulstrode Whitelocke; John Lisle; Richard Keeble
1654 Bulstrode Whitelocke; Sir Thomas Widdrington; John Lisle
1656 Nathaniel Fiennes; John Lisle

* The indispensable source for office-holders is F. M. Powicke and E. B. Foyde, *Handbook of British Chronology* (Royal Historical Society, 1961).

1659 (January) Nathaniel Fiennes; John Lisle; Bulstrode Whitelocke; (June) John Bradshaw; Thomas Terryll; John Fountain
1660 William Lenthall; Sir Thomas Widdrington; Thomas Terryll; John Fountain; Edward, Earl of Manchester

Charles II
1649 Sir Richard Lane, *Lord Keeper*
1653 Sir Edward Herbert, *Lord Keeper*
1658 Sir Edward Hyde (afterwards Lord Hyde, 1660, and Earl of Clarendon, 1661), *Lord Keeper*, later *Lord Chancellor* (1658)
1667 Sir Orlando Bridgeman, *Lord Keeper*
1672 Anthony Ashley Cooper, Earl of Shaftesbury, *Lord Chancellor*
1673 Sir Heneage Finch (afterwards Lord Finch, 1674, and Earl of Nottingham, 1681), *Lord Keeper,* later *Lord Chancellor* (1675)
1682 Sir Francis North (afterwards Lord Guildford, 1683), *Lord Keeper*

James II
1685 Sir George Jeffreys (afterwards Lord Jeffreys, 1685); *Lord Chancellor*

LORD TREASURERS AND LORD COMMISSIONERS OF THE TREASURY

James I
1603 Sir Thomas Sackville, Lord Buckhurst (afterwards Earl of Dorset, 1604), *Lord Treasurer*
1608 Robert Cecil, Earl of Salisbury, *Lord Treasurer*
1612 Henry Howard, Earl of Northampton, *First Lord*
1613 Sir Thomas Egerton, Lord Ellesmere, *First Lord*
1614 Thomas Howard, Earl of Suffolk, *Lord Treasurer*
1618 George Abbot, Archbishop of Canterbury, *First Lord*
1620 Sir Henry Montagu, Viscount Mandeville (afterwards Earl of Manchester, 1926), *Lord Treasurer*
1621 Lionel, Lord Cranfield (afterwards Earl of Middlesex, 1622), *Lord Treasurer*
1624 James, Lord Ley (afterwards Earl of Marlborough, 1626), *Lord Treasurer*

Charles I
1628 Richard, Lord Weston (afterwards Earl of Portland, 1633), *Lord Treasurer*
1635 William Laud, Archbishop of Canterbury, *First Lord*
      Henry, Earl of Manchester; Francis, Lord Cottington; Sir John Coke; Sir Francis Windebank: *commissioners*
1636 William Juxon, Bishop of London, *Lord Treasurer*
1641 Sir Edward Lyttleton (afterwards Lord Lyttleton), *First Lord*

Henry, Earl of Manchester; Sir John Banks; Edward, Lord Newburgh; Sir Henry Vane: *commissioners*

1643   Francis, Lord Cottington, *Lord Treasurer*

Civil War and Interregnum

(financial system in abeyance until 1654)

1654   Bulstrode Whitelocke; Sir Thomas Widdrington; John Lisle; Henry Rolle; Oliver St John; Edward Montagu; William Sydenham; William Matham: *commissioners*

1658   Bulstrode, Lord Whitelocke; Edward, Lord Montagu; William, Lord Sydenham; Sir Thomas Widdrington: *commissioners*

1659   John Disbrowe; William Sydenham; Richard Salway; Cornelius Holland; John Clerke; John Blackwell: *Parlt commissioners*

Charles II

1660   Sir Edward Hyde (afterwards Earl of Clarendon, 1661), *First Lord*
George Monck; Thomas, Earl of Southampton; John, Lord Robarts; Thomas, Lord Colepeper; General Edward Montagu; Sir Edward Nicholas; Sir William Morrice: *commissioners*

1660   Thomas, Earl of Southampton, *Lord Treasurer*

1667   George Monck, Duke of Albemarle, *First Lord*
Anthony, Lord Ashley; Sir Thomas Clifford; Sir William Coventry; Sir John Duncombe: *commissioners*

1669   Same, but without Sir William Coventry

1672   Thomas, Lord Clifford, *Lord Treasurer*

1673   Sir Thomas Osborne, Viscount Latimer (afterwards Earl of Danby, 1674), *Lord Treasurer*

1679   (March) Arthur, Earl of Essex, *First Lord*
Hon. Laurence Hyde; Sir John Ernley; Sir Edward Deering; Sidney Godolphin: *commissioners*
(November) Laurence Hyde (afterwards Earl of Rochester, 1682); *First Lord*
Sir John Ernley; Sir Edward Deering; Sidney Godolphin; Sir Stephen Fox: *commissioners*

1684   Sidney, Lord Godolphin, *First Lord*
Sir John Ernley; Sir Stephen Fox; Sir Dudley North; Henry Frederick Thynne: *commissioners*

James II

1685   Laurence, Earl of Rochester, *Lord Treasurer*

1687   John, Lord Belasyse, *First Lord*
Sidney, Lord Godolphin; Henry, Lord Dover; Sir John Ernley; Sir Stephen Fox: *commissioners*

SECRETARIES OF STATE

James I

1596 Sir Robert Cecil (afterwards Earl of Salisbury, 1605)
1600 John Herbert
1612 Robert Carr (afterwards Earl of Somerset, 1613)
1614 Sir Ralph Winwood
1616 Sir Thomas Lake
1618 Sir Robert Naunton
1619 Sir George Calvert
1623 Sir Edward Conway

Charles I

1625 Sir Albertus Morton
　　　Sir John Coke
1628 Dudley Carleton (afterwards Viscount Dorchester, 1628)
1632 Sir Francis Windebank
1640 Sir Henry Vane
1641 Sir Edward Nicholas
1642 Lucis Carey, Viscount Falkland
1643 George Digby (afterwards Earl of Bristol, 1653)

(Interregnum)

Charles II

1660 Sir Edward Nicholas – South
　　　Sir William Morice – North
1662 Sir Henry Bennet (afterwards Lord Arlington, 1665) – South
1668 Sir John Trevor – North
1672 Henry Coventry – North till 1674, then South 1674–80
1674 Sir Joseph Williamson – North
1679 Robert Spencer, Earl of Sunderland – North till 1680, then South 1680–1
1680 Sir Leoline Jenkins – North till 1681, then South 1681–4
1681 Edward, Viscount Conway – North
1683 Robert, Earl of Sunderland – North till 1684, then South 1684–8
1684 Sidney Godolphin – North; Charles, Earl of Middleton – North till 1688, then South 1688

James II

1688 Richard, Viscount Preston – North

LORD PRESIDENTS OF THE COUNCIL

Sep 1621　　　　Henry Montague, Viscount Manderville, Earl of Manchester, 1626

15 July 1628	James Ley, Earl of Marlborough
14 Dec 1628	Edward, Viscount Conway (until 3 January 1631)
21 Apr 1679	Anthony Ashley-Cooper, Earl of Shaftesbury
24 Oct 1679	John Robartes, Earl of Radnor
24 Aug 1684	Laurence Hyde, Earl of Rochester
18 Feb 1685	George Saville, Marquess of Halifax
4 Dec 1685	Robert Spencer, Earl of Sunderland

LORDS PRIVY SEAL

James I
1603 Sir Robert Cecil continued in office (afterwards Lord Cecil, 1603, and Earl of Salisbury, 1605)
1608 Henry Howard, Earl of Northampton
1614 Robert Carr, Earl of Somerset
1616 Edward Somerset, Earl of Worcester

Charles I
1628 (March) Sir John Coke
        (May) Sir Robert Naunton
        (July) Henry Montagu, Earl of Manchester
1643 Sir Edward Nicholas
1644 Henry Bourchier, Earl of Bath

(Interregnum)

Charles II
1660 William, Viscount Saye and Sele
1661 John, Lord Robarts
1669 Sir Edward Deering; Sir Thomas Strickland; Robert Milward: *commissioners*, during absence of Robarts
1673 Arthur Annesley, Earl of Anglesey
1682 George Saville, Marquis of Halifax

James II
1685 Henry Hyde, Earl of Clarendon
        Robert, Viscount Tiviot; Robert Phillips;
        John Evelyn: *commissioners*, during absence of Hyde
1686 Henry, Lord Arundell

CHANCELLORS OF THE EXCHEQUER

James I
1603 George, Lord Hume
Sir Fulke Greville
1620 Sir Richard Weston (afterwards Earl of Portland)
1622 Lionel, Lord Cranfield (afterwards Earl of Middlesex)
1624 Sir Richard Weston

Charles I
1628 Francis Cottington
1636 Edward, Lord Newburgh
1642 Sir John Colepeper
Sir Edward Hyde

(Interregnum)

Charles II
1660 Sir Robert Long
1667 Anthony, Lord Ashley (afterwards Earl of Shaftesbury)
1672 Sir John Duncombe
1679 Hon. Laurence Hyde (afterwards Earl of Rochester)
Sir John Ernley

James II
1685 Sir John Ernley

LORD LIEUTENANTS AND CHIEF GOVERNORS OF IRELAND

(*LL* = Lord Lieutenant; *LD* = Lord Deputy; *LJ* = Lord Justice; *LC* = Lord Chancellor)

James I
1603 Sir Charles Blount, *LL*
Sir George Cary, *LD*
1605 Sir Arthur Chichester, *LD*
1616 Thomas Jones and Sir John Denham, *LJ*s
Sir Oliver St John, *LD*
1622 Sir Adam Loftus, *LC*, and Richard, Viscount Powerscourt, *LJ*
Henry Cary, Viscount Falkland, *LD*

Charles I
1629 Adam, Viscount Loftus, *LC*, and Richard, Earl of Cork, *LJ*
1633 Thomas Wentworth (afterwards Earl of Strafford, 1640), *LD*

1640 Christopher Wandesford, *LD*
1641 Robert Sydney, Earl of Leicester, *LL*
1643 Sir John Borlase and Sir Henry Tichborne, *LJs*
1644 James, Marquis of Ormond, *LL* (apptd by King)
1646 Philip Sydney, Lord Lisle, *LL* (apptd by Parl.)
1647 Arthur Annesley; Sir Robert King; Sir Robert Meredith; Col. John Moore; Col. Michael Jones: *Parl. commissioners*
1648 James, Marquis of Ormond, *LL* (apptd by King)

Interregnum
1649 Oliver Cromwell, *LL*
1650 Ulick Burke, Marquis of Clanrickarde, *LD* (apptd by Charles II)
1652 Lt-Gen. Charles Fleetwood; Lt-Gen. Edmund Ludlow; Miles Corbett; John Jones; John Weaver: *Parl. commissioners*
1654 Charles Fleetwood, *LD*
1655 Henry Cromwell; Matthew Tomlinson; Miles Corbett; Robert Goodwin and (in 1656) William Steel: *Parl. commissioners*
1657 Henry Cromwell, *LD* then *LL* (1658)
1659 Edmund Ludlow; John Jones; Matthew Tomlinson; Miles Corbett; William Bury: *Parl. commissioners*
1660 Roger, Lord Boghill; Sir Charles Coote; Major Williams Bury: *Parl. commissioners*

Charles II
1660 Lt-Gen. George Monck, Duke of Albemarle, *LL*
      Sir Maurice Eustace, *LC*, and Roger, Earl of Orrery, *LJ*
1662 James, Duke of Ormond, *LL*
1669 Thomas, Earl of Ossory, *LD*
      John, Lord Robartes, *LL*
1670 John, Lord Berkeley, *LL*
1672 Arthur, Earl of Essex, *LL*
1677 James, Duke of Ormond, *LL*

James II
1685 Michael Boye, *LC*, and Arthur, Earl of Granard, *LJ*
      Henry, Earl of Clarendon, *LL*
1687 Richard, Earl of Tyrconnell, *LD*
1689 James II in person

LORD ADMIRALS AND FIRST LORDS OF THE ADMIRALTY

(*LA* = Lord Admiral; *FL* = First Lord of the Admiralty)

8 July 1585   Charles, Lord Howard of Effingham (Earl of Nottingham, 1597), *LA*

28 Jan 1619	George Villiers, Marquess of Buckingham, *LA*
20 Sep 1628	Richard Weston, Lord Weston (Earl of Portland, 1633), *FL*
10 Apr 1635	Robert Bertie, Earl of Lindsey, *FL*
16 Mar 1636	William Juxon, Bishop of London, *FL*
13 Apr 1638	Algernon Percy, Earl of Northumberland, *LA* to 19 Oct 1642, then *FL*
Dec 1643	Francis, Lord Cottington, *FL*
15 Apr 1645	*Parl. committee*: Arthur, Earl of Essex; Robert, Earl of Warwick; William, Viscount Say and Sele; Dudley, Lord North; William Earle; Philip Stapleton; J. Levelyn; C. Wray; J. Rolle; G. Greene; D. Hollis; J. Selden; F. Rouse; T. Eden; J. Lisle; Bulstrode Whitelocke
28 Apr 1645	Robert, Earl of Warwick; J. Bense; H. Pelham (*Parl. appointees*)
12 Feb 1649	J. Dean; F. Popham; R. Blake (*Parl. appointees*)
2 July 1660	James, Duke of York, *LA*
15 June 1673	King Charles II, *LA*
9 July 1673	Prince Rupert, Duke of Cumberland, *FL*
14 May 1679	Sir Henry Capell, *FL*
19 Feb 1681	Daniel Finch (Earl of Nottingham, 1682), *FL*
19 May 1684	King Charles II, *LA*
6 Feb 1685	King James II, *LA*

MASTERS OF THE MINT

James I
1603   Sir Richard Martin and Richard Martin
1615   Thomas, Lord Knyvet and Edward Doubleday
1619   Randal Cranfield
1623   Sir Edward Villiers
1624   Sir Henry Villiers and Henry Twedy
1625   Sir Henry Villiers

Charles I
1625   Sir Robert Harley
1635   Sir Ralph Freeman
1637   Thomas Bushell
1641   Sir William Parkhurst and Thomas Bushell
1643   Sir Robert Harley
1647   Henry Slingsby and John Faulkener

Interregnum
1649   Aaron Guerdain

Charles II
1660   Sir William Parkhurst and Sir Ralph Freeman
1660   Sir Thomas Vyner, Robert Vyner and Daniel Bellingham
1670   Henry Slingsby
1679   Thomas Neale and John Faulkener

James II
1685   Thomas Neale
1688   Office in commission

CHANCELLORS OF THE DUCHY OF LANCASTER

4 Nov 1601	Sir John Fortescue
23 Dec 1607	Sir Thomas Parry
5 June 1616	Sir John Dacombe
3 Feb 1617	Office in commission
23 Mar 1618	Sir Humphrey May
16 Apr 1629	Edward Barrett, Lord Barrett of Newburgh
10 Feb 1645	William, Lord Grey of Warke; and William Lenthall
4 Apr 1648	Sir Gilbert Gerrard
28 July 1649	John Bradshaw until the duchy jurisdiction ceased, on 10 October 1653
1 Jan 1655	Thomas Fell until the duchy jurisdiction again ceased, later in the year
14 Mar 1660	Sir Gilbert Gerrard
9 July 1660	Francis, Lord Seymour
21 July 1664	Sir Thomas Ingram
22 Feb 1672	Sir Robert Carr
21 Nov 1682	Sir Thomas Chicheley
15 Mar 1687	Office in commission
25 May 1687	Robert Phelipps

CHIEF JUSTICES OF THE KING'S BENCH

Mar 1603	John Popham	Feb 1627	Nicholas Hyde
June 1607	Thomas Fleming	Oct 1631	Thomas Richardson
Oct 1613	Edward Coke	Apr 1635	John Bramston
Nov 1616	Henry Montagu	Oct 1642	Robert Heath (disabled,
Jan 1621	James Ley		November 1645)
Jan 1625	Ranulphe Crewe		
	(removed, November 1626)		

Oct 1648	Henry Rolle	May 1678	William Scroggs
June 1655	John Glynne	Apr 1681	Francis Pemberton
Jan 1660	Richard Newdigate	Jan 1683	Edmund Saunders (died, June)
Oct 1660	Robert Foster	Sep 1683	George Jeffreys
Oct 1663	Robert Hyde	Oct 1685	Edward Herbert
Nov 1665	John Kelyng	Apr 1687	Robert Wright
May 1671	Matthew Hale		
Apr 1676	Richardson Rainsford		

MASTERS OF THE ROLLS

Mar 1603	Sir Thomas Egerton	Nov 1643	William Lenthall
May 1603	Edward Bruce, Lord Kinloss	Jan 1649	John, Lord Colepeper
Jan 1611	Sir Edward Phellips	Nov 1660	Sir Harbottle Grimstone
Sep 1614	Sir Julius Caesar		
Apr 1636	Sir Dudley Digges	Jan 1685	John Churchill (Sir John, February)
Mar 1639	Sir Charles Ceaser		
Jan 1643	Sir John Colepeper (Lord Colepeper, October 1644)	Oct 1685	Sir John Trevor

CHIEF BARONS OF THE COURT OF EXCHEQUER

Mar 1603	William Peryam	May 1655	William Steele
Oct 1604	Thomas Fleming	June 1658	Thomas Widrington
June 1607	Laurence Tanfield	Jan 1660	John Wilde
May 1625	John Walter (died, November 1630)	June 1660	Orlando Bridgeman
		Nov 1660	Matthew Hale
Jan 1631	Humphrey Davenport	May 1671	Edward Turnour
		Apr 1686	Edward Atkyns (resigned, October 1694)
Jan 1644	Richard Lane		
Oct 1648	John Wilde (till January 1654)		

CHIEF JUSTICES OF THE COURT OF COMMON PLEAS

Mar 1603	Edmund Anderson	Oct 1631	Robert Heath
Aug 1605	Francis Gawdy	Oct 1634	John Finch
June 1606	Edward Coke	Jan 1640	Edward Lyttelton
Nov 1613	Henry Hobart (died, December 1625)	Jan 1641	John Banks (died, December 1644)
Nov 1626	Thomas Richardson	Oct 1648	Oliver St John

Oct 1660	Orlando Bridgeman	Sep 1683	Thomas Jones
May 1668	John Vaughan	Apr 1686	Henry Bedingfield
Jan 1675	Francis North	Apr 1687	Robert Wright
Jan 1683	Francis Pemberton	Apr 1687	Edward Herbert

ATTORNEY GENERALS

Mar 1603	Edward Coke	Oct 1625	Robert Heath
July 1606	Henry Hobart	Oct 1631	William Noy
Oct 1613	Francis Bacon	Sep 1634	John Banks
Mar 1617	Henry Yelverton	Jan 1641	Edward Herbert
Jan 1621	Thomas Coventry (till March 1625)	Nov 1645	Thomas Gardner

PARL. APPOINTEES

Jan 1649	William Steele	May 1660	Geoffrey Palmer
Apr 1649	Edmund Prideaux	May 1670	Heneage Finch
1659	Robert Reynolds	Nov 1673	Francis North
(1649–53	Edward Herbert was the King's Attorney General)	Jan 1675	William Jones
		Oct 1679	Creswell Levinz
		Feb 1681	Robert Sawyer
		Dec 1687	Thomas Powys

SOLICITOR GENERALS

Mar 1603	Thomas Fleming	Oct 1625	Richard Shilton or Sheldon
Oct 1604	John Doderidge		
June 1607	Francis Bacon	Oct 1634	Edward Lyttleton
Oct 1613	Henry Yelverton	Jan 1640	Edward Herbert
Mar 1617	Thomas Coventry	Jan 1641	Oliver St John
Jan 1621	Robert Heath (till March 1625)	Oct 1643	Thomas Gardner
		Nov 1645	Geoffrey Palmer

PARL. APPOINTEES

(1643	Oliver St John continued in office)	May 1670	Edward Turnour
		May 1671	Francis North
Oct 1648	Edmund Prideaux	Nov 1673	William Jones
Jan 1649	John Cook	Dec 1674	Francis Winnington
1650	Robert Reynolds	Jan 1679	Hon. Heneage Finch
May 1654	William Ellis	Apr 1686	Thomas Powys
June 1660	Heneage Finch	Dec 1687	William Williams

3 A GLOSSARY OF CENTRAL GOVERNMENT

THE CENTRAL EXECUTIVE

The central executive consisted of the King, the two Secretaries of State and the Privy Council; it was responsible for efficient administration, execution of policies and communication between the King and his people.

THE KING AND HIS SEALS

ROYAL STYLE: after the union of the English and Scottish crowns (24 March 1603), James I used the style 'King of England, Scotland, France and Ireland, Defender of the Faith, etc.'

ACCESSION: since 1307 the theory has operated that the King never dies. In the seventeenth century, therefore, the accession of the monarch was assumed to take place on the day following the death of the old one.

REGENTS: the exercise of royal power during the absence of the monarch has, since the reign of Edward II, been mainly entrusted either to nominated members of the royal family or to the Lord Justices. In the seventeenth century, James I, Charles I, Charles II and James II were never absent from their dominions.

MASTERS OF REQUEST: four worked on a monthly rota at court to receive petitions from subjects; these petitions could be presented directly to the King without reference to the Privy Council or Secretaries of State. In practice petitions were often referred to the Council, the Attorney-General or the Lord Treasurer. Grants were normally authorised by the use of all three seals – the Signet Seal, the Privy Seal and the Great Seal.

SIGN MANUAL: the royal signature used to authorise the application of the signet seal on grants, etc.; also used on personal letters. Some sovereigns, unlike Charles I, employed wooden stamps for this purpose.

SIGNET SEAL: a single-sided seal bearing the royal arms; smaller than the Privy Seal; kept by the Secretaries of State; used not only for sealing major communications, but also more personal letters to subjects.

SIGNET OFFICE: consisted of the personal staff of the Secretaries of State (responsible for the King's personal correspondence and first drafts of documents requiring the Sign Manual), four Signet Clerks (responsible for the King's official correspondence and preparing documents for the Privy Seal), a French Secretary, a Latin Secretary and a German Interpreter.

PRIVY SEAL: a single-sided seal bearing the royal coat of arms; usually applied on red wax (not pendant); smaller than the Great Seal; kept by the Lord Privy Seal; letters of Privy Seal used by the King to answer certain petitions and to authorise certain money transactions.

PRIVY SEAL OFFICE: consisted of four Masters of Request, four Clerks of the Privy Seal and about four Deputy Clerks; responsible for receiving Signet documents and preparing documents for the Great Seal.

LORD PRIVY SEAL: the first Keeper of the Privy Seal appointed in 1311; Thomas Cromwell was the first to be styled Lord Privy Seal; responsible for the Privy Seal and for the Court of Requests.

GREAT SEAL: a circular and double-sided seal, showing on one side the sovereign enthroned and on the other the sovereign mounted; kept by the Lord Chancellor (or the Lord Keeper) or occasionally put in commission; used to authenticate most state documents on receipt of a Privy Seal warrant.

CHANCERY: the offices of the Lord Chancellor; a staff of nearly fifty secretaries and clerks responsible for the final issue of instruments authorised by the Great Seal. It had also become a popular equity court, dealing with petitions which were outside the scope of common law.

LORD CHANCELLOR: Keeper of the Great Seal, Speaker of the House of Lords, head of Chancery and judge in the equity court of Chancery; possessed the right to delay or veto the issue of instruments under the Great Seal, thus acting as a check on the advice given by the Secretaries of State.

LETTERS CLOSE: a document under the Great Seal addressed to one or more particular people; dealt with administrative or judicial matters which were less public and perhaps more transient; folded and sealed up.

LETTERS PATENT: a formal document under the Great Seal addressed to all who might be concerned; dealt with matters which were of greater public interest and importance (e.g. licences, commissions); left open with the seal hanging from the bottom.

CHARTER: a document under the Great Seal recording a grant of land, privileges, etc.; addressed to all people present and future.

PROCLAMATIONS IN COUNCIL: issued under the Great Seal or Privy Seal; used to supplement Parliamentary statutes on a wide range of subjects; enforced by Star Chamber. The Commons in 1610 petitioned against their too-frequent use — judges ruled that they must not change the common law.

SECRETARIES OF STATE

Responsibilities:

(a) administrative – dealing with the King's personal correspondence, preparation of official letters for the Sign Manual and documents for the Signet Seal;
(b) executive – dealing with many matters of state on their own initiative;
(c) advisory – as members of the Council, advising the King on foreign and domestic matters.

From 1540 two Secretaries of State were appointed; from 1640 their work in foreign affairs was formally shared out between them into a Northern Department (i.e. responsibility for Protestant countries) and a Southern Department (for Catholic countries), although this division became more apparent after the Restoration. The Northern Secretary was always 'promoted' to the more senior Southern Department on the retirement of the former holder. During the absence of the Lord President, they were responsible for the Council's agenda and its staff. By the seventeenth century, the office of Secretary of State had grown in stature (especially under powerful personalities such as Robert Cecil) to rival that of Lord Treasurer and Lord Chancellor.

PRIVY COUNCIL

DEVELOPMENT: By the late fourteenth century this smaller body of court advisers had emerged out of the King's Council (or Parliament); by Tudor times it had developed important political, administrative and judicial functions. Not only did the Council offer advice to the sovereign: it also undertook much of the actual business of central government (in particular that concerning the Treasury, Admiralty, plantations, foreign policy and local matters). Because of its increased size during the seventeenth century, an 'inner cabinet council' gradually evolved. This took the form of the Standing Committee on Foreign Affairs (consisting of senior officers of state), although its advice to the King extended to other confidential and important matters. Individuals were occasionally referred to as 'chief minister' (e.g. Danby, Clarendon, Buckingham), but the office of Prime Minister had not yet developed.

SIZE

1605	16	1630	42	1670	41
1610	19	1635	32	1675	50
1615	22	1640	35	1679	47
1620	28	1660	29		
1625	30	1664	40		

SOURCES: G. E. Aylmer, *The King's Servants; the Civil Service of Charles I 1625–1642* (1961); E. R. Turner, *The Privy Council of England*, vols I and II (1927–8).

MEMBERSHIP: In 1625 Sir John Coke, Secretary of State, listed the principal officers of state who 'are by place and office so interested in the businesses of state as they are of the Council' (i.e. the *ex officio* members of the Council), as follows.

Lord President: office is first mentioned in 1497; an Act of 1529 gave the Lord President official status above the Keeper of the Privy Seal, but below the Chancellor and Treasurer; office not regularly filled until after 1679.

Archbishop of Canterbury.

Secretaries of State (see above).

Lord Chancellor (see above).

Lord Treasurer: title first used in twelfth century by the chamberlain who controlled the Winchester treasury; from the reign of Henry I, he also presided over the Exchequer, a central financial organisation dealing with Crown revenue; by Tudor times, when he received the title of Lord Treasurer, he had become an important officer of state and adviser to the King. In 1653 the office was put in commission, only to be revived in 1660.

Lord Privy Seal (see above).

Lord Steward: responsible for organising the Royal Household below stairs, which provided food, fuel, transport and lodging for the court; together with the Treasurer and Comptroller, known as the 'Whitestaves'.

Lord Admiral (or First Lord of the Admiralty): title 'Admiral of England' first used in 1412, lasting unchanged until 1540, when the style 'Lord Admiral' appeared. From 1546 the Navy Board became responsible for the regular maintenance of royal ships, but it was not until 1619 that the Lord Admiral assumed control over the Navy Board. After 1628 the office was frequently put into commission under the leadership of the First Lord of the Admiralty.

Lord Chamberlain: regarded as the head of the whole Royal Household, above and below stairs; but primarily responsible for the Chamber (i.e. the King's Household above stairs), which organised ceremonial and entertainment at Court.

Treasurer of the Household: with the Comptroller, Cofferer, Clerks of the Greencloth, Clerk Comptrollers and Master of the Household made up the Board of Greencloth, which was responsible for the financial organisation of court; with the Lord Steward and Comptroller known as the 'Whitestaves'.

Comptroller of the Household: a member of the Board of Greencloth, responsible for financial organisation; in charge of the Compting House with a staff of nine; one of the 'Whitestaves'.

Chancellor of the Exchequer.

Chancellor of the Duchy of Lancaster: presided over the Duchy Council.

The following were, in addition, frequently members of the Privy Council.

Lord Great Chamberlain: office revived by Charles I in 1626.

Queen's Lord Chamberlain: head of Queen's Household at court.

Earl Marshal: originally a senior member of the Royal Household; office revived by James I in 1621.

Lord Treasurer of Scotland.

Archbishop of York.

Master of the Horse.

Master of the Wards.

Master of the Rolls.

STANDING COMMITTEES: During the seventeenth century certain types of business were handed over to standing committees of the Privy Council for preliminary consideration. A few prominent Council members (e.g. the Lord Chancellor, Lord Treasurer, Chancellor of Exchequer, Lord Privy Seal, Secretaries of State) tended to be members of several committees. However, the oldest committee, the Committee on Foreign Affairs, gradually became increasingly powerful as the main organ of executive government under the Crown. After 1679, as the Council slowly declined in activity and greatness, the importance of these standing committees dwindled. Additional committees, as first mentioned in Council registers, were as follows (membership numbers in parentheses).

1617 Committee 'for the State of Ireland' (9)
      Committee 'for the Household' (6)
      Committee 'for the Navy' (7)
      Committee 'for the Wardrobe and Robes' (8)
      Committee 'for the Works, Castles and Forts' (8)
      Committee 'for the Book of Rates, Impositions, Exportation and Importation' (10)
      Committee 'for putting Laws into execution concerning Strangers' (2)
      Committee 'for separable Debts' (2)
      Committee 'for the Fishing' (10)
      Committee 'for Enfranchising Copyholders and improving Rents' (6)
      Committee 'for Gifts, Grants and other Things' (2)
      Committee 'for Grievances in General'
1623 Committee on 'The Church' (4)
      Committee on 'New Patents, Monopolies etc.' (11)
      Committee on 'The Army' (13)

1629   Committee 'for Trade' (13)
        Committee 'for the Trayned Bands' (18)
        Committee 'for the Order of Knighthood' (19)
1630   Committee 'for the Poor' (10)
1632   Committee 'for New England' (12)
        Committee 'about Pirates' (6)
1634   Committee 'for Foreign Plantations' (12)
        Committee 'for the Ordinance' (7)
        Committee 'for the Treasury' (5)
1639   Committee of the North

ASSOCIATED COUNCILS AND COMMISSIONS: With the increase of business by the seventeenth century, the Privy Council found it necessary to seek additional assistance in specialised fields. Members of these associated councils and commissions were not always members of the Council.

Council of War (first established in 1621)
Commission to Inquire into the Decay of the Clothing Trade (1622)
Commission to Study Manufactures (1622)
Commission on Matters Concerning Virginia (1623)
Commission on Matters Concerning the Somers Islands (1624)
Commission of Trade (1625)
Commission on Virginia Affairs (1631)
Committee on New England Affairs (1632)
Committee on Scottish Affairs (1640)
Council of Trade (1660)
Council for Foreign Plantations (1660)

EXTENSIONS OF THE CENTRAL EXECUTIVE

IRELAND: ruled through a Lord Deputy or Lord Lieutenant, who in the seventeenth century exercised wide powers; assisted by a Privy Council based in Dublin.

SCOTLAND: controlled by the King through a Scottish Privy Council (dominated by the Scottish Secretary of State, the Lord Treasurer of Scotland and an inner group of councillors).

COUNCIL IN THE NORTH: a regional council based on York under the Lord President and Vice-President with a Secretary and Keeper of the Signet, Attorney, Clerk of the Bills, Clerk of the Tickets, etc., responsible for administration and both civil and criminal justice.

COUNCIL IN THE MARCHES OF WALES: a regional council concerned with Wales, Monmouth and the border counties of Hereford, Gloucester, Shropshire and Worcester; under the Lord President and Vice-President (usually Chief Justice of Chester) with a Clerk of the Council, Deputy Clerk, Attorney, Solicitor,

Remembrancer, Examiners, etc.; responsible for aspects of administration and both civil and criminal justice (although a separate administration and judiciary existed for Wales apart from the Council).

REPRESENTATIVES ABROAD: responsible to Secretaries of State.

Resident Ambassadors: at the Courts of Spain, France, the Empire, Turkey and the United Provinces.

Regular Agents: in Paris, The Hague, Vienna, Madrid, Brussels, Copenhagen, Danzig, Warsaw, Hamburg, Stockholm, Venice, Turin, Florence, Genoa and Moscow, and on the Barbary Coast.

Consuls: in chief European, North African and Levantine ports.

THE ROYAL HOUSEHOLD

In the Middle Ages the Royal Household had played an important part in the government of the country, the Wardrobe acting as a supply department in time of war and the Chamber rivalling the Exchequer as a treasury. By the seventeenth century this influence outside the court had declined, although the leading officers in the Household (Lord Chamberlain, Lord Steward, Treasurer and Comptroller) were also members of the Privy Council, while the Secretaries of State and Lord Privy Seal frequently dined at court. The costs of maintaining the Household had increased alarmingly under the influence of inflation, amounting under Charles I, to over 40 per cent of the total expenditure. Staff numbered at least 1800. The Household was growingly under attack for its wastefulness, inefficiency and corruption.

HOUSEHOLD ABOVE STAIRS (the 'Chamber'): responsible for the routine, ceremony and entertainment of Court; sub-departments included Works (construction and maintenance of buildings), Revels, Tents, Robes, Jewels, Toils, King's Guard, Privy Chamber, and Bedchamber (under the Groom of the Stole); Chamber directed by the Lord Chamberlain, the Vice-Chamberlain, the Treasurer and the Keeper of the Privy Purse, with a total staff of between 580 and 620 under Charles I.

HOUSEHOLD BELOW STAIRS (the 'Household'): responsible for supply of food, fuel, lighting, transport and accommodation outside court; directed by the Lord Steward; Board of Greencloth (Treasurer, Comptroller, Cofferer, Clerks of Greencloth and Clerk Comptrollers) responsible for organisation and financing of supply; Master of the Household responsible for control of staff; sub-departments included the Compting House, Kitchen, Poultry, Buttery, Cellar, Bakehouse, Laundry, Spicery, Scullery, Pastry, Confectionery, Almonry, Chandlery, Larder, Ewery, Woodyard and Acatry (meat); total staff of about 305.

GREAT WARDROBE: responsible for supply of royal clothing and furnishings; directed by the Master of the Great Wardrobe with a staff of about sixty; independent of the Chamber and Household.

ROYAL STABLES: directed by the Master of the Horse and Master of the Queen's Horse with a staff of about 263.

QUEEN'S HOUSEHOLD AND CHAMBER: directed by the Lord Chamberlain with a staff of about 180 and an organisation similar to that of the King's Household.

PRINCE'S HOUSEHOLD: directed by the Governor and Groom of the Stole with a staff of about thirty-two.

FINANCE

REVENUE DEPARTMENTS IN 1603

THE COURT OF WARDS: independent of the Exchequer; administered profits produced by wardship and livery (see below); also responsible for the management of estates and personal welfare of wards, where wardship had not been sold to an outside purchaser; directed by a Master, a Receiver General, a Surveyor, an Attorney, two Auditors, a Clerk and a Clerk of the Liveries.

THE DUCHY OF LANCASTER: responsible for the finance and estate management of all the royal estates; directed by a Chancellor, a Receiver General, two Auditors, an Attorney and a Clerk.

THE EXCHEQUER: the country's chief financial organisation; divided into

(1) the Upper Exchequer (the Exchequer of Audit) – responsible for auditing all government revenue and expense accounts (except those of the Court of Wards, the Duchy of Lancaster and the Queen's Household), and
(2) the Lower Exchequer (the Exchequer of Receipt) – responsible for all actual receipts and payments and for keeping records.

The Exchequer was presided over by the Lord Treasurer; the Chancellor (of the Upper Exchequer) was also Under-Treasurer of the Lower Exchequer.

THE CUSTOMS SERVICE: a vital part of Crown finance with strong links to the Exchequer; customs usually leased out to 'customs farmers' (City financiers and merchants). The service was under the control of the Surveyor-Generals, two Co-Surveyors of London and a Surveyor of the Outports, responsible to the Lord Treasurer.

THE ALIENATIONS OFFICE: responsible for revenue raised from fines on sale of land held by Crown tenants; directed by a Clerk, a Receiver and three Deputies for Compositions.

SOURCES OF REVENUE IN 1603

CROWN LANDS, FEUDAL RIGHTS AND PREROGATIVE: Purpose of these sources was, in theory, to provide the costs of internal administration; regarded as 'ordinary revenue' of the Crown.

Crown lands: although rent was an important part of the 'ordinary' revenue, because of inefficiency, yields under the Stuarts never reached their true potential.

Wardship: the King's right to act as guardian to those tenants who inherited estates as minors; wardship *either* undertaken directly by the King, who supervised and educated the wards, administered the estates and enjoyed their proceeds, *or* sold to an outsider for an agreed sum.

Marriage: the King's right to arrange the marriage of female heirs of his tenants or the remarriage of widows who held land from him.

Livery: the King's right to mulct those who inherited any of his land, including wards when they came of age.

Purveyance: the King's right to purchase food, supplies, etc., for his court at prices below market value.

Monopolies: the King's prerogative to grant to companies and individuals the exclusive right to produce, sell or trade in specified merchandise; very unpopular under Elizabeth I.

Proceeds of justice: fines, court fees, etc.

CUSTOMS DUTIES: A tax on imports and exports – the most flexible part of the King's 'ordinary' revenue; purpose, in theory, to provide for maintenance of the navy, defence of the realm and protection of trade; not regarded as a national tax, but as a toll on consumers to safeguard their merchandise; also used to control foreign trade in the interests of home production.

Tunnage and poundage: customs duties on wine and wool, normally granted to the monarch for life by the first parliament of the reign.

'New Impositions' (or new import duties): traditionally the Crown was entitled to raise or extend import duties for protection of English trade and industry; in 1601 Elizabeth I had first levied a duty of 5s. 6d. per cwt on imported currants, later extending it to tobacco; in 1608 Robert Cecil imposed the tax on most imports (except food, ships' stores and munitions), much to the anger of the Commons.

DIRECT TAXES: The 'extraordinary' revenue raised by order of Parliament to provide for specific national needs (e.g. war); imposed selectively according to an individual's means; very poor people usually exempt. These seventeenth-century taxes were not often very productive, because assessments were outdated and took little account of inflation. From 1640 the standard for direct taxation increasingly became income rather than movable property, with growing concern for a man's ability to pay.

The fifteenth and tenth: originated in the thirteenth-century; a tax on movable goods (except personal clothing, etc.) paid by all.

The subsidy: a tax on income for landowners, office-holders and wage-earners and on movable property for merchants, artisans and tenant farmers.

Poll tax: a tax on individuals; that of 1641 fixed contributions according to rank, occupation or income from £100 for a Duke to 6d. per head for poorer people.

Ship money: the King's right in wartime to collect money from coastal towns and counties for the building and provision of ships.

OTHER SOURCES

Benevolences (or forced loans); a compulsory levy, in theory, illegal.

Loans from financiers: especially from wealthy customs farmers.

Sale of crown assets: land, timber, valuables, titles, offices, honours, etc.

MAIN DEVELOPMENTS IN FINANCE

1604   (March) Conference between the Lords and the Commons, arranged by Cecil, to discuss wardship and purveyance ended in stalemate.

1606   Bate's Case: John Bate, a merchant, imprisoned after refusing to pay the imposition on currants. Chief Baron Fleming, in giving judgement for the Crown, stressed the King's right to levy duty on any merchandise.

1606   (March) Commons petition against monopolies and purveyance increased customs duties and impositions.

1608   (July) Impositions extended by Robert Cecil, Earl of Salisbury, to most imports, except food, ships' stores and munitions.

1610   The 'Great Contract' designed by Salisbury to grant the King regular taxation (e.g. excise or land tax) in return for his surrender of impositions and feudal rights (especially purveyance and wardship). Negotiations broke down (November).

1610   (July) Commons petition the King against impositions, etc., in a Petition of Grievances, but these continued until 1641.

1612   James I renewed policy of granting patents of monopoly.

1621   Commons and Lords, in James I's third parliament, launched an attack on monopolies; impeachment of monopolists Mitchell and Mompesson, but Coke failed to make monopolies illegal.

1621   James I granted two subsidies by Parliament.

1624   Monopolies Act: the King's right to grant monopolies limited to new inventions.

1624   Subsidy Act: granted King three subsidies and three fifteenths and tenths; but subsidies only to be spent on defence and assistance to the Dutch.

1625   The Commons, in Charles I's first parliament, granted the King tunnage and poundage for one year only (contrary to the normal tradition of granting it for life). Charles nevertheless continued to collect it.

1626   After the dissolution of Parliament (July), Charles I resorted to extracting money to pay for war through forced loans.

1626   (July) Privy council stated (following Parliament's protest against the King's illegal collection of tunnage and poundage) that the duty was an established part of the monarch's revenue and that it was not subject to Parliamentary approval.

1627   (November) The Five Knights' Case: Lord Chief Justice Hyde ruled on the King's bench that those detained for refusal to pay forced loans could not be released on bail.

1628   John Rolles and other merchants refused to pay tunnage and poundage; their goods were confiscated by order of the Council.

1628   (June) The Commons reacted to Charles I's insistence that tunnage and poundage was outside their jurisdiction by passing a remonstrance that unauthorised collection of the duty was 'a breach of the fundamental liberties of this Kingdom'; subjects encouraged to refuse payment.

1628   (June) The Petition of Right included a request by the Commons that the King should not levy taxes without consent of Parliament.

1628   (December) Commission for Defective Titles appointed (December) to compound with Crown tenants who lacked an effective title to their land or who could not prove continuous occupation for the last sixty years; also with those who had illegally enclosed wastes or commons, or who had encroached on royal forest.

1629   (March) The Three Resolutions, passed prior to dissolution, with the Speaker held down in his chair, included clauses against those who advised the collection of unauthorised tunnage and poundage and those who willingly paid it.

1629   (March) Charles I issued a proclamation reiterating his right to collect 'those duties that were received by the King our father, which we neither can nor will dispense withal' (i.e. tunnage and poundage).

1630   London merchants attempted a boycott of trade in protest against the King's collection of tunnage and poundage.

1630   Commission for Defective Titles reappointed.

1630   (January) Forced knighthood: a commission appointed (January) to compound with those holding land worth £40 per annum who had failed to take up knighthood at the King's coronation (according to feudal custom). £165,000 raised by this device (1630–5).

1634   Commission of Justice in Eyre appointed to compound with those who had encroached on royal forests.

1634   Ship money: Charles I exercised his right to collect tax from coastal towns and counties for protection against pirates and enemy shipping.

1635   Inquiry into the state of royal finances by the Treasury Commissioners; Crown debts estimated at nearly two years' 'ordinary' revenue.

1635   Cottingham became Master of the Wards, Chancellor of the Exchequer and Under-Treasurer.

1635   Commission for Defective Titles reappointed.

1635   The Crown's 'ordinary' revenue since 1631 averaged £618,376 per annum, including £53,866 from the Court of Wards and Liveries and £53,091 from the 'New Impositions'. 'Extraordinary' revenue since 1625 averaged £240,000 per annum.

1635   Ship money extended to inland counties. The Privy Council assessed counties and towns according to size and wealth. Levied for six successive years (1635–40), yielding an average of approx. £107,000 per annum.

1636   John Hampden refused to pay ship money.

1637   The trial of John Hampden.

1638   Hampden's Case: judgement in favour of the King's right to impose ship money.

1639   Ship money: only £43,417 paid out of £214,000 assessed.

1640   (January) Crown mortgaged its revenues from sugar and alum until 1645 and from wine licences until 1651. (Known as 'assignment' or 'anticipation'.)

1641   Crown's 'ordinary' revenue since 1636 averaged £899,482 per annum, including £75,088 from the Court of Wards and Liveries and £119,583 from the 'New Impositions'.

1641 The Tunnage and Poundage Act granted Charles I these duties and all current impositions for two months. (Renewed bimonthly until 1642.)

1641 Parliament ruled that ship money was illegal, defined the legal limits of royal forest and banned the collection of fines for failure to assume knighthood.

1641 Poll tax introduced, to raise money for disbandment of the army; contribution fixed according to rank, occupation or income, from £100 for a duke to 6d. for a poorer person.

1642 (March) Act to raise £4 million by a subsidy for the payment of debt in Scotland and war in Ireland. County committees appointed to be responsible for collection of the sum to which each county assessed.

1642 (June) Ordinance to raise plate, money and horses by voluntary contributions 'for the preservation of the public peace, and for the defence of the King and both Houses of Parliament'.

1642 (November) Ordinance to assess all those who had not yet contributed to Parliament's call for money, plate, horses, etc.

1643 Committee for the Advance of Monies established at Haberdashers' Hall; responsible for raising supplies for the army and for taxing those (royalists or neutrals) who had not given freely to Parliament's cause.

1643 Ordinances empowering county committees to tax those who had not yet given freely to Parliament's call for contributions – or to seize goods to the value of one-twentieth of their estate.

1643 (January) Ordinance for continuing subsidy of tunnage and poundage.

1643 (February) Ordinance established the Weekly Assessment. Each county to pay a specified sum to be raised by the county committee according to local assessments on individuals. Became a type of land tax.

1643 (March) Ordinance for sequestering 'notorious Deliquents' estates' established local committees to confiscate and manage the estates of all known royalists.

1643 (July) The Excise Ordinance, proposed by Pym, authorised a 'New Impost' on home-produced ale, beer, cider and perry, and on imported tobacco, figs, raisins, wine, currants, sugar, pepper, silks, leather, lace and furs. Eight commissioners appointed in London, with deputies in the provinces to collect the tax; granted powers of search and examination of suspects. Duties on beer of 2s. per barrel of strong beer and 6d. per barrel of small beer. The introduction of excise was without precedent in England. Although the tax was justified as being easy to collect, productive in time of need and equitable in distribution, it was bitterly attacked for its threat to the cost of basic necessities and to personal liberty.

1643   (September) Excise duty extended to cloth, paper and imported glass.

1644   (January) Excise duty imposed on salt ($\frac{1}{2}$d. per gallon) and meat (1s. per lb.), and (July) on alum, copper, hats, hops, starch, saffron and English silks, etc.

1644   (September) The Goldsmith's Hall Committee began compounding with royalists for their estates (i.e. imposing a fine which could total up to two-thirds of their estates).

1645   (February) The Monthly Assessment replaced the Weekly Assessment, but was based on similar principles.

1645   (November) Excise duty imposed on lead, gold, silver, glass, oil and woollens, etc.

1646   Ordinances for the sale of Bishops' land to raise money for payment of the Scots; contractors appointed to be responsible for the sale, trustees for the profits.

1646   (February) Ordinance ending wardship and the Court of Wards.

1647   Committee for Taking the Accounts of the Kingdom (established 1644) reconstituted with members who were not members of Parliament; other committees later similarly affected (a consequence of the Self-Denying Ordinance, 1645).

1647   (February) In face of anti-excise riots, Parliament issued an ordinance to justify continuance of the tax until the army had been disbanded and to establish procedure for dealing with complaints against officials.

1647   (June) Excise on meat and salt abolished.

1649   Monthly Assessment: the 'pound rate' introduced to charge men of personal property 5 per cent of their stock (thus bringing their tax more into line with that paid by landowners on rent or yearly value). Continued until 1653, but not greatly successful.

1649   Committee of Regulars appointed (consisting of navy commissioners and London merchants) to investigate the suitability of all customs and navy officers.

1649   (June) Ordinance for the sale of the lands of deans and chapters.

1649   (July) Acts for the sale of goods, lands and personal estate of the late King, and of the Queen and Prince.

1649   (December) Excise on salt re-established.

1650   Seven professional Compounding Commissioners appointed to replace Parliament's Compounding Committee (Chairman, John Ashe), thus allowing MPs more time on Parliamentary business; to be responsible for sequestrations, compounding with royalists and advance of money.

1652   Seven full-time Obstruction Commissioners appointed to replace Parliament's Obstructions Committee; to be responsible for speeding up the sale of remaining lands of the Crown, deans and chapters and sequestered royalists.

1653   The Commonwealth largely dependent on the following for revenue.

(1) The Assessment – organised by the Army Committee and War Treasurer, but collected and often assigned locally by county commissioners; used chiefly to finance the army.

(2) The customs – organised by customs commissioners; used to finance the navy.

(3) The excise – organised by excise commissioners; chiefly used to finance the navy.

(4) Land sales – used chiefly to service the public debt.

(5) Royalist sequestrations and compositions – organised by Goldsmiths' Hall Committee; chiefly used for the minor costs of government.

(6) Other revenue (Crown land, Duchy of Lancaster, alienations, sale of forests, advance of monies) – used for costs of government.

1653   (December) The Instrument of Government granted Cromwell, as Lord Protector, £200,000 per annum to cover the military and administrative costs of government, plus the benefits of all remaining Crown lands.

1654   (March) Excise duty extended to most merchandise.

1655   (August) Decision taken that costs of the Major-Generals and their cavalry-militia to be raised by a decimation tax' (10 per cent on the estates of royalists).

1657   Monthly Assessment reduced to its lowest ever, £35,000 per month (as opposed to £120,000 at its peak). In June the Humble Petition and Advice (amended) granted the Lord Protector £1.3 million per annum, including £1 million for the armed forces (not to be raised by a land tax).

1660   The Convention Parliament abolished purveyance and feudal dues.

1660   In the Restoration, the Excise was retained as a method of taxation (especially on beer, spirits, tea, coffee, etc., although duties on other commodities were abolished).

1660   Poll tax introduced – a 2 per cent tax on income on those not rated by rank or calling.

1661   Commons granted Charles II tunnage and poundage for life; the Hereditary Excise (on beer, cider, mead, spirits, coffee, chocolate, tea and sherbert) granted to the King and his successors for ever (in lieu of wardship, purveyance and feudal dues); the Additional Excise (on all other merchandise) granted for life. Estimated total yield of King's revenue amounted to £1.2 million to cover government and peace-time military expenses, but this was never actually achieved.

1662   The hearth tax introduced (a duty of 2s. per hearth per annum on the occupier of each house).

1665   The Supply Act (amid suspicions of corruption) ruled that tax receipts and payments were to be strictly logged in an Exchequer register and that repayment of loans was to be made by the government in chronological order.

1666   The Supply Act stipulated that £380,000 of the total grant (£1,256,347) should be devoted to seamen's wages, thus commencing the practice of 'appropriation'.

1667   Amid widespread fears of excessive corruption, a commission appointed (for three years) to inspect public accounts, with powers to view all records and to examine all officials under oath.

1670   (June) Treaty of Dover with France. Charles II, as part of the agreement, received subsidies from France (five subsidies received between 1670 and 1678, totalling £741,985).

1672   (January) Stop of the Exchequer: payments to royal creditors suspended for one year in the face of a financial crisis.

1673   Parliament granted £1.2 million over three years for the Dutch War on condition that Charles II cancel the Declaration of Indulgence (1672).

1678   Parliament's grant of money (£206,462) was strictly made for the disbandment of the Flanders army, and 'to no other intent, use or purpose whatsoever' (i.e. appropriation).

1685   Parliament voted James II additional impositions on sugar, wine, tobacco and vinegar for eight years without strict control of their application (i.e. no appropriation).

OTHER DEPARTMENTS OF STATE

THE MINT: responsible for coinage of the realm: directed by two Wardens, a Master, a Comptroller, an Assay Master, two Auditors, a Teller, a Surveyor of the Melting House, a Chief Graver, a Provost, etc.

THE ORDNANCE OFFICE: responsible for the supply and control of munitions for both army and navy; answerable to the Privy Council; directed by a Master, a Lieutenant, a Surveyor, a Clerk, a Storekeeper, a Clerk of Deliveries, etc.

THE ARMOURY: responsible for hand weapons (pikes, swords, etc.); a sub-department of the Ordnance; directed by a Master, two Surveyors, a Clerk, etc.

THE NAVY: responsible to the King and Privy Council; directed by the Lord High Admiral, a Lieutenant, a Treasurer, a Comptroller, a Surveyor, a Victualler, a Clerk, etc.

THE TOWER OF LONDON: directed by the Lieutenant of the Tower and the Keeper of the Records.

THE COLLEGE OF ARMS AND COURT OF CHIVALRY: responsible for checking number and entitlement of gentry: directed by the Earl Marshal, a Lieutenant, the Garter King of Arms, the Clarenceux King of Arms, the Norroy King of Arms, etc.

CENTRAL GOVERNMENT, 1603–89: GLOSSARY OF TERMS

ADDLED PARLIAMENT, 1614: called by James I, on Bacon's advice, to secure financial aid; met between 5 April and 7 June. The failure of the 'Undertakers' to ensure the success of favourable candidates by tampering with the elections led to the return of a hostile Commons dominated by Phelips, Hakewill, Sandys, Wentworth, Eliot and Pym; in the face of vociferous complaints against impositions, monopolies, deprived clergy, undertakers etc., James dissolved Parliament before it had achieved anything.

AGREEMENT OF THE PEOPLE, 1647: a statement of Leveller views drawn up by representatives of the army's regiments (known as Agitators) and presented to the Army Council at the Putney Debates (28 October). It proposed (1) dissolution of the present parliament on 30 September 1648; (2) equal electoral areas; (3) biennial parliaments; (4) sovereignty of the Commons; (5) freedom of conscience in religion; (6) equality of all citizens before the laws; and (7) an end to impressment for military service. It was amended by the Army Council and presented to the Rump (January 1649).

APOLOGY OF THE COMMONS, 1604: a statement made by the Commons in June 1604 (called, in full, the Form of Apology and Satisfaction), but never formally presented to James I. Reaffirmed Parliament's rights to free speech, freedom from arrest and free elections – privileges which were of right, not of grace; the King should have no power to make alterations in religion without the consent of Parliament.

BAREBONES PARLIAMENT, the PARLIAMENT OF THE SAINTS, NOMINATED PARLIAMENT or LITTLE PARLIAMENT, 1653: so called after one of its members, Praise-God Barebones. Following the dismissal of the Rump, Cromwell accepted Major-Gen. Harrison's advice to establish a 'godly' parliament (4 July 1653) 140 members were selected by the Council of Army Officers from lists submitted by Independent congregations, throughout the country; their reckless targets for reform, including the law and tithes, quickly alienated the moderates, who met early one morning to dissolve themselves (12 December 1653).

BATE'S CASE, 1606: John Bate, a merchant, was imprisoned after refusing to pay the imposition on currants; Chief Baron Fleming, in giving judgement for the Crown in the Court of the Exchequer, stressed the King's right to levy duty on any merchandise for the purpose of controlling trade, but not for the purpose of increasing taxation.

BILL OF RIGHTS, 1689: contained the clauses submitted for acceptance by William and Mary in the Declaration of Rights; the Bill further stipulated that the throne must only be occupied by a Protestant; that the succession was to rest with (1) the heirs of Mary, (2) Anne and her heirs; that subjects were to take an oath of allegiance to the new rulers.

BILLETING: the system, used extensively by Charles, I, of accommodating troops with private citizens, who were usually unwilling and often unpaid; this caused great resentment and frequent disturbances, resulting in the imposition of martial law in those areas affected (especially in 1627-8, after the return of the unsuccessful expedition to Rhé). The practice was condemned in the Petition of Right (1628) and made illegal (1679), but was revived by Charles II and James II; again made illegal in the Bill of Rights (1689).

BLOODY ASSIZES, September 1685: Judge Jeffreys, the Lord Chief Justice, and four other judges on the Western Circuit tried those implicated in Monmouth's Rebellion; the trials, noted for their brutality and lack of justice, condemned an estimated 320 people to death and a further 800 to transportation to Barbados.

BOOK OF ORDERS, 1631: a scheme of eight orders introduced by Charles I, for the supervision of local government. Once a month, justices of the peace were to meet singly in petty sessions in each hundred to check on the operation of the poor law and the state of vagabondage; this information would be passed on first to the sheriff, then to the Assize judges and then to a special county commission of the Privy Council. A proclamation of 1632 ordered the gentry to leave their houses in London and return to their counties to assist with local government and the protection of their tenants.

BOOK OF RATES, 1608: issued by the Lord Treasurer, Robert Cecil, Earl of Salisbury, following the favourable ruling in Bate's Case (1606). After consultation with merchants, impositions were now extended to most imports (except food, ship's stores and munitions) and the rates increased; Cecil's aim was to increase the non-Parliamentary income of the Crown by an estimated yield of £70,000. Bitterly opposed by Parliament when it reassembled in 1610.

BOOK OF SPORTS, 1633: puritan pressure to maintain strict observance of the Sabbath had resulted in an attempt by Lancashire magistrates, in 1617, to suppress Morris dancing and other sports after the service on Sundays; James I thereupon issued a declaration legalising these recreations and ordered it to be read from the pulpit throughout the country (1618). An attempt by Puritans in Somerset to ban church ales, wakes and other such celebrations on Sundays (1633) caused Charles I to reissue the Book of Sports, as it was called, and to reorder its proclamation from the pulpits. This bitterly offended the Puritan conscience. Clergy who refused were removed from their livings.

BYE PLOT, 1603; a scheme, designed by a Roman Catholic priest named William Watson, to kidnap James I and compel him to redress grievances; betrayed to the Council by a Jesuit. The conspirators were tried with organisers of the Main Plot; Watson was executed.

CABAL, 1667–73; Charles II's inner group or ministers – Clifford, Arlington, Buckingham, Ashley-Cooper, Lauderdale – appointed after Clarendon's fall; divided by personal rivalry, they favoured toleration, encouraged English trade and opposed the Dutch. The Cabal collapsed through Parliamentary resistance to the Declaration of Indulgence (1672) and the French Alliance (1670).

CASE OF THE ARMY TRULY STATED, 1647: the first of the two documents drawn up in October by Levellers in the army and drafted by John Lilburne; it demanded payment of arrears, war indemnity, biennial parliaments elected by all free-born males over twenty-one, an end to the present parliament, sovereignty of the people (with the House of Commons as the only legislative body) and the removal of social grievances (including the oppressive excise and its replacement with a duty on foreign goods).

CAVALIER PARLIAMENT, 1661: met in May, after elections had returned a huge royalist majority; contained only sixty Presbyterians/Independents and no Irish or Scottish MPs. Finally dissolved in 1679.

CESSATION, 1643: an agreement made (15 September) by the Marquess of Ormonde, on behalf of Charles I, with the Irish Catholic rebels; this provided for a year's suspension of hostilities, pending fuller negotiations and a permanent settlement. The immediate effect of this was to release the King's English army in Ireland, which had been fighting the rebels, for service against Parliament. Many people bitterly complained that Charles was employing Irish Papists to fight for his cause; but, although the rebels granted him £30,000, they refused to send their own forces to England.

CLARENDON CODE, 1661–5: a series of four Acts, passed by the Cavalier Parliament, to check the influence of nonconformists; consisted of the Corporation Act (1661), the Act of uniformity (1662), the Conventicle Act (1664) and the Five Mile Act (1665); named after the Chancellor, Clarendon, although not drafted or even entirely approved by him.

COMMITTEE OF BOTH KINGDOMS, 1644: set up (16 February) as a result of the agreement between Parliament and the Scots in 1643 (i.e. the Solemn League and Covenant), it was composed of fourteen members of the Commons, seven members of the Lords and four Scottish commissioners, and its function was to direct the joint war effort. It was replaced in 1648 by the Derby House Committee.

COMMONWEALTH: after abolishing the monarchy (17 March 1649) and the

House of Lords (19 March) the Rump went on to declare England a 'Commonwealth and Free State' (19 May). The new republic was to be governed by the Rump, with a Council of State of forty-one members chosen by them; the first President of the Council was John Bradshaw. The Commonwealth ended after Cromwell's dismissal of the Rump (20 April 1653) and of its successor, the Barebones Parliament (12 December). It was replaced by the Protectorate, established on 16 December 1653 by the Instrument of Government.

COVENTICLE ACT, 1664: aimed to prevent ejected clergy from holding their own separate services with members of their previous congregations; prohibited religious meetings of more than five people (except families) which did not conform to Prayer Book regulations.

CONVENTION PARLIAMENT, 1660: met (25 April), after the dissolution of the Long Parliament, to work out a settlement; resolved that the government should be by King, Lords and Commons and that Charles II had been King 'by inherent birthright' since 1649; invited Charles to resume the throne; confirmed the legislation passed in 1641; dissolved on 9 December.

CONVENTION PARLIAMENT, 1689: summoned by William of Orange and, therefore, not strictly speaking a 'parliament'; met (22 January) and declared that James II, by breaking the original contract between King and people and by fleeing abroad, had abdicated; the vacant throne was offered jointly to William and Mary on their acceptance of the Declaration of Rights (formerly undertaken, 23 February); the Convention also passed the Mutiny Act, the Toleration Act and the Bill of Rights.

CORPORATION ACT, 1661: passed by the Cavalier Parliament in an attempt to exclude Presbyterians, Roman Catholics and other dissenters from membership of corporations, thus helping to ensure the return of Anglicans to Parliament; all office-holders in boroughs were to renounce the Covenant, swear oaths of allegiance, non-resistance and supremacy, and receive the sacrament of the Church of England.

DARNEL'S CASE, 1627: see Five Knights' Case.

DECLARATION OF BREDA, 1660: issued by Charles II from Breda for the Convention of Parliament (4 April) on the advice of Monck, and drafted by Hyde; promised indemnity and pardon to former enemies (apart from those excepted by Parliament), arrears of pay for the army, religious toleration and a land settlement to safeguard earlier purchases of delinquents' estates; each clause to be ratified by Parliament, thus making it responsible if promises were not fulfilled.

DECLARATION OF RIGHTS, 1689: outlined the conditions to which William and Mary were to agree before being offered the throne – i.e. acceptance of Parliamentary freedom of speech, free elections and freedom to petition the King, and rejection of ecclesiastical courts, standing armies in peacetime (without Parliament's permission), the suspending power, the dispensing power ('as it hath been assumed and exercised of late'), excessive fines and the levying of unauthorised taxes. Having accepted these terms, William and Mary were then proclaimed King and Queen (23 February). The Declaration was later formed into a Bill of Rights.

DECLARATIONS OF INDULGENCE, 1662, 1672, 1687, 1688: the 1662 Declaration was a promise by Charles II to remove the laws against nonconformists; Parliament rejected the idea. The 1672 Declaration suspended the penal laws, and allowed Protestant dissenters freedom to worship in public and Roman Catholics freedom in private. It was withdrawn on Parliament's objection and was quickly followed by the Test Act (1673). The 1687 Declaration by James II suspended all penal laws and granted freedom to worship in public to both Protestant dissenters and Roman Catholics alike. The 1688 Declaration repeated the terms of 1687 with the injunction that it was to be read in churches; the ensuing protest by clergy led to the trial of seven bishops (*see* Seven Bishops' Case).

DERBY HOUSE COMMITTEE: established by Parliament (January 1648) to take over direction of all military affairs from the Committee of Both Kingdoms. This resulted from Charles I's engagement with the Scots. The Committee, which met at Derby House in London, now consisted entirely of English representatives.

DIGGERS (or TRUE LEVELLERS): a small party of radicals, who set up an agricultural community on St George's Hill in Surrey; led by Winstanley and Everard, they believed that social revolution was the basis on which political revolution should be secured, that the welfare of the masses was of paramount importance and that the land should be given back to the people; their ideas of economic equality were expressed in Winstanley's book *Law of Freedom*. Reluctant to use physical violence, their opposition to the Rump was quickly crushed – their huts were destroyed, their cattle confiscated and their community dispersed.

DISPENSING POWER: the use of the royal prerogative to dispense with a law for the benefit of a particular person. James II granted dispensations from the Test Act to allow certain Catholics to hold high office – e.g. Sir Edward Hales (Governor of Dover), the Earl of Tyrconnell (Lord Lieutenant of Ireland) and Sir Roger Strickland (Commander of the Fleet). The dispensing power 'as it hath been assumed and exercised of late' was made illegal in the Bill of Rights (1689).

DIVINE RIGHT OF KINGS: the theory that Kings were appointed by and, therefore, only answerable to God for their actions. It was advocated strongly by James I in his writings and speeches (e.g. *True Law of Free Monarchies*, 1598), but was finally rejected in England by the Glorious Revolution and the Bill of Rights (1688–9).

'EIKON BASILIKE' (or *The Pourtraicture of His Sacred Majestie in His Solitudes and Sufferings*, 1649): this document was in circulation shortly after the execution of Charles I and was thought to be the work of the King, expressing 'the private reflections of my conscience, and my most impartial thoughts'. Although its real authorship remains a mystery, it has been closely associated with John Gauden, later Bishop of Exeter. Widely circulated, with translation in several languages, the book helped to create the legend of the martyred King; Council of State, unable to suppress its publication, countered by persuading Milton to write an answer to it, the *Eikonoklastes*, or 'Image-Breaker'.

ELEVEN YEARS' TYRANNY: Charles I's 'Personal Rule' or government without Parliament (10 March 1629 to 13 April 1640); it was characterised by the raising of money by disputed methods (*see also* Forced knighthood, Monopolies, Enlargement of royal forests, Ship Money, Forced loans), by the High Church policies of Archbishop Laud and by Strafford's policy of Thorough in Ireland.

ENGAGEMENT, 1647: fearing for his own safety, Charles I fled from the army's custody at Hampton Court (12 November) to Carisbrooke Castle on the Isle of Wight; from there he continued to intrigue with the Scots until a secret Engagement was signed on 26 December. It was agreed that the King should establish Presbyterianism for a trial period of three years, that the two kingdoms should be united and that the Scots would forcibly disband the English army, suppress the Independent sects and restore Charles to the throne. Parliament immediately passed a Vote of No Address; the Second Civil War became inevitable.

'ENGLAND'S NEW CHAINS DISCOVERED', 1649: a pamphlet attacking the policies of the Rump, written by John Lilburne (26 February).

EXCLUSION BILLS, 1679, 1680, 1681: Shaftesbury's 'Country Party' of Whig opponents to the court of Charles II won the elections of 1679, pledging themselves to exclude the Roman Catholic James, Duke of York, from the succession. The first Exclusion Bill failed when the King dissolved Parliament (July 1679); the second Bill passed the Commons, but was rejected by the Lords by sixty-three votes to thirty (October 1680); the third Bill, introduced to the Oxford Parliament, brought about its immediate dissolution (April 1681). Shaftesbury made the mistake of advocating James, Duke of Monmouth (Charles II's illegitimate son), as his candidate for the throne.

EXECUTION OF CHARLES I, 1649: took place on Tuesday 30 January at 2 p.m. outside the Banqueting House in Whitehall; he was accompanied to the scaffold by Bishop Juxon, Colonel Tomlinson, etc. He made a short speech in which he claimed that he was a martyr for the people, whose 'liberty and freedom consists in having of government', not in 'having a share in government'; 'a subject and a sovereign', he said, 'are clean different things'. The King's body was later embalmed and buried in St George's Chapel, Windsor.

FIFTH MONARCHY MEN: a Puritan sect who believed that the 'Saints' should take over government to prepare for the rule on earth of Jesus Christ himself; ideas were based on Nebuchadnezzar's dream, which prophesied the collapse of four kingdoms before the 'fifth monarchy' appeared. Their greatest success was the establishment of the Barebones Parliament, or the Parliament of the Saints, 1653. After its dissolution, they became bitter enemies of Cromwell, planning an abortive rising under Thomas Venner (April 1657); also opposed to the Restoration, they staged an armed rising in London (6 January 1661), which was firmly crushed. Their most influential figure was Major-Gen. Thomas Harrison.

FIVE KNIGHTS' CASE, 1627: to pay for the war against France, Charles I had imposed a forced loan amounting to five subsidies (£350,000); about eighty gentry were imprisoned on command of the King for refusing to pay. Five of these (Darnel, Erle, Hevingham, Hampden and Corbet) brought an action against the Crown before the King's Bench; they contended that they should either be charged with a specific offence or released on bail. When Lord Chief Justice Hyde ruled that they could not be released, it was generally interpreted that the judges had accepted the legality both of the loan and of indefinite imprisonment at the King's command. They were released in 1628.

FIVE MEMBERS, 1642: Charles I, angered by the threat of impeachment against the Queen, attempted to impeach five members of the Commons (Pym, Holles, Hampden, Strode and Haslerig) and Lord Mandeville, who were charged with high treason. The House of Lords refused to order their arrest (3 January) and immediately set up a committee to investigate the legality of the King's action . Charles unsuccessfully sent a sergeant-at-arms to arrest the five members in the Commons. Next day, urged on by the Queen and accompanied by 300 troops, the King went down to the Commons to arrest them himself; but the five members had escaped by boat into the City of London, whose Council was now under Puritan control. They returned to Parliament, amid great rejoicing, on 11 January.

FIVE MILE ACT, 1665: nonconformist clergy were forbidden to come within five miles of a corporate town or a place where they had previously been employed as ministers; they were also forbidden to teach.

FORCED KNIGHTHOOD: a device used by Charles I, during the Eleven Years' Tyranny, to raise money. A commission was appointed in January 1630 to compound with those holding land worth £40 per annum who had failed to take up knighthood at the King's coronation (according to feudal custom); £165,000 was raised by this process (1630–5). The device was made illegal by Parliament in 1641.

FORCED LOANS (or BENEVOLENCES): a method used by the Crown to raise money from wealthy subjects for emergencies, especially war; most Tudor monarchs had taken such levies, as did James I. The loans imposed by Charles I in 1626 and 1627, however, caused considerable opposition and resulted in the Five Knights' Case. Another levy was taken in 1640, in spite of the protest that the Commons made against forced loans in the Petition of Right (1628).

GODDEN V. HALES, 1686: Sir Edward Hales, a Roman Catholic and

Governor of Dover, was sued by his servant Godden for failure to take the oaths and sacrament as specified in the Test Act. Eleven out of twelve Appeal Judges on the King's Bench upheld the King's right to grant dispensations to particular people. Hales was later made Governor of the Tower of London and Master of the Ordnance.

GOLDSMITH'S HALL COMMITTEE, 1644: in March 1643, a Parliamentary ordinance had ordered the sequestration of the estates of 'notorious Delinquents'; local committees were established to undertake this confiscation and management of royalist property. From September 1644 the Goldsmith's Hall Committee in London, under its Chairman, John Ashe, began to compound with royalists for the return of their estates (i.e. to impose a fine, which was normally one-tenth, one-sixth or one-third of the value of their estates, but could extend to two-thirds). In 1650 the Committee was replaced by seven professional Compounding Commissioners.

GOODWIN V. FORTESCUE, 1604: the election of Sir Frances Goodwin, an outlaw, for Buckinghamshire had been declared void by the Court of Chancery. Although Sir John Fortescue had won the by-election, the Commons instructed Goodwin to take his seat. This resulted in the first clash over the Crown's prerogative and the privilege of the Commons. James claimed that all privileges were derived from him and that the Commons should not interfere with returns. Finally, however, he accepted their right to be arbiters of disputed elections.

GRAND REMONSTRANCE, 1641: an address to the King, drawn up by Pym, but intended as an appeal to the country, it listed the King's misdeeds and the recent reforms of the Long Parliament; it demanded that the King should only appoint ministers approved by Parliament and that the Church should be reformed along lines suggested by an Assembly of Divines. The Remonstrance, fiercely debated in the Commons, was passed by only 159 votes to 148 (22 November); presented to Charles I on 1 December, it served to unite many moderates behind the King.

GREAT CONTRACT, 1610: designed by Lord Salisbury, the Treasurer, to grant the King regular taxation worth £200,000 per annum (in the form of land tax or excise) in return for his surrender of feudal rights (especially purveyance and wardship) and impositions (which would be controlled henceforth by statute). Negotiations broke down in the face of renewed disputes over religion (November). Parliament was dissolved before agreement could be reached (February 1611).

GUNPOWDER PLOT, 1605: a scheme, organised by Robert Catesby, to blow up Parliament at the King's opening of it. His accomplices, Tresham, Digby and Rookwood, were to lead a Catholic rising in the ensuing chaos. They were betrayed to Cecil by Lord Monteagle, who had been unwisely informed by Tresham; Guido Fawkes, who was to light the fuse to gunpowder stored beneath the House of Lords, was arrested on the spot. The failure of the plot led to the execution of the conspirators and the strict enforcement of the Penal Laws against Roman Catholics.

HABEAS CORPUS AMENDMENT ACT, 1679: declared illegal various devices, which had enabled officers of the Crown to evade the implications of the *Habeas Corpus* writ – i.e. that a person could not be imprisoned indefinitely without being properly charged in a court of law; regarded as a vital safeguard to personal liberty against intrusions by the royal prerogative.

HAMPDEN'S CASE, 1637: the annual levy of ship money (1634–40) and its extension to the inland counties (1635), caused many to fear that the government would use it as a permanent tax. A group of opponents, led by Lord Saye and Sele, decided to fight a test case through John Hampden, who refused to pay a tax of 20s; seven out of twelve judges in the Exchequer of Pleas ruled that the King had the right, in times of danger, to levy a tax for the defence of the country and that the King had the sole right to decide when danger existed. Many people became alarmed that this was a precedent for unlimited taxation. (*See also* Ship money.)

HAMPTON COURT CONFERENCE, 1604: called by James I in response to the Millennary Petition. John Reynolds and three Puritan ministers disputed with Archbishop Whitgift and eight bishops in the presence of the King and his Council. The Puritan case for moderate reform was cut short by the King's misunderstanding of their use of the word 'presbytery'. He, fearing a challenge to his supremacy in the Church, insisted there should be 'one doctrine and one discipline, one religion in substance and in ceremony'; they must conform, or he would 'harry them out of the land'.

HEADS OF PROPOSALS, 1647: strained relations between Parliament and the army caused army leaders to attempt direct settlement negotiations with Charles I. These proposals, drawn up chiefly by Henry Ireton and approved by the Army Council, suggested (1) a definite end to the Long Parliament; (2) biennial parliaments thereafter lasting at least 120 days, with control over the army and navy for ten years; (3) equal electoral areas, free elections and reform of the franchise; (4) a Council of State to conduct foreign policy for seven years; (5) removal of coercive powers from bishops; (6) repeal of acts enforcing the use of the Prayer Book; (7) end of insistence on the Covenant; (8) disqualification of royalists from state office for five years; and (9) grant of easy terms of composition to royalists for their delinquency. The King refused.

HUMBLE PETITION, 1648: a comprehensive statement of Leveller views, drafted by Lilburne in the form of a petition to Parliament from the citizens of London (11 September). It stated that the Commons were 'the supreme authority of England' and that 'the King was but at most the chief public officer of this Kingdom, and accountable to the House'; it complained that Parliament had attempted to make a treaty with the King after the Second Civil War; and it listed all the unfulfilled expectations that the Levellers had of the present Parliament.

HUMBLE PETITION AND ADVICE, 1657: the original petition, presented to Cromwell on 31 March 1657, begged the Protector to accept the Crown and to re-establish the House of Lords in an attempt to end arbitrary rule and to restore the familiar constitution; Lambert, Fleetwood, Desborough and other senior officers strongly opposed this. Cromwell finally rejected the Kingship on 8 May for the sake of the common soldier, the 'people of God', instead. He accepted the amended petition (25 May), which gave him the right to nominate his successor and the members of an Upper House; Parliament, which was to meet at least once every three years, had greater control over the membership of the Council and absolute control over the admission or exclusion of elected members.

IMPEACHMENT: a method of bringing a person to face criminal charges in a trial before the House of Lords, on a petition from the Commons. These powers, last used in 1459, were revived in 1621 to bring ministers and others in high places to justice, where ordinary courts could not be trusted. Mitchell, Mompesson and Bacon were impeached in 1621, Cranfield in 1624, Buckingham in 1626, Strafford and Laud in 1640; by then the process was becoming abused through its use against countless minor offenders.

IMPOSITIONS: the 'New Impositions' or new import duties were based on the Crown's traditional right to impose import duties for the regulation of trade and the protection of home industry. Elizabeth I had introduced a levy on currants and tobacco (1601). James I extended this in 1608 to most imports; after Parliament's protests in 1610, James revised the tax so that its greatest weight fell on foreign merchants. (*See also* Bate's Case *and the* Book of Rates.)

INDEMNITY AND OBLIVION, ACT OF, 1660: passed by the Convention Parliament to express one of the clauses contained in the Declaration of Breda; a general pardon granted to all those involved in the Civil War or later republican governments, except fifty named persons. Sir Henry Vane and thirteen regicides were executed.

INDEPENDENTS: the collective name given to religious sects most prominent during the civil War and Interregnum. In religion, they believed in freedom of conscience and freedom of congregations to choose their own forms of worship; they opposed the organisation of Anglican bishops, as well as that of the Presbyterians. The most prominent sects were the Baptists and the Congregationalists. Politically, the Independents were usually identified with the 'war party; which stood for vigorous prosecution of the war and the defeat of the King; they were also responsible for Pride's Purge and the trial of Charles I. Although represented in the Long Parliament, their main strength was in the army.

INSTRUMENT OF GOVERNMENT, 1653: England's first written constitution, drafted by John Lambert and the Council of Officers after the failure of the Barebones Parliament. Published on 16 December, when Cromwell was installed as Lord Protector, it provided for a Lord Protector, triennial parliaments (sitting for at least five months) reform of the franchise and electoral areas, exclusion of royalists from the first four parliaments and a Council of State. The protector was granted £200,000 per annum for civil administration and a further sum for an army of 30,000, and he was given a veto on any attempt to change the Instrument. Parliament, consisting of 460 MPs, was first to meet on 3 September 1654. The Lord Protector could issue ordinance when Parliament was not in session. Freedom of worship was granted, except to papists and prelatists.

INTERREGNUM: the period in English history between the execution of Charles I (30 January 1649) and the restoration of Charles II (8 May 1660); consisting of the Commonwealth (19 May 1649 to 16 December 1653) and the Protectorate (to 25 May 1659).

INVITATION TO WILLIAM OF ORANGE, 1688: following the trial of the Seven Bishops (June) and the birth of a son to James II's Catholic Queen, Mary of Modena (1 July), an invitation was sent to William of Orange requesting his intervention; it was carried over to Holland by Arthur Herbert (late Vice-Admiral) and signed by Russell, Devonshire and Henry Sidney (Whigs), Danby and Bishop Compton (Tories), Lumley and Shrewsbury (ex-Catholics). William accepted, and landed at Torbay (15 November).

KILLING NO MURDER', 1657: A Leveller pamphlet calling for the death of the apostate, Oliver Cromwell.

LEVELLERS: a party of extreme radicals, whose power was based initially on the London mob. Led by John Lilburne, John Wildman, Col. Rainborough etc., they gradually extended their influence to the army in 1647; their political programme, outlined in their documents *The Case of the Army Truly Stated*, *The Agreement of the People* and *The Humble Petition*, demand social reform, sovereignty of the people, manhood suffrage, abolition of the monarchy and House of Lords, and liberty of conscience and equality before the law. Leveller Agitators, elected from each regiment, debated these beliefs with Cromwell and other senior officers in the Putney Debates; alarmed at Cromwell's negotiations with the King (1647), some Leveller regiments mutinied at Ware (15 November), but were crushed. The influence of the Levellers declined after the execution of the King in 1649.

LICENSING ACT, 1662: set up censorship to prevent heretical and seditious writings; master printers were to be reduced to twenty; books were not to be published without a licence from the appropriate censor; printing presses were only to be authorised in Oxford, Cambridge, London and York.

LONG PARLIAMENT, 1640: summoned by Charles I on 3 November 1640 to raise money to free the North from the Scottish army, sat throughout the Civil War (though without its royalist members). Its Presbyterian members were excluded in Pride's Purge, organised by the Independent army officers on 6 December 1648. The remnant or Rump made arrangements for Charles I's trial and execution, thereafter establishing the Commonwealth (19 May 1649). The

Rump was forcibly ejected by Cromwell (20 April 1653), but was recalled after Richard Cromwell's failure as Protector (7 May 1659). General Monck gained the reinstatement of those members excluded in Pride's Purge (21 February 1660). Having made arrangements for the Convention Parliament, the Long Parliament finally dissolved itself (16 March 1660).

MAIN PLOT, 1603: a scheme, designed by Lord Cobham, to overthrow James I and set up Lady Arabella Stuart (a descendant of Mary Tudor and the Earl of Angus). Cobham, who turned King's evidence, implicated Walter Raleigh, an outspoken critic of the new government. Conspirators were tried with the organisers of the Bye Plot; some were executed, some imprisoned; Raleigh was reprieved after being condemned to death.

MAJOR-GENERALS: following the failure of his first Protectorate parliament (dissolved 22 January 1655) and the outbreak of Penruddock's Rising, Cromwell decided on direct rule by the army. The country was divided into ten (later eleven) areas, each controlled by a major-general with a cavalry-militia. The cost was raised by a 'decimation tax' on royalists (i.e. a 10 per cent levy on land). The Major-Generals were responsible for collecting the decimation, keeping law and order, searching out plots and suppressing vice and encouraging virtue. The men chosen were Lambert, Worsley, Berry, Desborough, Goffe, Kelsey, Boteler, Fleetwood, Whalley, Skippon and Barkstead; unpopular with local justices and gentry, they worked efficiently and protected the interests of the poorer people. Their rule ended in the autumn of 1656.

MARCH ON LONDON, 1647: on 29 May the army, under Parliament's threat of disbandment without the settlement of pay arrears, mutinied; the King was captured from Holmby House (4 June). The Declaration of the Army, outlining its political programme, was rejected by the Presbyterian majority in Parliament. The army then moved towards London, camping first at St Albans and then on Hounslow Heath (with Cromwell's cavalry in Hyde Park). Under this pressure, Denzil Holles and ten other Presbyterian members withdrew from Parliament.

MARTIAL LAW: the maintenance of law and order by the armed forces during periods of civil confusion, when regular law courts had been suspended by royal proclamation. Became a grievance in 1627–8, when Charles I imposed martial law on certain areas, following disturbances caused by billeting of soldiers returning from the Rhé expedition. The practice was condemned in the Petition of Right (1628).

MEAL TUB PLOT, 1679: designed to discredit Presbyterians and Whigs, this 'plot' to obstruct the Duke of York's succession to the throne was revealed by Thomas Dangerfield. The evidence had, allegedly, been found under a meal tub belonging to Mrs Cellier; it was soon shown to be false.

MILITIA ACTS, 1662–3: command of the militia had been given to the King (1661); dominance locally was regained by the landowners. Lord lieutenants were required to recruit cavalry and infantry from the ranks of the wealthier citizens; substitutes were permitted, but service could be demanded anywhere in the country.

MILITIA BILL, 1642: aimed to give Parliament control of the county trained bands by assuming the power to nominate the lord lieutenant for each county. Passed the Commons (31 January); the Lords associated themselves with it by agreeing to a list of lord lieutenants; Charles I refused his assent. The two Houses therefore passed the Militia Ordinance (5 March), which gave the measure the force of law without the King's assent; Charles retaliated with a proclamation (27 May) which forbade the militia to observe the ordinance.

MILLENNARY PETITION, 1603: a petition, claiming to represent the views of over a thousand ministers, presented to James I on his way to London; contained moderate Puritan demands for reform of certain Catholic practices in liturgy and worship – the sign of cross in baptism, the ring in marriage, bowing to the altar, the positioning and ornamentation of the altar, the wearing of the cap and surplice, etc. James summoned both Puritan ministers and Anglican bishops to the Hampton Court Conference to adjudicate on the issue.

MONMOUTH'S REBELLION, 1685: an attempt by James, Duke of Monmouth to seize the succession after the death of Charles II. Landing at Lyme Regis (11 June), he failed to take Bridport before advancing to Taunton, where he was proclaimed King. Disappointed at the poor response to his cause he was eventually defeated at Sedgemoor (6 July) by Feversham's army, captured near Ringwood (7 July) and executed on Tower Hill (15 July). Judge Jeffreys dealt with many of his accomplices in his 'Bloody Assizes'.

MONOPOLIES: the exclusive right, purchased by royal favour, to produce or sell specific merchandise, or to issue licences. They were extremely unpopular both inside and outside Parliament; but in spite of frequent protests, James I renewed the policy of granting patents of monopoly (1612). Monopolies for the manufacture of gold and silver thread and for the licensing of inns and ale-houses were granted to relatives of the Duke of Buckingham; two of them, Mitchell and Mompesson, were impeached by the Commons for extortion in 1621. The Monopolies Act, 1624, made monopolies illegal except for inventors, boroughs and trading companies. Charles I issued new monopolies (1632), but withdrew them later (1639).

NEW MODEL ARMY: established, at the suggestion of Waller and Cromwell, by ordinance (15 February 1645). Consisting of twelve infantry regiments, eleven cavalry regiments, a regiment of dragoons, two regiments of fusiliers, a company of pioneers and a powerful artillery, its total strength numbered 22,000. Although remnants of the armies of Waller, Essex and Manchester formed its nucleus, additional recruits were pressed into service through county quotas; the new army was more professional, well disciplined, regularly paid, better trained, properly equipped and more mobile. Sir Thomas Fairfax was appointed

Commander-in-Chief, with Philip Skippon as Commander of Infantry and Oliver Cromwell as Commander of Cavalry.

NEWPORT TREATY, 1648: after the ending of the Second Civil War, negotiations between the Presbyterian majority in Parliament and the King reopened at Newport, Isle of Wight (18 September), much to the anger of the army. Discussions broke down, however, over the question of religion.

NINETEEN PROPOSITIONS, 1642: delivered to Charles I at York on 1 June, they summarised Parliament's political demands; these, in effect, amounted to the seizure of sovereignty and included Parliamentary control of the appointment of Privy Councillors and officers of state, Parliamentary control of the education and marriage of the King's children, and Parliamentary control of Church reform and foreign policy. In addition the King was to sign the Militia Ordinance, to apply the laws against Roman Catholics and to hand over 'delinquents' to the justice of Parliament. Rejecting these proposals, Charles declined to surrender either his royal power or the Church of England.

OXFORD NEGOTIATIONS, 1643: Parliamentary commissioners (led by the Earl of Northumberland) visited the King in Oxford in March to put forward terms for a settlement – the abolition of episcopacy, the strict application of penal laws against Catholics and the punishment of leading royalists. Charles I countered with his own demands: the disbandment of all Parliament's forces, the handing over of all fortified places and the transfer of Parliament from Westminster to a neutral area, free from the pressure of the mob. The negotiations ended in deadlock.

PENRUDDOCK'S RISING, 1655: part of a plan for a general Royalist rising in England (8 March) to coincide with an invasion from Scotland and a landing by Charles II, supported by foreign troops. The rising, organised by the Sealed Knot and led by the Earl of Rochester, was a dismal failure, thanks to betrayals and the work of Thurloe's spies. The rising in the West, however, took place on 12 March, when 200 troops seized the Sheriff and Assize judges in Salisbury; led by Wagstaffe, Penruddock, Jones and Grove, the rebels failed to rally support for their cause and were finally caught at South Molton. Although Wagstaffe escaped, Penruddock, Jones and Grove were later executed. One result of the rising was the rule of the Major-Generals.

PETITION OF RIGHT, 1628: the four resolutions presented to Charles I by both Houses at the meeting of the new Parliament, before the granting of subsidies. These resolutions requested the King to reaffirm the old statutes which protected their rights and liberties and to redress their particular grievances: forced loans, arbitrary imprisonment, billeting and martial law. The King, in need of money, gave his assent to a Bill incorporating these resolutions (June 1628).

POPISH PLOT, 1678: rumours spread by Titus Oates and Israel Tonge of a Roman Catholic conspiracy, with French and Irish support, to massacre Protestants, burn down London, assassinate Charles II and enthrone James, Duke of York.

The ensuing panic resulted in the Test Act, the fall of Danby, the dissolution of the Cavalier Parliament, the rise of Shaftesbury's 'Country Party' and the introduction of Exclusion Bills to remove the Duke of York from the succession. In the meantime, Lord Chief Justice Scroggs and others had sentenced thirty-five men to death for treason and all Catholic recusants had been banned from within ten miles of London. The scare lasted until 1681, during which times Oates was maintained at public expense; he was later convicted of perjury.

PRIDE'S PURGE, 1648: angry at the attempt made by the Presbyterian majority in the Commons to reopen negotiations with Charles I (the Newport Treaty), army leaders ordered the removal of the King from Carisbrooke Castle to Hurst Castle – and later to London. Meanwhile, on 6 December, Colonel Pride, with a body of musketeers, 'purged' the Commons of 143 of its Presbyterian members, leaving a remnant or Rump of about fifty who were sympathetic to the army. The Rump immediately set up a court for the trial of the King.

PROPOSITIONS OF NEWCASTLE, 1646: nineteen clauses sent to the King in captivity with the Scots in Newcastle (14 July), outlining Parliament's terms for a settlement and a return to the throne. These demanded that he should take the Covenant, agree to the abolition of episcopacy and the reform of the Church, permit Parliament to control the army and foreign policy for twenty years and accept the punishment of his supporters. Charles I delayed his reply, but found the proposals totally unacceptable.

PROTECTORATE: established by the Instrument of Government (16 December 1653); government to consist of a Protector, a Council of State and the House of Commons. After the Humble Petition and Advice (25 May 1657), a Second Chamber was added and the Protector given the right to nominate his successor. The first Protectorate parliament met in 1654; the second in 1656–8. After Oliver Cromwell's death (3 September 1658), his son Richard succeeded, but later abdicated (25 May 1659).

PROTESTATION, 1621: the Commons attempted to reverse James I's foreign policy by advising him to declare war on Spain and find a Protestant wife for his son. James deeply resented this intrusion into the royal prerogative, which traditionally had exclusive control of foreign policy and royal marriages; he threatened to punish those who meddled with matters which did not concern them. The Commons angrily claimed their privileges of freedom of speech and on 18 December entered the Protestation in their Journal; their privileges and liberties were 'the ancient and undoubted birthright and inheritance of the subjects of England'. Parliament was dissolved, Coke and Phelips imprisoned – and James tore out the page from the Journal.

PUTNEY DEBATES, 1647: discussions, held in Putney church, by the Army Council (as envisaged by the Solemn Engagement, with two officers representatives and two Agitators from each regiment joining the general officers). The Leveller documents, *The Case of the Army Truly Stated* and *The Agreement of the*

People were debated for a fortnight (28 October to 8 November), revealing deep differences between the more conservative senior officers and the Levellers. At the end of the debates, the representatives were sent back to their regiments (8 November).

REGICIDES: the fifty-nine commissioners who signed the death warrant of Charles I (January 1649). Of these, twenty-nine were tried and convicted of treason (October 1660), being excepted by Parliament from the general amnesty in the Act of Indemnity and Oblivion; only thirteen, however, were executed. In addition, the bodies of Cromwell, Ireton and Bradshaw were exhumed for ceremonial hanging and quartering at Tyburn.

REMONSTRANCE OF THE ARMY, 1648: presented by the Council of Army Officers to Parliament (20 November); drafted by Ireton, it reflected Leveller views much more noticeably than earlier documents from the Council; it demanded the sovereignty of the people, payment of soldiers' arrears, the removal of all Presbyterians from Parliament and the trial of the King. It was rejected by Parliament, thus precipitating Pride's Purge.

RESTORATION, 1660: the Convention Parliament, after receiving the Declaration of Breda, invited back Charles II (entered London 29 May). The Restoration settlement gave the King the right to appoint ministers, to dissolve Parliament, to veto legislation, to command the forces and to conduct foreign policy; but he lost the right to raise taxes without Parliament's consent, to modify the law by proclamation, and to use the Courts of High Commission and Star Chamber.

ROOT AND BRANCH BILL, 1641: based on a petition of some 15,000 London citizens (11 December 1640) that episcopal government 'with all its dependencies, roots and branches', should be abolished. The debate on the petition (February 1641) revealed wide divisions of opinion over the question of bishops. The Root and Branch Bill was introduced into the Commons on 27 May 1641, proposing the abolition of bishops, deans and chapters and the establishment of joint commissions of laymen and clergy in each county to control church affairs. It was eventually dropped.

ROYAL FORESTS, ENLARGEMENT OF: a device, used by Charles I in the 1630s, to raise additional revenue by reviving the Crown's jurisdiction over forests. Large fines were imposed on people whose ancestors had encroached on the boundaries of royal forests, fixed in 1297 (i.e. the Forests of Epping, Dean, Rockingham and Waltham, and the New Forest). Great bitterness was caused: seventeen whole villages were now included in the Forest of Dean; Rockingham Forest increased from 6 square miles to 60; etc. In 1641 Parliament defined the legal limits of royal forest.

RUMP PARLIAMENT: on 6 December 1648, Pride's Purge removed Presbyterians and their adherents from the Commons, leaving a remnant of about fifty who were sympathetic to the army; this 'Rump', even with later additions, never exceeded 125. It established a Commonwealth (19 May 1649), after the abolition of the monarchy, and ruled, with a Council of State, until its removal by Cromwell (20 April 1653). It was recalled after Richard Cromwell's failure as Protector (7 May 1659).

RYE HOUSE PLOT, 1683: a plot to assassinate Charles II and James, Duke of York, on their return from the Newmarket Races (April); devised by Richard Rumbold and a group of 'lesser conspirators', who planned an ambush outside Rye House, near Hoddesdon. Foiled by the premature return of the royal party, following a serious fire in Newmarket. Conspirators were betrayed by Josiah Keeling; also implicated (unjustly) were the Council of Six – including the well known Whig Exclusionists Lord Grey, the Earl of Essex, Algernon Sydney, the Duke of Monmouth, Lord Russell and Lord Havard.

SAVOY CONFERENCE, April–July 1660: met at the Savoy Palace to discuss the Prayer Book in the light of Charles II's wishes for a comprehensive settlement, expressed in his Declaration on Ecclesiastical Affairs (1660). The twelve bishops and twelve Presbyterians who attended failed to reach agreement: the Savoy Liturgy and modifications to the Prayer Book put forward by the Presbyterians were rejected.

SELF-DENYING ORDINANCE, 1645: in the face of mounting criticism in Parliament of inefficient army commanders and their direction of the war (especially Cromwell's attack on the Earl of Manchester in December 1644), this ordinance of 3 April stipulated that all members of both Houses should resign every civil office or military command granted since 20 November 1640 within forty days; they might, however, be reappointed. This measure enabled the New Model Army to be officered by the best available commanders.

SEVEN BISHOPS' CASE, 1688: James II reissued his Declaration of Indulgence (May), ordering it to be read in all churches for two successive Sundays. Archbishop Sancroft and six bishops petitioned the King to withdraw his instructions in view of Parliament's declarations against the legality of his dispensing power. James ordered the prosecution of the bishops for seditious libel; they were acquitted amidst general rejoicing (30 June).

SHIP MONEY: in 1634 Charles I exercised his right to collect this tax from coastal towns and counties for protection against pirates and enemy shipping; in 1635 the tax was extended to inland counties and towns, which were assessed according to wealth and size. Levied for six successive years (1635–40) and yielding an average of £107,000 per annum, it met with increasing opposition. In 1639 only £43,417 was paid out of £214,000 assessed. (*See also* Hampden's Case.) Ship money made illegal in 1641.

SHIRLEY'S CASE, 1604: Sir Thomas Shirley, a Member of Parliament, had been arrested for debt and imprisoned in the Fleet; the Commons took up his case and gained royal assent for Bills which confirmed the members' privilege of freedom from arrest during sessions of Parliament (except for felony, treason or breach of the peace). The Warden of the Fleet was sent to the Tower; Shirley was freed.

SHORT PARLIAMENT, 1640: called by Charles I on 13 April, on the advice of Strafford, to secure supplies for the war against the Scots. Under the influence of John Pym, the Commons insisted on first discussing the infringement of their liberties and the recent abuse of the royal prerogative; they rejected the King's offer to surrender ship money for twelve subsidies and petitioned for a treaty with the Scots to enable full consideration of their grievances. Charles dissolved Parliament on 5 May.

SOLEMN ENGAGEMENT, 1647: threatened by Parliament's attempt at disbandment without pay arrears, the army mutinied (29 May) and staged a rendezvous at Newmarket. There the Solemn Engagement was unanimously adopted, pledging the troops to resist disbandment until satisfactory terms had been negotiated by a council (consisting of the general officers with two representative officers and two men from each regiment).

SOLEMN LEAGUE AND COVENANT, 1643: an alliance between the English Parliament and the Scots (25 September), engineered by Pym in the face of Royalist victories in the north and west. They agreed to preserve the Church of Scotland and to reform the Church of England and Ireland 'according to the Word of God, and the example of the best reformed Churches'; an assembly of divines was to work out a plan for organising the Church on Presbyterian lines; and in return for £30,000 per month the Scots were to send an army to fight for Parliament in the war, which would be directed by a Committee of Both Kingdoms.

STOP OF THE EXCHEQUER, 1672: in view of its serious debt (caused by the Cabal's unsound handling of public finance and the cost of the Dutch War), the government withheld interest on part of its outstanding loans from bankers, using the money to buy war supplies; this caused the bankruptcy of five City financiers, which resulted in a total loss of confidence. The government later restored what it had thus diverted, at 6 per cent interest.

SUSPENDING POWER: the use of the royal prerogative to suspend a particular law from operation. James II's Declaration of Indulgence (1687) suspended the penal laws against Roman Catholics and nonconformists, thus permitting them to practise their own religion freely; the Bill of Rights (1689) made illegal any application of the suspending power without Parliament's agreement.

TEST ACTS, 1673, 1678: in the 1673 Act all civil or military office-holders were required to receive the sacraments in accordance with the Anglican rite, to swear the oaths of supremacy and allegiance and to take a declaration against transubstantiation. The 1678 Act, passed against the background of the Popish Plot, banned Roman Catholics from sitting in Parliament (with the exemption of the Duke of York).

THOROUGH: the name given to a system of government which Strafford and Laud attempted to operate during the Eleven Years' Tyranny (1629–40). It was based on vigorous discipline, order and efficiency in the interests of King and state. These attitudes were ruthlessly applied by Strafford as President of the Council of the North (1628–33) and Lord Deputy of Ireland (1632–9), and by Laud, as Bishop of London (1628–33) and Archbishop of Canterbury (1633–45). The poor benefited from just application of the law, but others resented the high-handed use of the royal prerogative.

THREE RESOLUTIONS, 1629. In the face of renewed attacks in the Commons against Wentworth, Weston and the Arminians, Charles I ordered an adjournment of the spring session. Amid angry scenes, Eliot persuaded the Commons to lock out the King's bodyguard; then, with an unco-operative Speaker held down in his chair, the Three Resolutions were carried by acclamation against (1) innovation in religion or extension of Popery; (2) levying of unauthorised tunnage and poundage; (3) payment of unauthorised tunnage and poundage. Charles I immediately dissolved Parliament.

TRIAL OF CHARLES I, 1649: after Pride's Purge, the Rump formally decided on a trial of Charles I (2 January). An ordinance established a court of 135 commissioners (in spite of the opposition of the Lords); John Bradshaw was appointed as president of the court and John Cook as prosecutor. The trial, which opened in the Painted Chamber of Westminster Hall on 20 January lasted eight days; the charge was that the King had 'traitorously and maliciously levied war against the present Parliament, and the people therein represented'. Charles, refusing to acknowledge the authority of that court or the right of any court to try the King, declined to plead. He was sentenced to death (27 January) 'as a tyrant, traitor, murderer and public enemy'; the death warrant was signed by fifty-nine commissioners, after some persuasion.

TRIENNIAL ACT, 1641: passed by the Long Parliament and given reluctant assent by Charles I (16 February); obliged the King to meet Parliament for a session of at least fifty days every three years; also set up machinery for the automatic summoning of Parliament (through writs issued by the Lord Chancellor and the Lord Keeper) if the King should disregard the Act.

TRIENNIAL ACT, 1664: repealed the Act of 1641 (which established the procedure for calling a Parliament, if the King should fail to do so after three years); stated that Parliament should meet at least once every three years, but left it entirely to the King to ensure this.

TUNNAGE AND POUNDAGE: of medieval origin, tunnage was a tax on each imported tun of wine and poundage a tax of 3d. per £ value on all merchandise either imported or exported; traditionally granted by Parliament to sovereigns as subsidies for life (from the fifteenth century). Although Charles I's 1625 Parliament made the grant for one year only, he continued to collect it, much to Parliament's annoyance (see the Petition of Right, 1628, and the Three Resolutions, 1629). The Tunnage and Poundage Act (1641), granting the duties for two months, was renewed bimonthly to 1642. Tunnage and poundage were granted to Charles II for life (1661).

UNIFORMITY, ACT OF, 1662: passed in May to enforce use of the Prayer Book, recently revised by the Convocations, it required all clergy and schoolmasters to swear an oath agreeing to use the Prayer Book, denouncing rebellion and rejecting the Covenant. All clergy holding livings were to be properly ordained by a bishop or be ejected; all schoolmasters were to be licensed by a bishop. As a result, about 2000 clergy were ejected.

UXBRIDGE NEGOTIATIONS, January–February 1645: discussions for a settlement between the King's commissioners (led by the Duke of Richmond), Parliament's commissioners (led by Vane and St John) and the Scots' commissioners (led by Chancellor Loudoun) at Uxbridge. The terms of the so-called Uxbridge Treaty were to include the establishment of a Presbyterian church system, control of the forces by a commission appointed by Parliament, control of foreign and Irish affairs by Parliament, and the punishment of named leading royalists. Charles I refused to surrender 'the Church, my crown and my friends', and the negotiations broke up in deadlock (22 February).

VOTE OF NO ADDRESSES, 1648: passed by the Long Parliament (17 January) on hearing about the likelihood of an Engagement between the King and the Scots. No further offers of settlement were to be made to Charles I; the Committee of Both Kingdoms was to be replaced by the Derby House Committee. The Vote was repealed in September, when Parliament recommenced negotiations, after the ending of the Second Civil War.

WESTMINSTER ASSEMBLY, 1643–9: established by an ordinance of the Long Parliament to discuss matters of liturgy, discipline and government of the Church of England, as referred to it by Parliament. Consisting of 120 clergy and thirty laity, including members of both Houses, it was joined by eight Scottish commissioners; it eventually issued the Directory (to replace the Prayer Book) and the Confession of Faith, together with a plan for Presbyterian government.

GLOSSARY OF LEGAL TERMS

ADMIRALTY, COURT OF: from later medieval times, this exercised jurisdiction over the activities of the mercantile class, including foreign traders. The court increased its strength under the Tudors, and gained a near monopoly in all important commercial cases. A campaign by common law lawyers against the power of this royal prerogative court extended into the seventeenth century.

ARCHES, COURT OF: in medieval ecclesiastical jurisdiction, appeals were passed to the consistory courts of the archbishops, in Canterbury known as the Court of Arches. These survived the Reformation in modified form.

The Ecclesiastical Commission Act of 1661 restored all church courts, except the High Commission, but their coercive powers over the laity gradually disappeared.

ASSIZES: a medieval term of judicial procedure, which in time was used to denote the periodical sittings of professional judges of the High Court at the various towns they visit on their circuits. This helped to enforce central government throughout the kingdom.

CHANCERY, COURT OF: the consistory court of the Archbishop of York, which heard appeals from the church courts. The institution was restored in 1661. (*See* Court of Arches.)

COMMON PLEAS, COURT OF: this developed in the 13th century, independent from king and council, to deal with civil suits between subjects. It became the busiest and slowest of the common law courts, losing many of its cases to the King's Bench.

COUNCIL OF THE MARCHES OF WALES: originally formed in the fifteenth century, revived and strengthened in Tudor times, and its powers defined in 1543, this exercised judicial and administrative authority in Wales and the Marches (Gloucester, Worcester, Hereford and Shropshire).

Abolished along with the prerogative courts in 1641, by the Long Parliament, the Council was re-established after the Restoration but disappeared again in 1689.

COUNCIL OF THE NORTH: created in the fifteenth century, and a permanent body from 1537, as a court based at York to deal with the special problems of law and order in the border counties of York, Durham, Northumberland, Cumberland and Westmorland. Retained long after achieving its original purpose, the council was dominated by crown-appointed lawyers and clerics who used Star Chamber techniques to exercise authority. Attacked by upholders of common law after 1600, identified as an instrument of arbitrary rule and increasingly unpopular, it was also weakened by internal scandals. The Earl of Strafford, Viscount Wentworth, used the Council when he was president (1628–31) for his policy of 'Thorough', by which loyalty to king and country, order and rule of law were sought through misuse of the royal prerogative. In 1641 the Long Parliament abolished the council.

DELEGATES, HIGH COURT OF: an appeal court for civil and canon law, first set up by the king in 1534 to hear appeals from church courts previously sent to Rome. It was not a permanent institution, but judges were appointed to each case by special commission.

EXCHEQUER: orginally the crown's financial department, which in the middle ages expanded to assume judicial responsibilities. In 1579 the Court of Exchequer (or Exchequer of Pleas) became formally the common law court dealing with financial cases.

The Court of Exchequer Chamber was a separate device, both from 1585 a court of appeal from the King's Bench and from 1589 a body to investigate complaints about the workings of the Court of Exchequer.

HIGH COMMISSION, COURT OF: a Tudor device with powers delegated by the

Crown as Supreme Head of the Church. The ecclesiastical courts survived the Reformation, but rights of appeal now lay not to the Pope but to the Crown, as represented more and more by the High Commission, which became a formal court after about 1580.

In 1641 the Long Parliament abolished the court which had become increasingly hated by champions of common law and by the Puritans. Its powers covered heresy, recusancy, and other ecclesiastical crimes, divorce and sexual offences etc., as defined in 1611, but its main use by Archbishop Laud was against Puritans. A new Ecclesiastical Commission, with similar powers, was revived by James II in 1686, until 1688.

KING'S BENCH, COURT OF: the highest common law court, originating as the court of the King in Council. By Tudor times, it was a sort of appeal court in criminal cases and in some civil matters.

REQUESTS, COURT OF: this prerogative court offered cheap and speedy justice to the poor. A popular alternative to the common law courts. Requests emerged from the King's Council to deal with civil cases, trade and land holding. Though it ceased to sit from the outbreak of the Civil War in 1642, the court was not abolished by statute.

STANNARIES, COURT OF THE: originating in the reign of King John (c. 1201) the court emanated from the royal prerogative and exercised jurisdiction over the tin miners of Devon and Cornwall.

STAR CHAMBER, COURT OF: a fifteenth century practice whereby the Royal Council met for judicial purposes in the Star Chamber at the Palace of Westminster, to deal mainly with political cases and matters of public order. More expeditious than the common law courts, it was enlarged by the Tudors through successive measures and, under Elizabeth, it emerged as a district court, separate from but closely connected with the Privy Council.

In 1641 the Long Parliament abolished the court which had gained a bad reputation as an instrument of arbitrary rule, independent from common law and used by the king to inflict savage punishments on Puritans and his political opponents, e.g. William Prynne (1634) and Henry Burton (1636).

WARDS AND LIVERIES, COURT OF: a Tudor institution, whereby the king increased his personal finances (the Chamber revenues) by strictly enforcing feudal rights of wardship etc.

Parliamentary pressure against this increasingly unpopular court led to its abolition in 1645–6, a measure confirmed after the Restoration.

4 SELECTED BIOGRAPHIES

Duke of Albermarle (1608–70)–*see* Gorge Monck.

Francis Bacon (1561–1626)   Born 22 January 1561; son of Lord Keeper Bacon; nephew of Lord Burghley. Educated at Trinity College, Cambridge, and Gray's Inn; called to the Bar (1582). MP for Melcombe Regis (1584), Taunton (1586), Liverpool (1589), Middlesex (1593), Southampton (1597). Friendship with the Earl of Essex (from 1591) gained him influence at court, but his opposition in the subsidy debates (1593) delayed his advancement. Appointed one of the Queen's learned Counsel (1596); gave Essex little support in his Star Chamber trial (1600) or in his treason trial (1601). Knighted by James I (July 1603); hoped to influence the King in favour of church reform and reconciliation between Crown and Parliament. Married Alice Barnham (May 1606). Made a great speech in the Commons supporting proposals for Union with Scotland (February 1607). Appointed Solicitor General (June 1607), Attorney General (October 1613), Privy Councillor (June 1616), Lord Keeper (March 1617) and Lord Chancellor (January 1618). Hoped to influence James through his support of George Villiers (Duke of Buckingham). Involved in the prosecution of Somerset (1616), Raleigh (1618), Suffolk (1619), Yelverton (1620). Supported James in his quarrel with Coke: judges should be 'lions, but yet lions under the throne', not arbiters of the constitution. Created Baron Verulam (July 1618) and Viscount St Albans (January 1621). As a supporter of the monarchy, he was attacked in the Commons and charged with bribery as Chancellor (1621). Dismissed from office, he was fined £40,000, imprisoned and disabled from sitting in Parliament. The King immediately granted a pardon. Died 9 April 1626. His writings include *Advancement of Learning* (1605), *Novum Organum* (1620), *Essays* (1597), *History of Henry the Seventh* (1622), *A Confession of Faith* (1603), *Maxims of the Law* (1630).

   BIOGRAPHIES: J. Spedding, *An Account of the Life and Times of Francis Bacon* (1880); J. G. Crowther, *Francis Bacon: The First Statesman of Science* (1960); B. Farrington, *Francis Bacon, Philosopher of Industrial Science* (1950).

Robert Blake (1599–1657)   Born in Bridgwater, August 1599; eldest son of Humphrey Blake, merchant. Educated Bridgwater Grammar School, St Alban Hall and Wadham College, Oxford. MP for Bridgwater in Short Parliament

(1640) and in Long Parliament (from 1645). On the outbreak of civil war joined Sir John Horner's force (1642); distinguished himself by brave conduct at the siege of Bristol (1643). Appointed member of the Somerset Committee of Ways and Means; lieutenant–colonel of Popham's regiment (1643). With a garrison of 500 brilliantly defended Lyme against Prince Maurice's siege (1644); promoted to an independent command; seized Taunton, holding it for a year against royalist attack (1644–5); stayed on as Governor to rebuild the town after its relief. Appointed to share chief command of the fleet (27 February 1649); blockaded Prince Rupert's fleet at Kinsale; became Warden of the Cinque Ports. Appointed sole commander of the winter fleet based at Plymouth. Blockaded Rupert in the Tagus (March 1650); pursued him to the Mediterranean, destroying most of his fleet at Malaga (January 1651). Appointed commander of the Irish Seas Squadron (March 1651); successfully reduced the Scilly Isles and Jersey (which were bases for royalist pirates); prevented foreign help reaching Scotland and Ireland. Member of the Council of State (December 1651). In the First Dutch War, after two indecisive battles against Tromp off Dover (May 1652) and the Kentish Knock (September 1652), Blake was defeated in the battle off Dungeness (November 1652), which gave Tromp control of the Channel for three months. Blake's victories off Portland (February 1653) and the Gabbard (June 1653), however, ensured England's ultimate success in the war. In the Spanish War he was appointed to command the Mediterranean Fleet (1656); captured a large fleet of Spanish galleons in Tenerife harbour (1657). Died at sea in 1658. Buried in Westminster Abbey. His body was disinterred by royalists at the Restoration and hung from the gallows at Tyburn.

BIOGRAPHY: J. R. Powell, *Robert Blake* (1972).

Duke of Buckingham (1592–1628)–*see* George Villiers.

James Butler, 12th Earl and 1st Duke of Ormonde (1610–88)   Born 19 October 1610 at Clerkenwell; eldest son of Thomas, Viscount Thurles. As a royal ward, after the death of his father (1619), educated under Archbishop Abbot at Lambeth. Married Elizabeth Preston (September 1629). Succeeded to the earldom of Ormonde and Ossory (1632); took up residence in Ireland (1633); befriended Wentworth (later Strafford); became Commander-in-Chief in Ireland during his absence (1640). Appointed Lieutenant-General of the King's forces in Ireland on the outbreak of rebellion (1641); won victories at Killsalghen, Kilrush and Ross. Concluded the Cessation with the rebels on instructions from Charles (15 September 1643), sending 5000 men under Byron to serve the King in England. Made Lord Lieutenant of Ireland (January 1644); tried hard to bring about a general peace in the province; finally surrendered Dublin to Parliamentarian forces and concluded a treaty with their commissioners (June 1647). Surrendered his office; fled to France (February 1648). After execution of King (1649), reappointed Lord Lieutenant by Charles II, but his attempt to retake Dublin was frustrated by the arrival of Cromwell (August

1649). Returned to France and remained with Charles II in exile as a member of his Privy Council. Commanded the King's regiment on active service for Spain (1656–7). At the Restoration created Baron Butler and Earl of Brecknock (1660); Duke of Ormonde and Lord High Steward (1661). Reappointed Lord Lieutenant of Ireland (1661–8 and 1677–85); encouraged internal peace and Irish trade. Appointed Chancellor of Oxford University (1669). Carried the crown at the coronations of Charles II and James II, but opposed the latter's attempt to assume dispensing power (1687). Died 21 July 1688; buried in Westminster Abbey.

BIOGRAPHY: T. Carte, *The Life of James Duke of Ormonde* (1735–6).

William Cavendish, Duke of Newcastle (1592–1676)   Son of Sir Charles Cavendish; educated St John's College, Cambridge; married Elizabeth Bassett (c. 1617; she died in 1643) and Margaret Lucas (1645). Made Knight of the Bath (1610), Viscount Mansfield (1620), Earl of Newcastle (1628), Privy Councillor and Governor of Prince of Wales (1638). Twice entertained Charles I lavishly at Welbeck, costing a total of £20,000. On outbreak of Scottish rebellion, raised a troop and lent King £10,000 (1639). On the approach of civil war in 1642, appointed Governor of Hull (January), but then sent by King to command the four northern counties; raised an army and secured the valuable port of Newcastle; defeated Hotham at Piercebridge (November) and Fairfax at Tadcaster (December); occupied Pontefract and Newark. In 1643 driven out of Bradford and the West Riding (January); welcomed Queen Henrietta Maria to York with money and arms from the continent (March); defeated the Fairfaxes at Adwalton Moor (June), captured Bradford and controlled all Yorkshire (except Hull); took Gainsborough (July) and Lincoln (August), but refused the King's request to march south for an attack on London; returned to besiege Hull (September–October) without success. Created Marquis (October). On entry of Scots (January 1644), marched north to defend Newcastle, but eventually retreated to York, in which he was besieged (April–July) by Leven, Fairfax, Manchester and Cromwell; siege raised by Rupert (1 July). Defeated at Marston Moor, after a disagreement with Rupert; fled abroad to Hamburg (8 July). Spent exile in Paris (1645–8), Rotterdam (1648) and Antwerp (1648–60). Impoverished, was a member of Charles II's Privy Council, devoted himself to riding and wrote a book on horsemanship, *La Méthode et invention nouvelle de dresser les chevaux* (1657). At the Restoration, regained some of his estates (though his losses estimated at £940,000); appointed Chief Justice in Eyre north of Trent (1661), Duke of Newcastle (1665); played no part in political affairs; devoted his time to riding and writing poetry and comedies. At various times a friend or patron of Jonson, Shirley, Davenant, Dryden, Shadwell, Descartes and Hobbes. Died 25 December 1676; buried in Westminster Abbey.

BIOGRAPHY: Margaret Cavendish, *The Life of William Cavendish, Duke of Newcastle*, ed. C. H. Firth (1886).

Robert Cecil, Earl of Salisbury (1563–1612)   Son of William Cecil, Lord Burghley; educated St John's College, Cambridge; married Elizabeth Brooke (1589). Member of Lord Derby's embassy negotiating peace with Spain (1588); MP for Hertfordshire and High Sheriff (1589); knighted and made Privy Councillor (1591); became Secretary of State for Elizabeth I (1596); led embassy to France to prevent its alliance with Spain (1598). Death of his father (1598) reduced his influence at court, faced with the rivalry of the Queen's favourite, the Earl of Essex; took part in the trial of Essex for insurrection (1601); corresponded with James I in preparation for his succession; successfully obtained subsidies for the Spanish War from Elizabeth's last parliament. Read proclamation declaring James I King (23 March 1603); continued as Secretary of State; made Lord High Steward to the Queen (1603), Baron Cecil of Essingden (1603), Viscount Cranbourne (1604), Earl of Salisbury (1605), Knight of the Garter (1605), Lord Treasurer (1608). An able speaker and gifted financier, he virtually controlled the whole government. Reconstructed Hatfield House. Died exhausted 24 May 1612.

BIOGRAPHY: A. Cecil, *A Life of Robert Cecil, the First Earl of Salisbury*.

Charles I (1600–49)   Born 19 November 1600 at Dunfermline; second son of James I and Anne of Denmark. Created Duke of York (1605), Knight of the Garter (1611), Duke of Cornwall (1613), Prince of Wales (1616) and Privy Councillor (1621). Visited Spain with Buckingham in unsuccessful attempt to marry the Spanish Infanta (1623). Succeeded to throne (27 March 1625); married Henrietta Maria of France (1625); pursued policy of war with Spain – failure of Mansfeld's expedition and Cadiz expedition (1625). Dissolved first parliament after dispute over tunnage and poundage (1625). Declared war on France (1627) – failure of Buckingham's La Rochelle expedition (1627). Quarrelled with his third parliament, which passed the Petition of Right (1628) and the Three Resolutions (1629). Decided to rule without parliament (1629–40); made peace with France (1629) and Spain (1630); adopted various expedients to raise money – forced knighthood, forced loans, monopolies, fines for breach of forest laws, ship money; appointed Laud Archbishop of Canterbury (1633) and supported his introduction of High Church practices, together with his use of the Court of High Commission and Court of Star Chamber; appointed Wentworth (later Earl of Strafford) Lord Deputy of Ireland (1632); attempted to force new Prayer Book on Scotland (1637), resulting in the First and Second Bishops' Wars (1639, 1640); called the abortive Short Parliament (April 1640); called the Long Parliament (November 1640) after Scottish invasion and defeat of forces at Newburn. Reluctantly agreed to the execution of Strafford, the Triennial Act and the abolition of prerogative courts (1641). Unsuccessfully attempted to arrest the Five Members (January 1642); left London for York (March 1642); issued commissions of array (June 1642); raised standard at Nottingham (22 August 1642). Fought drawn battle at Edgehill (October 1642); established headquarters at Oxford; failed in his plan to retake London (1643); unsuccessfully besieged Gloucester and defeated at Newbury (1643); established his own parliament at Oxford (1644); defeated Waller at Cropredy Bridge and Essex at Lostwithiel (1644); convincingly beaten by the New Model Army at Naseby (1645); surrendered to the Scots at Newark (1646); handed over to Parliament (January 1647); captured by army from Holmby House (June 1647); escaped to Carisbrooke Castle (November 1647); concluded Engagement with the Scots (December 1647) thus bringing about the Second Civil War (1648); negotiated with Parliamentary commissioners at Newport (September 1648); arrested by army and moved to Hurst Castle (November 1648): conducted to Windsor (December 1648); tried in Westminster Hall (20–27 January 1649); executed (30 January 1649).

BIOGRAPHIES: F.M.G. Higham, *Charles I: A Study* (1932); E. John, *King Charles I* (1952 edn); Margaret Toynbee, *King Charles I* (1968).

Charles II (1630–85) Born 29 May 1630; son of Charles I and Henrietta Maria; created Prince of Wales (1639); married Catherine of Braganza (1662). In the Civil War, present with his father at Edgehill; appointed commander of the royalist Western forces (1644); fled to the Scilly Isles, Jersey and France. Attempted to blockade the Thames with ships which had revolted from Warwick's Parliamentary fleet (1648). In desparation asked the regicides to name their own conditions for the release of his father. Assumed the title of King of England (January 1649); proclaimed King of Scotland (February 1649) – took the Covenant and crowned at Scone (January 1651). Defeated at Worcester (September 1651); escaped after a flight of forty-four days; set up his own court in exile, living in France, Germany and Holland (1651–60). Invited to return as King, after the action of General Monck; signed the Declaration of Breda; entered London (29 May 1660). With Clarendon as Lord Chancellor (1660–7), adopted a policy of war against Dutch (1665–7) and persecution of Puritans. With the Cabal ministry of Clifford, Arlington, Buckingham, Ashley-Cooper and Lauderdale (1667–73), he abandoned the Triple Alliance and signed the secret Treaty of Dover (1670) in return for a French pension; attempted to secure toleration for dissenters and Roman Catholics by the Declaration of Indulgence (1673); forced to accept the Test Act (1673). With Danby as chief minister (1673–9), veered towards a Dutch alliance: agreed to marriage of Princess Mary to William of Orange (1677). Forced by public opinion to agree to severe punishment of Roman Catholics following revelation of the 'Popish Plot' by Titus Oates (1678), and to the Parliamentary Test Act (1678); refused to accept the Exclusion Bill advocated by Shaftesbury and the Whig opposition (1679–81). Survived the Rye House Plot (1683). Died 6 February 1685.

BIOGRAPHIES: A. Bryant, *King Charles II* (1955); O. Airy, *Charles II* (1901); M. Ashley, *Charles II* (1971).

Earl of Clarendon (1609–74) – *see* Edward Hyde.

Sir Edward Coke (1552–1634) Born 1 February 1552 at Mileham, Norfolk;

educated Norwich Free School, Trinity College, Cambridge, and Clifford's Inn; called to the Bar (1578). Married (1) Bridget Paston (1582) and (2) Lady Elizabeth Hatton (1598). MP for Aldborough (1589), Norfolk (1592), Coventry (1624), Norfolk (1625), Buckinghamshire (1628). Recorder of Norwich (1586), Bencher of Inner Temple (1590), Solicitor General (1592), Recorder of London (1592), Speaker (1592–3), Attorney General (1593–4); Treasurer of Inner Temple (1596), knighted (1603), Chief Justice of the Common Pleas (1606), Chief Justice of the King's Bench (1613), Privy Councillor (1613), High Steward of Cambridge University (1614). Conducted the prosecutions against Essex (1600), Southampton (1600), Raleigh (1603), the gunpowder plotters (1605). Attracted the hostility of Ellesmere, Buckingham and Bacon by attempting to oppose the extension of James I's prerogative. Refused to stay the action against the Bishop of Coventry and Lichfield in the case of Commendams, in spite of the King's request (1616). Summoned before the Council, charged with remarks derogatory to the royal prerogative; suspended from the Council, removed from the Bench and from the post of Chief Justice (1616). After the marriage of his daughter to Buckingham's brother (1617), gradually regained favour; recalled to the council; sat in the Star Chamber and on commissions of inquiry. Led the Popular party in the 1620–1 parliament; opposed monopolies and the Spanish marriage; spoke vigorously in favour of the liberties of Parliament; arrested with other leaders; imprisoned in Tower for nine months. Spoke in favour of Middlesex's impeachment and against oppressive taxation (1624). In the 1628 parliament, largely responsible for the Petition of Right; bitterly attacked the forced loan, illegal taxation and Buckingham's influence. Spent retirement at Stoke Poges. Wrote *Reports* (1600–15) and *Institutes* (1628). Died 3 September 1634.

BIOGRAPHIES: C. D. Bowen, *The Lion and the Throne: The Life and Times of Sir Edward Coke* (1957); S. E. Thorne, *Sir Edward Coke 1552–1634* (1957).

Anthony Ashley Cooper, 1st Earl of Shaftesbury (1621–83)   Born 22 July 1621; son of John Cooper of Wimborne St Giles, Dorset; educated Exeter College, Oxford, and Lincoln's Inn; married (1) Margaret Coventry (1639) and (2) Lady Frances Cecil (1650). MP for Tewkesbury (1640). In the Civil War sided at first with the King; appointed by the Marquis of Hertford to the rank of colonel and commander of Weymouth garrison (1643), but changed sides on being relieved of his command (1644); made Field Marshal and commander of Parliamentary forces in Dorset. Appointed High Sheriff of Wiltshire (1646) and JP for Wiltshire and Dorset (1649). MP for Wiltshire in the Barebones Parliament (1653) and first Protectorate parliament (1654); member of the Council of State (1653); but quarrelled with Cromwell over rule without Parliament and excluded from sitting in 1656; joined the opposition of Presbyterians and republicans. MP for Wiltshire in Richard Cromwell's parliament (1659); member of the Council of State when the Long Parliament restored; opposed Lambert's designs (1659); joined the delegation to The Hague which invited Charles II to return. A member of the Convention Parliament (1660): appointed Chancellor of the Exchequer and created Lord Ashley (1661); a member of the Cabal ministry (1672); created Earl of Shaftesbury and Lord Chancellor (1672); supported the Declaration of Indulgence (1672) and Test Act (1673); fell from power with the Cabal (1673) and became leader of the opposition; began to intrigue with the Duke of Monmouth for the succession to the throne. Imprisoned in the Tower after clash with the King over the prorogation of Parliament (1677); supported the attacks on Catholics and the Duke of York during the Popish Plot scare (1678). Appointed President of Temple's new Council (1679), but dismissed for his support of the Exclusion Bill; successfully secured the passing of the Habeas Corpus Act (1679). Failed in his attempt to impeach the Duke of York as a Popish recusant (1680). Took part in the Oxford parliament and in the heated debates on the Exclusion Bill (1681); indicted for high treason, but released (1681). Discovered in new plot to overthrow government (with Russell and Sydney); fled to Holland (November 1682); died 21 January 1683.

BIOGRAPHIES: L. F. Brown, *The First Earl of Shaftesbury* (1933); K. H. D. Haley, *The First Earl of Shaftesbury* (1968).

Oliver Cromwell (1599–1658)   Born 25 April 1599 at Huntingdon; son of Robert Cromwell; educated at Huntingdon Free School and Sidney Sussex College, Cambridge: married Elizabeth Bourchier (1620). MP for Huntingdon (1628) and Cambridge (1640); attacked bishops (1629) and opposed fen drainage (1636); moved the second reading of the Triennial Bill (1640). On the outbreak of civil war raised a cavalry troop at Huntingdon; criticised the conduct of the Parliamentarian cavalry at Edgehill (1642); appointed colonel and raised a double regiment of cavalry (January 1643); defeated royalists at Grantham (May), Gainsborough (July) and Winceby (October); appointed Lieutenant-General in Manchester's Eastern Association (January 1644); successfully stormed Lincoln (May); commanded the left wing of the cavalry at Marston Moor (July); fought at Newbury (October); attacked the conduct of Manchester and supported the Self-Denying Ordinance (December); appointed Lieutenant-General in the New Model Army under Fairfax (June 1645); commanded the right wing at Naseby (June); saw action at Bridgwater (July), Bristol (September), Winchester (October), Basing House (October). After the end of the war (June 1646), moved to London to take up his seat in Parliament; supported the army in its quarrel with the Presbyterians in Parliament (1647); one of the commissioners sent to negotiate with the army (May); rejoined it when it mutinied (May); approved of the seizure of King from Holmby House (June); helped to draw up the Heads of Proposals (July), which the King rejected; led march on London to remove Presbyterian leaders from Parliament (August); chaired the Putney Debates and argued against the Levellers (October); during Second Civil War, besieged Pembroke Castle and won the Battle of Preston (August 1648); approved of Pride's Purge and the trial of the King (January 1649); signed the death warrant. Appointed member of the Council of State

(February); commanded the army sent to Ireland to crush rebels (August 1649); stormed Drogheda (September) and Wexford (October); took Ross (October), Cashel (February 1650) and Clonmel (May). Appointed Captain-General of the army to be sent to Scotland (June 1650); won at Dunbar (September), took Edinburgh, pursued the royalists and won the Battle of Worcester (September 1651). Expelled the Rump Parliament (April 1653); addressed the Barebones Parliament (July); appointed Lord Protector under the Instrument of Government (December); addressed the first Protectorate parliament (September 1654); sent military expedition to fight the Spanish in the West Indies (December); dissolved Parliament (January 1655); put down Penruddock's Rising (March); appointed Major-Generals to control the country (May); outbreak of war against Spain (October); signed treaty with France (March 1657); rejected offer of the crown, made in the *Humble Petition and Advice* (May) accepted proposal for new Upper House, which first met January 1658; gained Dunkirk after defeat of the Spanish at the battle of the Dunes (June). Died 3 September 1658; body disinterred from Westminster Abbey and hanged at Tyburn (January 1661).

BIOGRAPHIES: Antonia Fraser, *Cromwell our Chief of Men* (1973); Christopher Hill, *God's Englishman* (1970); C. H. Firth, *Cromwell and the Rule of the Puritans in England* (1900); C. V. Wedgwood, *Oliver Cromwell* (1973 edn); M. Ashley, *The Greatness of Oliver Cromwell* (1957); John Wroughton, *Cromwell and the Roundheads* (1969).

Richard Cromwell (1626–1712)   Third son of Oliver Cromwell; born 4 October 1626; educated Felstead School and Lincoln's Inn. Served in Parliament's army during the Civil War. Married Dorothy Mayor (1649). MP for Hampshire (1654) and Cambridge (1656). Member of the Committee of Trade and Navigation (1655). After his father's acceptance of the amended Humble Petition and Advice with the right to nominate his own heir (1657), took a more active part in government; appointed Chancellor of Oxford University (1657), member of the Council of State (1657), commander of a regiment (1658) and member of the new Upper House (1658). Nominated by his father as successor shortly before death; proclaimed Protector (3 September 1658); received general approval at home and abroad; new Parliament voted their official recognition (February 1659) after his statesmanlike opening speech. But Fleetwood's army became hostile after attack in Parliament on the Major-Generals; demanded that the army command should be independent. Cromwell ordered officers back to their regiments, when they delivered grievances from the Army Council; refused to arrest leaders when they disobeyed – 'I will not have a drop of blood spilt for the preservation of my greatness, which is a burden to me.' After rendezvous of the army at St James, agreed to dissolve Parliament and surrender office in return for protection (April 1659); refused French help or suggestion of a restoration. The revived Rump voted to pay his debts of £29,000 and grant an income of £8700, but never made this effective. Fled to Paris in poverty under the name of John

Clarke (1660); moved to Italy (1666); returned to England (1680); lived at Cheshunt. Died 12 July 1712.

BIOGRAPHY: R. W. Ramsey, *Richard Cromwell, Protector of England* (1935).

Earl of Danby (1632–1712) – *see* Sir Thomas Osborne.

Robert, Devereux, 3rd Earl of Essex (1591–1646)   Son of Robert, 2nd Earl, and Frances, daughter of Sir Francis Walsingham; educated Eton and Merton College, Oxford, Married (1) Frances Howard (1606) – divorced; (2) Elizabeth Paulet (1631). Military service under Vere in the Palatinate (1620), in Holland (1622–3), in Mansfeld's expedition (1624); Vice-Admiral in the Cadiz expedition (1625). MP and member of the Council of War (1621); refused to pay forced loan; gave support to the Popular party in the Petition of Right (1628). Appointed Lieutenant-General in the English army in the First Bishops' War (1639). Supported Pym and St John in the Long Parliament (1640) – in favour of Strafford's execution. Appointed by Charles I Lord Chamberlain, Privy Councillor and commander of forces south of the Trent (1641) in an attempt to gain his support. Warned the Five Members of their imminent arrest; refused to accompany the King to York (1642). Appointed member of Parliament's Committee of Safety, and General of Parliament's army (July 1642). Commanded at the battles of Edgehill (October) and Turnham Green (November). Captured Reading (April 1643), relieved Gloucester (September) and won the First Battle of Newbury (September). Failed to take Oxford (May 1644); campaign in south-west ended with defeat by the King at Lostwithiel and surrender of the whole infantry (September). Appointed commander of a newly raised army (October). Opposed Cromwell's attack on Manchester in Parliament (December) and the formation of the New Model Army (April 1645); anticipating the Self-Denying Ordinance, resigned his command (2 April 1645). As Commander-in-Chief, lacked resolution, initiative and tactical ability; but hampered by existence of independent armies under Waller and Manchester; an honest and loyal supporter of Parliament. Died 14 September 1646.

BIOGRAPHIES: W. B. Devereux, *Lives and Letters of the Devereux, Earls of Essex, 1540–1646* (1853); V. F. Snow, *Essex the Rebel* (1970).

Sir John Eliot, (1592–1632)   Born 20 April 1592 at Port Eliot, Cornwall; son of Richard Eliot; educated Exeter College, Oxford, and Inns of Court; married Rhadagund Gedie (1611). MP for St Germans in the Addled Parliament (1614); knighted (1618); appointed Vice-Admiral of Devon (1619); MP for Newport (Cornwall) in the 1624 parliament – supported the Spanish War. In the 1625 parliament in favour of strict application of laws against Roman Catholics and against further taxation for foreign wars. MP for St Germans (1626) – became a leader of the Popular party; demanded inquiry into Cadiz expedition; made a bitter attack on Buckingham and commenced his impeachment; introduced remonstrance claiming the right of Parliament to question ministers; arrested and sent to the Tower (May), but Commons refused to transact business until he was set free; the King dissolved Parliament. Refused to pay the forced loan (1627) – imprisoned in the Gatehouse. MP for Cornwall (1628) – led resistance to illegal taxation; with Coke responsible for the Petition of Right; made a further attack on Buckingham's policies. During the 1629 session spoke strongly against the illegal collection of tunnage and poundage, the confiscation of the goods of MPs who refused to pay customs duties and the activities of the Arminians. Under the threat of adjournment, read out the Three Resolutions with the Speaker held down in the chair (2 March 1629). Arrested and sent to the Tower with eight other leaders; tried (January 1630), fined £2000 and imprisoned. Wrote *Negotium Posterorum* (an account of Charles I's first parliament) and *The Monarchy of Man* (his views on constitutional monarchy). A brilliant orator. Died in prison 27 November 1632.

BIOGRAPHIES: H. Hulme, *The Life of Sir John Eliot, 1592–1632* (1957); J. Forster, *Sir John Eliot: A Biography* (1864).

Thomas Fairfax, 3rd Lord Fairfax (1612–71)   Born 17 January 1612 in Denton, Yorks; son of Ferdinando, 2nd Lord; educated St John's College, Cambridge; married Anne Vere (1637). Fought in Netherlands under Vere (1629); commanded troop in the First Bishops' War (1639). Knighted (January 1640); presented the King with petition from the gentry of Yorkshire (June 1642); assisted his father as leader of Parliament's forces in Yorkshire on the outbreak of civil war (August 1642). In 1643 recaptured Leeds and Wakefield, defeated at Adwalton Moor, helped to garrison Hull and assisted Cromwell in victory at Winceby, Lincs. In 1644 defeated royalists at Nantwich and Selby, established control over Cheshire, commanded the right wing of the cavalry at Marston Moor and completed the reduction of enemy fortresses in Yorkshire. Appointed commander of the New Model Army (January 1645); defeated the King at Naseby (June) and Goring at Langport (July); captured Bridgwater, Bath, Bristol and Tiverton. Completed conquest of the West with the surrender of Exeter (April 1646); took Oxford (June) and Raglan (August) to end the war. Supported the army in its quarrel with Parliament (1647), including the expulsion of the eleven MPs. In the Second Civil War (1648), won battle at Maidstone and took Colchester after siege. Agreed to the trial and deposition of the King, but refused to be a member of the High Court of Justice. Resigned his commission (June 1650), being unwilling to lead invasion of Scotland. Played no active part in military or political affairs under Cromwell. MP for Yorkshire in Richard Cromwell's parliament (1659); appointed member of the Council of State by the revived Rump but failed to take part; negotiated with Monck (November 1659) after Lambert's forced expulsion of Parliament; raised volunteers and occupied York (January 1660) when Monck marched into England; declared for a free Parliament and the restoration of the King; MP in the new parliament (March) – appointed leader of commission sent to the King at The Hague. Played no part in public affairs after the Restoration. Died 12 November 1671.

BIOGRAPHIES: M. A. Gibb, *The Lord General: A Life of Thomas Fairfax* (1938); C. R. Markham, *Life of Thomas Fairfax* (1870).

Charles Fleetwood (d. 1692) Son of Sir Miles Fleetwood of Aldwinkle, Northants; educated Gray's Inn, married (1) Frances Smith (2) Bridget Cromwell (1652) and (3) Mary Hartopp (1664). On the outbreak of civil war, joined the life guard of the Earl of Essex (1642); captain in Tyrrell's regiment in the First Battle of Newbury (1643); appointed Receiver of Court of Wards (1644); commanded regiment under Manchester (1644), containing many sectaries; commanded cavalry regiment in the New Model Army at Naseby (1645). MP for Marlborough (1646). Supported the army in its quarrel with Parliament (1647); one of the four commissioners sent by Parliament to negotiate with the army; partly responsible for the capture of the King at Holmby House; but played no part in the Second Civil War or the trial of the King. Appointed Governor of the Isle of Wight (1649). Accompanied Cromwell to Scotland as Lieutenant-General of Horse (1650) – fought at Dunbar. Appointed to the Council of State (1651) and commander of forces in England; played major role in the defeat of Charles II at Worcester (3 September 1651). Appointed commander-in-chief in Ireland (1652–5), a commissioner for the civil government and Lord Deputy (1654); persecuted Catholic priests and transplanted Catholic landowners to Connaught. A keen supporter of Cromwell in the Protectorate; member of the Council of State (1654); appointed Major-General of Norfolk, Suffolk, Buckingham, Cambridge, Oxford, Essex and Huntingdonshire; against the offer of the crown to Cromwell, but supported the amended Humble Petition and Advice; became a member of the new Second House. Supported the accession of Richard Cromwell (1658), but led the demands of army officers to make him Commander-in-Chief with powers independent of the Protector; Richard's order that officers should return to their regiments he defied by staging a military demonstration, which resulted in the dissolution of Parliament (22 April 1659). Appointed member of both the Committee of Safety and the Council of State as well as Commander-in Chief by the restored Rump; but after further disagreements, the army expelled the Rump by force (12 October 1659). Deprived of his command when Parliament was again called on the advance of Monck into England (December 1659). At the Restoration banned for life from all offices of trust (August 1660); played no further part in public affairs. Died 4 October 1962.

SEE M. Ashley, *Cromwell's Generals* (1954).

Marquis of Halifax (1635–95) – *see* George Savile.

John Hampden (1594–1643) Son of William Hampden of Great Hampden, Bucks; educated Thame Grammar School, Magdalen College, Oxford, and Inner Temple; married (1) Elizabeth Symeon and (2) Letitia Knollys. MP for Grampound (1621), Wendover (1626) and Buckinghamshire (1640). Refused to pay forced loan (1627)—imprisoned; supported Eliot's opposition to the King's policies in Parliament. Refused to pay ship money for inland counties (1637). In the Short Parliament (1640) served on committees to discuss ship money, Parliamentary privileges and recent changes in religious practice; made major speech in the supply debate (May); briefly arrested on the dissolution of

Parliament. In the Long Parliament (1640) worked closely with Pym; helped to draw up the indictment of Strafford; one of the managers of his impeachment; against the use of a Bill of Attainder. Favoured settlement with the King and reform of episcopacy. Survived the King's attempt to arrest him with four other MPs (January 1642); proposed that the Tower and the militia should be controlled by Parliament. Appointed to the Committee of Safety (July 1642); raised regiment of green-coats at start of the Civil War; seized control of Buckinghamshire; not present at Edgehill, but criticised the retreat of the Earl of Essex. Became a member of the 'war' party: opposed the King's peace proposals and advocated a vigorous attack on Oxford. Present at the siege of Reading; mortally wounded at Chalgrove Field in seeking to prevent royalist cavalry from returning to Oxford (18 June 1643).

BIOGRAPHIES: G. G. Nugent, *Some Memorials of John Hampden, His Party and His Times* (1831); H. R. Williamson, *John Hampden* (1933); J. Adair, *John Hampden the Patriot* (1976).

Edward Hyde, Earl of Clarendon (1609–74)   Born 18 February 1609; son of Henry Hyde of Dinton, Wilts; educated Magdalen Hall, Oxford, and Middle Temple; married (1) Anne Ayliffe and (2) Frances Aylesbury. Appointed Keeper of Writs and Rolls of the Common Pleas (1634). MP for Wootton Bassett in the Short Parliament (1640); for Saltash in the Long Parliament (1640); actively supported the Popular party in its attacks on ship money and the Star Chamber; assisted in the preparation of Strafford's impeachment, but opposed 'root and branch' measures against episcopacy, fearing an attempt to impose Presbyterianism. Became leader of the King's party in the Commons (1641), hoping to restrain Charles from further unconstitutional actions. Disagreed with his attempted arrest of the Five Members, but joined him in York (1642). Knighted, appointed Privy Councillor and Chancellor of the Exchequer (1643); recommended the establishment of the Oxford Parliament (December 1643); became the King's negotiator in all peace proposals. Accompanied the Prince of Wales to the West of England (1645), the Scilly Isles and Jersey (1645). Ambassador of the exiled court to Madrid (1649–51); chief minister of Charles II in exile (1652–60) – appointed Lord Chancellor (1658). Helped to draw up the Declaration of Breda (1660), suggesting that the precise details should be referred to the wisdom of Parliament. At the Restoration became head of government; appointed Chancellor of Oxford University (1660) and Earl of Clarendon (1661); his daughter, Anne, married the Duke of York. Supported persecution of Puritans in the Corporation Act (1661), the Act of Uniformity (1662), the Conventicle Act (1664) and the Five Mile Act (1665). Continued the French alliance; sold back Dunkirk to Louis XIV (1662); opposed the outbreak of the Dutch War, but took the blame for its indecisive conduct. Unpopular, dismissed as Chancellor (1667) and impeached by the Commons for corruption, arbitrary government and treachery in the late war. Fled to France; sentenced to exile for life. Died on 9 December 1674. During his exile wrote *History of the Great Rebellion* and *The Life of Edward, Earl of Clarendon*. An honest, loyal statesman with great respect for the constitution, the royal prerogative and the Church.

BIOGRAPHIES: T. H. Lister, *Life and Administration of Edward, First Earl of Clarendon* (1837–8); C. H. Firth, *Edward Hyde, Earl of Clarendon* (1909); B. H. G. Wormald, *Clarendon: Politics, History and Religion, 1640–1660* (1951).

Lawrence Hyde, Earl of Rochester (1641–1711)   Born March 1641; second son of Edward Hyde, Earl of Clarendon; married Harrietta Boyle (1665). MP for Newport, Cornwall (1660), Oxford University (1661–79) and Wootton Bassett (1679). Appointed Master of the Robes (1662–75), ambassador to John III of Poland (1676), commissioner at Peace of Nimeguen (1677), First Lord of the Treasury (1679). Created Viscount Hyde (1681) and Earl of Rochester (1682). Became very influential after the fall of Shaftesbury; defended the Duke of York in Exclusion Bill debates; negotiated with Barillon the secret subsidy treaty with France; supported policy of close alliance with France in opposition to Halifax, who preferred a Triple Alliance; dismissed from the Treasury (1684). Under James II, created Lord Treasurer and Knight of the Garter (1685); controlled the ministry; served on the ecclesiastical commission and voted for the suspension of Henry Compton, Bishop of London (1686); but, as a loyal Anglican, opposed the King's plans to restore Catholicism; struggled for influence with the more amenable Sunderland; dismissed on refusal to change his religion (1667). Appointed Lord Lieutenant of Hereford (1687). Favoured a regency in the revolution (1688), but supported William III and Mary after their accession. Readmitted to the Privy Council (1692) and to the cabinet, as leader of the High Church party (1700); appointed Lord Lieutenant of Ireland (1700). Under Anne, opposed the war with France; resigned (1703); opposed the Regency Bill (1705) and Act of Union (1707); appointed Lord President in Harley's ministry (1710). Published his father's *History of the Great Rebellion* (1702–4). Died 1 May 1711.

Henry Ireton (1611–51)   Born November 1611; son of German Ireton of Attenborough, Notts; educated Trinity College, Oxford, and Middle Temple; married Bridget Cromwell (1646). Led the Parliamentarians in Nottinghamshire on the outbreak of civil war (1642); captain of troop of horse at Edgehill (1642); major in Thornhalgh's regiment at Gainsborough (1643); appointed Deputy Governor of Isle of Ely (1643); quartermaster-general in Manchester's army at the Second Battle of Newbury (1644); supported Cromwell's criticism of Manchester in Parliament, which led to the Self-Denying Ordinance; appointed Commissary General of Horse in the New Model Army (1645); commanded the left wing of the cavalry at Naseby (1645); took part in the sieges of Bristol (1645) and Oxford (1646). MP for Appleby (October 1645); supported the army in its quarrel with Parliament (1647); one of the commissioners sent by Parliament to negotiate with the army; partly responsible for the seizure of the King at Holmby House. Drew up the declaration of the Army (5 June 1647), the Remonstrance of the Army (14 June 1647) and the Heads of Proposals (23 July 1647). In the Putney Debates (October–November 1647), opposed the Levellers' extreme demands outlined in the Agreeement of the People; urged moderation. In the Second Civil War (1648) fought with Fairfax in Kent and Essex; now favoured the trial of the King; instrumental in Pride's Purge and the removal of the King from Hurst Castle (December 1648); a member of the High Court of Justice and a signatory of the death warrant. Drew up the final version of the Agreement of the People (January 1649); member of the Council of War and the Derby House Committee, but not elected to the Council of State. Accompanied Cromwell to Ireland as second-in-command (June 1649); appointed President of Munster (January 1650) and Lord Deputy of Ireland on Cromwell's return to England (May 1650); conducted a successful military campaign (1650–1); adopted policy of replantation with English colonists; no toleration for Catholics. Died 26 November 1651; buried in Westminster Abbey; but disinterred at the Restoration and hanged at Tyburn.

BIOGRAPHY: R. W. Ramsey, *Henry Ireton* (1649).

James I (1566–1625)   Born 19 June 1566; son of Mary, Queen of Scots, and Lord Darnley; became James VI of Scotland (24 July 1567); childhood supervised by the Earl of Mar and Alexander Erskine; assumed personal power with the conclusion of Morton's regency (1578). Captured by nobles at the Raid of Ruthven (1582); unable to prevent the abolition of episcopacy by the General Assembly. Signed treaty with Elizabeth I and assisted in preparations against the Spanish Armada, despite the execution of his mother (1587). Married Anne of Denmark (1589). Survived Bothwell's assassination attempts (1591, 1593). Won victory at Glenlivet against the Catholic nobility (1594). Published *Basilikon Doron* (c.1598), advocating episcopacy and banishment of leading Presbyterians; reappointed bishops (1599). Survived Ruthven's Gowrie Conspiracy (1600). Succeeded to the English throne (24 March 1603). Favoured the Anglican religion; Puritans rebuffed at Hampton Court Conference (1604); Jesuits expelled (1604); survived the Gunpowder Plot (1605). Under Cecil's influence, followed a policy of hostility to Spain. Alleviated financial problems by forced loans and increased customs (new Book of Rates, 1608). Suffered the death of Henry, Prince of Wales (1612); arranged the marriage of his daughter, Elizabeth, to Frederick V, Elector Palatine. George Villiers (later Duke of Buckingham) replaced Robert Carr (Earl of Somerset) as court favourite (1615). Commencement of peace policy with Spain (1615). Failed in his attempt to control the Addled Parliament through 'managers' (1614). Resorted to raising money through benevolences, sale of peerages and monopolies. Alienated public opinion by the execution of Raleigh and refused to enter the Thirty Years War on behalf of the Elector Palatine (1618). Dissolved the 1621 parliament after its impeachment of Bacon and its criticism of his foreign policy and financial expedients. Attempted to marry Prince Charles to the Spanish Infanta (1635), but declared war on Spain after the failure of the visit by Charles and Buckingham; Mansfeld raised troops to fight in Germany. Planned marriage between Charles and Henrietta Maria of France. Died 27 March 1625.

BIOGRAPHIES: D. H. Wilson, *King James VI and I* (1956); M. G. Strafford, *James VI of Scotland and the Throne of England* (1940); D. Mathew, *James I* (1967).

James II (1633–1701)   Second son of Charles I and Henrietta Maria; married (1) Anne Hyde (1660) and (2) Mary of Modena (1673); created Duke of York (1633). Remained in the company of his father during the Civil War, captured by Fairfax at Oxford (1646), but escaped to Holland (1648); served in French and Spanish armies on the continent. Appointed Lord High Admiral at the Restoration (1660); ably commanded fleet against the Dutch (1665); converted to Roman Catholicism (1669) and resigned command on passing of Test Act (1673). Subject of Exclusion Bill to prevent his succession, organised by Lord Shaftesbury and the Whigs; sent abroad by Charles II to avoid public hostility; returned as Lord High Commissioner to Scotland; survived attempt to impeach him as Popish recusant (1680) and attempt to assassinate him in the Rye House Plot (1683); reappointed Lord High Admiral and member of the Council (1684). Succeeded to the throne (6 February 1685); survived Monmouth's rebellion in England and Argyll's in Scotland (1685). Aimed to restore Catholicism; used dispensing power to appoint Catholics to office, freeing them from the conditions of the Test Act; established a new Court of Ecclesiastical Commission (1686), which suspended the Bishop of London; appointed a Roman Catholic president of Magdalen College, Oxford, and introduced monks to Cambridge (1686); persuaded judges to agree to the legality of dispensing power; assembled an army of 13,000 on Hounslow Heath under Catholic officers; issued the Declaration of Indulgence (1687) to relieve dissenters and ordered it to be read in churches (1687); ordered the trial of seven bishops who refused to enforce the Declaration (1688). Public dismayed at birth of his son (1688); invitation sent to William of Orange to overthrow the King. In face of William's arrival James attempted to mend his ways: some counsellors dismissed, the Bishop of London restored to office. Deserted by his own army; escaped to France; supported by Louis XIV in expedition to Ireland (1689); suffered setback by the raising of the siege of Londonderry and defeat at the Boyne (1690). Returned to St Germain where he remained till his death (16 September 1701).

BIOGRAPHIES: F. C. Turner, *James II* (1948); F. M. G. Higham, *James the Second* (1934), J. Haswell, *James II, Soldier and Sailor* (1972).

John Lambert (1619–83)   Born 17 September 1619 at Calton, Yorks; married Francis Lister (1639). Fought in the Civil War for Parliament under Lord Fairfax; saw action at Hull (1643), Nantwich (1644), Bradford (1644), Marston Moor (1644) and Pontefract (1645); commanded infantry regiment in the New Model Army. Played major part in arranging the Treaty of Truro and the surrender of Exeter and Oxford (1646). Led the army protest in the quarrel with Parliament (1647). Assisted Cromwell in the Battle of Preston (1648) and successfully pursued Hamilton to Uttoxeter. Sent to Scotland in support of the Duke of Argyll (1648). Spoke in favour of bringing the King to trial.

Accompanied Cromwell to Scotland as major-general and second-in-command (1650) – fought at Dunbar; pursued Charles II to his defeat at Worcester; rewarded by Parliament with a grant of land worth £1000 per annum. Refused appointment as commander-in-chief in Ireland, after his new post as Lord Deputy had been abolished (1652). Strongly urged Cromwell to dissolve the Rump (1653); a member of the Council of State. Helped to draw up the Instrument of Government, which offered Cromwell the position of Protector (1653). Loyally supported Cromwell (1653–7), but opposed the offer of kingship. Refused to take the oath required from Councillors (1657) and resigned all offices in consequence. Supported the accession of Richard Cromwell (1658); MP for Pontefract (1659); played little active part in the dissolution of Parliament (April 1659) and recall of the Rump; appointed to the Committee of Safety and the Council of State (May 1659); restored to his army command; played major part in the forcible dissolution of the Rump (October 1659); marched north to prevent Monck's march on London from Scotland; deprived of his command by the restored Parliament; imprisoned in the Tower (March 1660), but escaped to lead an abortive rising (April 1660); tried and condemned for treason (1662), but reprieved by Charles II; exiled to Guernsey.

BIOGRAPHY: W. H. Dawson, *Cromwell's Understudy: The Life and Times of General John Lambert* (1938).

William Laud (1573–1645)   Born 7 October 1573; son of William Laud, a Reading clothier; educated Reading Free School and St John's College, Oxford; ordained (4 January 1601). Appointed chaplain to the Earl of Devonshire (1603); vicar of Stanford, Northants (1607); preached before the King (1608) and became a King's chaplain; vicar of Caxton, Kent (1610); Archdeacon of Huntingdon (1615); Dean of Gloucester (1616); accompanied James I to Scotland (1617); Prebendary of Westminster and Bishop of St David's (1621). Became a close friend of the Duke of Buckingham. Gained real influence on the accession of Charles I (1625): supported the King in his disputes with Parliament, drafted his speeches in defence of Buckingham and advised the promotion of Arminian clergy only. Appointed Dean of the Chapel Royal and Bishop of Bath and Wells (1626); Privy Councillor (1627); Bishop of London (1628); Chancellor of Oxford University (1630). Worked hard to end Puritan lectures, to restore uniformity in the Church, to revive the wearing of full canonical robes and the practice of bowing to the altar. Attacked immorality through the Court of High Commission. Appointed Archbishop of Canterbury (1633): revived metropolitan visitations (1634); all communion tables to be fixed at the east end, all clergy to conform to the Prayer Book; inquiry made into the conduct of clergy; supported Charles I in his issue of the 'Book of Sports' (1633) – opposed the Puritan Sabbath. Played prominent part in the prosecution of Prynne in the Court of Star Chamber (1634 and 1637). Became a member of both the Commission of the Treasury and the Committee for Foreign Affairs (1635). Supported the enforcement of the new canons and Prayer Book in Scotland and the recall of Parliament to supply money for the Scottish war

(1639). Regarded by public opinion as the source of all evil; impeached by the Long Parliament (December 1640); imprisoned in Tower for over two years without trial. Tried (March 1644) for endeavouring to subvert the laws and overthrow the Protestant religion; condemned to death by ordinance; executed 10 January 1645.

BIOGRAPHY: H. R. Trevor-Roper, *Archbishop Laud, 1573–1645* (1962 edn).

John Milton (1608–74) Born 9 December 1608 at Cheapside, London; son of John Milton, scrivener; educated St Paul's School and Christ's College, Cambridge; married (1) Mary Powell (1643), (2) Catherine Woodstock (1656) and (3) Elizabeth Minshull (1663). Travelled abroad in France and Italy (1638–9); took pupils at his home in Aldersgate Street, London. Wrote pamphlets attacking episcopacy, 1641–2 (*The Reason of Church Government*; *Of Reformation Touching Church Discipline in England*) – involved him in controversy with Joseph Hall, Bishop of Exeter. Sympathetic to Parliament's cause, but did not join the army on the outbreak of civil war. Wrote controversial book on divorce (1643) and *Areopagitica* on the censorship of the press (1644). Supported Parliament's victory in the war; favoured the army in their quarrel with Parliament (1647). Approved of the King's execution; wrote *Tenure of Kings and Magistrates* (1649), advocating the people's right to judge their rulers. Appointed Latin Secretary to the Council of State (1649); wrote at the request of the Council *Eikonoklastes* (1649 – a reply to Gauden's *Eikon Basilike*), *Pro Populo Anglicano* (1650 – a reply to Salmasius's *Defensio Regia pro Carolo I*) and *Defensio Secunda* (1654 – a reply to Moulin's *Regii Sanguinis Clamor ad Coelum*). Lost his sight (1652); moved to Westminster; assisted in official duties by Philip Meadows and Andrew Marvell; loyal to the Protectorate; supported the accession of Richard Cromwell; favoured the separation of Church and State. At the Restoration (1660) lived in hiding; his *Defensio* burnt by the common hangman; arrested, but pardoned under Indemnity Act. Wrote his most famous works in retirement at Bunhill Fields: *Paradise Lost* (1667), *Paradise Regained* (1671), *Samson Agonistes* (1671). Died 8 November 1674.

BIOGRAPHIES: D. Mason, *The Life of John Milton* (1946 edn); J. H. Hanford, *John Milton* (1949); E. M. W. Tillyard, *Milton* (1966 edn).

George Monck, Duke of Albemarle (1608–70) Born 6 December 1608 at Potheridge, Devon; son of Sir Thomas Monck. Took part in expeditions to Cadiz (1625) and the Isle of Rhé (1627); fought for the Dutch in Oxford's regiment (1629); present at the siege of Breda (1637). Returned to England on the outbreak of the Scottish rebellion (1639); served in Scotland as lieutenant-colonel of Newport's regiment (1640); served in Ireland against rebels as commander of Leicester's regiment; fought in victory at Kilrush (1642); after the Cessation, sent back to England to assist Charles I (1643); met the King at Oxford; appointed Major-General (January 1644), but taken prisoner in defeat by Fairfax at Nantwich; accused by the Commons of high treason (July); imprisoned in the Tower for two years. After the Civil War, persuaded by Lord Lisle to take the Covenant and serve Parliament in Ireland; appointed commander of forces in Ulster (1647–9), where he skilfully consolidated his position; forced to make truce with rebels under O'Neill, for which censured by the Commons. Accompanied Cromwell to Scotland as commander of new regiment (1650); led brigade of foot at Dunbar; appointed Lieutenant-General of Ordnance and commander-in-chief in Scotland on Cromwell's departure (1651); completed reduction of Scotland by the capture of Stirling, Dundee, Aberdeen, etc.; appointed one of the commissioners responsible for civil settlement (November 1651); returned to England (February 1652). On outbreak of the Dutch War, appointed as one of three generals of the fleet (November 1652); took part in victories off Portland (February 1653) and the Gabbard (June 1653). MP for Devon (1653). Returned to command the army in Scotland (1654–8). Supported the accession of Richard Cromwell as Protector (1658). With the outbreak of disorder following the forcible expulsion of Parliament by Lambert's English army, marched into England (January 1660); Lambert imprisoned; made member of the Council of State and Commander-in-Chief all forces; insisted on the election of a new parliament (April); opened negotiations with Charles II and advised him on contents of the Declaration of Breda (4 April); presented the King's letters to Parliament, which voted the Restoration (1 May); received commission as Captain-General; met the King at Dover (25 May); granted the Order of the Garter; created Baron Monck and Duke of Albemarle (7 July); supervised the government of London during the plague (1665) and the Great Fire (1666); joined Rupert and the navy in war against the Dutch (1666–7); appointed First Lord of the Treasury (May 1667). Died 3 January 1670.

BIOGRAPHIES: J. S. Corbett, *Monck* (1889); J. D. G. Davies, *Honest George Monck* (1936); O. M. W. Warner, *Hero of One Restoration* (1936).

Duke of Monmouth (1649–85) – *see* James Scott.

Duke of Newcastle (1592–1676) – *see* William Cavendish.

Earl of Nottingham (1647–1730) – *see* Daniel Finch.

Duke of Ormonde (1610–88) – *see* James Butler.

Sir Thomas Osborne, 1st Earl of Danby (1632–1712)   Born 20 February 1632; son of Sir Edward Osborne of Kiveton, Yorks; married Lady Bridget Bertie (1654). Appointed High Sheriff of Yorkshire (1661); MP for York (1665); Treasurer of the Navy (1668); Privy Councillor (1673); Lord High Treasurer (1673); Lord Lieutenant of the West Riding (1674); Knight of the Garter (1677). Created Viscount Osborne (February 1673), Baron Osborne (August 1673) and

Earl of Danby (June 1674). Chief minister of Charles II (1673–8); a High Tory; gained support of the Commons through bribery and trade in offices; renewed persecution laws against Roman Catholics and dissenters (1676); ended the Dutch War; opposed the aggressive designs of Louis XIV; arranged the marriage of Princess Mary to William of Orange (October 1677); consented to secret agreements between Charles II and Louis XIV for England's neutrality in return for cash. His fall engineered by Louis through Montagu (the ambassador in Paris), who betrayed his part in the secret negotiations. Impeached (1678) and imprisoned without trial until 1684; bitterly attacked by public opinion and pamphleteers. Impeachment removed (May 1685). Greatly distrusted James II's Catholic tendencies and arbitrary actions; signed the invitation to William of Orange (June 1688); seized control of York for William (November); chief advocate of the view that James had abdicated by implication and that the throne was vacant; urged the Lords to support the Commons' joint offer of the crown to William and Mary. Created Marquis of Carmarthen (1689); President of the Council (1689); Lord Lieutenant of the Three Ridings (1692); Duke of Leeds (1694). After the retirement of Lord Halifax (1690), almost solely in control of government. Impeached (1695) for receiving a bribe from the East India Company; escaped punishment, but gradually lost influence. Nicknamed 'Tom the Tyrant'. Resigned offices (1699); died 26 July 1712.

BIOGRAPHY: A. Browning, *Thomas Osborne, Earl of Danby and Duke of Leeds, 1632–1712* (1944–51).

William Prynne (1600–69)   Born at Swainswick, Somerset; son of Thomas Prynne; educated Bath Free School, Oriel College, Oxford, and Lincoln's Inn. Wrote an attack on stage plays, *Histriomastix* (1632); tried before the Star Chamber for his implied criticism of the Queen; sentenced to life imprisonment, £5000 fine, expulsion from Lincoln's Inn, loss of degree and both ears (1634). Wrote pamphlets in the Tower attacking bishops, especially Wren, Bishop of Norwich, in *News from Ipswich* (1636); again tried before the Star Chamber; sentenced to life imprisonment, £5000 fine, loss of the remainder of his ears and branding with the letters 'SL' ('Seditious Libeller'); deprived of books and pens. Released by the Long Parliament (1640), which declared the former sentences illegal (1641). Wrote pamphlets again attacking bishops (e.g. *The Antipathy of the English Lordly Prelacy*, 1641) and in favour of Parliament (e.g. *The Sovereign Power of Parliaments and Kingdoms*, 1643). Played leading part in the prosecution of Nathaniel Fiennes, Governor of Bristol (1643), and of Archbishop Laud (1645); wrote pamphlets on Laud's trial – *Hidden Works of Darkness* (1644), *Canterburies Doom* (1646). Wrote pamphlets against Independency, calling on Parliament to defeat the sectaries (e.g. *Independency Examined, Unmasked and Refuted*, 1644). Supported the Presbyterians in Parliament in their quarrel with the army (1647). Appointed member of the Committee of Accounts (1644), commissioner for visitation of Oxford University (1647), Recorder of Bath (1647), MP for Newport, Cornwall (1648).

Spoke vigorously against the army and in favour of settlement with the King; expelled and arrested in Pride's Purge; opposed the trial. On release (January 1649) wrote bitterly against the new Commonwealth (*A Legal Vindication of the Liberties of England*, 1649); arrested and imprisoned without trial (1650–3). Resumed seat (February 1660) on recall of the Long Parliament; speeded passing of the Militia Bill, which hastened the Restoration. MP for Bath in the Convention Parliament (1660); conducted campaign against the regicides; tried to restrict the Act of Indemnity. Reprimanded for his pamphlet against the Corporation Bill (1661); a manager in Mordaunt's impeachment (1667); opposed the banishment of Clarendon. Appointed Keeper of Records in the Tower (1660–9). Wrote *Brevia Parliamentaria Rediviva* (1662). Died 24 October 1669.

BIOGRAPHIES: E. W. Kirby, *William Prynne: A Study in Puritanism* (1931); W. M. Lamont, *Marginal Prynne, 1600–1699* (1963).

John Pym (1584–1643)   Eldest son of Alexander Pym of Brymore, Somerset; educated Broadgates Hall, Oxford, and Middle Temple; married Anna Hooker. Appointed Receiver General for Gloucestershire, Hampshire and Wiltshire (1607–38); MP for Tavistock (1620); advocated strict enforcement of the laws against Roman Catholics (1625); a manager of Buckingham's impeachment (1626); supported the Petition of Right and provided a major contribution to the bitter attack on Buckingham (1628). Became leader of the Popular party in the Short Parliament (1640); made memorable speech summarising the nation's grievances: helped to draw up petition demanding the trial of the King's advisers. In the Long Parliament, played leading part in the impeachment and trial of Strafford (1641); moved the impeachment of Laud (1640); supported the Root and Branch Bill (1641), although opposed to Presbyterian church system. Largely responsible for the Grand Remonstrance (1641); supported Haslerig's Militia Bill (1641). Offered the position of Chancellor of Exchequer by King in an attempt to win his support (January 1642). One of the Five Members (with Hampden, Holles, Haslerig and Strode) whose impeachment and arrest were unsuccessfully attempted by the King (January 1642). Appointed member of Parliament's Committee of Safety (July, 1642) to organise the war; proposed that Parliament should assume powers of taxation (November 1642); proposed imposition of the excise, after breakdown of the Oxford negotiations (March 1643). Became leader of the 'war party'; criticised Essex's lack of vigour in pursuing the war; successfully mediated in the dispute between Essex and Waller; advocated the alliance with Scotland; appointed Lieutenant-General of Ordnance (November 1643). Died of an internal abscess (8 December 1643). An able debater and a clever Parliamentary tactician.

BIOGRAPHIES: S. R. Brett, *John Pym: The Statesman of the Puritan Revolution* (1940); J. H. Hexter, *The Reign of King Pym* (1941); C. E. Wade, *John Pym* (1912).

Prince Rupert (1619–82)   Born 17 December 1619 in Prague; son of Elizabeth,

Queen of Bohemia, and Frederick V, Elector Palatine. Fled with parents to Berlin and Holland (1621); sent to live in Leyden (1623); fought with the Prince of Orange in the siege of Rhynberg (1633), invasion of Brabant (1635) and siege of Breda (1637); visited Charles I in England (1636–7); accompanied his father in the invasion of Westphalia (1638) – taken prisoner at Vlotho; released (1641) and returned to his parents at The Hague. On the outbreak of civil war, landed with Prince Maurice at Tynemouth and joined the King at Nottingham (1642); appointed General of the Horse; offended courtiers by his rough manner and arrogance. In 1642 commanded the right wing at Edgehill, captured Reading, defeated Parliamentarian infantry at Brentford before being forced back at Turnham Green. In 1643 took Cirencester, Birmingham, Lichfield and Bristol; besieged Gloucester; fought at Aldbourne Chase and Newbury. In 1644 created Earl of Holderness and Duke of Cumberland; given an independent command as Captain-General of Chester, Lancashire, Worcester, Shropshire and the six northern Welsh counties; relieved Newark and York; routed at Marston Moor; appointed Commander-in-Chief of the royal army; relieved Donnington Castle. In 1645 relieved Chester, captured Leicester, but defeated at Naseby; became Governor of Bristol, but surrendered it to Fairfax; banished by the King in anger, but brought about a reconciliation. Taken at the surrender of Oxford; ordered by Parliament to leave the country; fled to St Germain (July 1646). Served in the French army under Gassion at the sieges of Landrécy and La Basse (1647). Sailed with Prince Charles from Holland with the rebellious ships from Warwick's fleet (1648); went as commander of the royalist fleet to assist Ormonde in Ireland; brought relief to Kinsale and the Scilly Isles (1649); captured merchant ships off Portugal and in Mediterranean; pursued by Blake, who blockaded him in the Tagus and destroyed most of his fleet in Cartagena; sailed with the remainder to the West Indies (1652); returned to the court of Charles II in Paris (1653); lived in Germany (1654–60). At the Restoration made Privy Councillor (1662). Appointed Admiral of the White Fleet under the Duke of York at the Battle of Solebay (1665); joint commander of the fleet with Monck in battles against the Dutch (1666); Constable of Windsor Castle (1668); member of the Council for Trade and Plantations (1670); Vice-Admiral (1672) and Admiral (1673) of the fleet in the Third Dutch War; First Lord of the Admiralty (1673–9). Died 29 November 1682.

BIOGRAPHIES: E. Scott, *Rupert, Prince Palatine* (1899); B. E. Fergusson, *Rupert of the Rhine* (1952).

Earl of Salisbury (1563–1612) – *see* Robert Cecil.

George Savile, Marquis of Halifax (1633–95)   Born 11 November 1633: son of Sir William Savile of Thornhill, Yorks; educated Shrewsbury School; married (1) Dorothy Spencer (1656) and (2) Gertrude Pierrepont (1672). MP for Pontefract in Convention Parliament (1660); captain in Prince Rupert's regiment of horse

(1667); created Baron Savile and Viscount Halifax (1668); appointed Commissioner of Trade (1669) and Privy Councillor (1672). Opposed the Test Act (1673) and the policies of the Cabal; member of the new Council of Thirty (1679) and Committee for Foreign Affairs; created Earl of Halifax (1679), Marquis of Halifax and Lord Privy Seal (1682). Opposed the Exclusion Bill in the Lords (1680), but uneasy about James's increasing influence. Wrote *Character of a Trimmer* and *Character of King Charles II* (1685). Under James II made President of the Council, but dismissed after his opposition to the repeal of the Test and Habeas Corpus Acts (1686). Wrote *Letter to a Dissenter* (1686). After the invasion by William of Orange, sent by James II to negotiate. Pledged his support to William (December 1688); elected Speaker of the Lords in the Convention Parliament and Lord Privy Seal (1689). Resigned offices after fierce criticism (1689–90); continued to attend the House of Lords and opposed the renewal of press censorship (1692). Died 5 April 1695.

BIOGRAPHY: H. C. Foxcroft, *The Life and Letters of Sir George Savile* (1898).

James Scott, Duke of Monmouth (1649–85)   Born in Rotterdam; illegitimate son of Charles II by Lucy Walter; during the exile of the royalist court, adopted the name of James Crofts; married Lady Anne Scott (1663). After the Restoration returned to England (1662); created Duke of Monmouth and Orkney (1663); officially recognised by the King as his son. Followed military career: fought at sea against the Dutch (1665), appointed captain in the Life Guards (1668), commanded troops in the Dutch War (1672), served under Prince William of Orange (1678), fought at Bothwell Bridge against the Scottish Covenanters (1679). Advocated as the next heir to the throne by Shaftesbury and the Protestant party; banished to Holland by Charles II, who proclaimed his illegitimacy (1679). Returned without authority (1680) and made a triumphant tour through England; arrested at Stafford, but reconciled to the King; joined the plot to mount a revolution (1683); again banished to Holland, from which he was expelled on the accession of James II. Landed at Lyme Regis with small invasion force (11 June 1685); proclaimed his own legitimacy and right to the throne; marched through Chard, Taunton, Bridgwater, Keynsham, Norton St Philip, Frome and Wells, but disappointed at the lack of popular support; routed by the King's troops under Feversham and Churchill at Sedgemoor (5 July 1685); captured near Ringwood; executed 15 July 1685.

BIOGRAPHIES: G. Roberts, *The Life, Progresses and Rebellion of James, Duke of Monmouth* (1844); E. D'Oyley, *James, Duke of Monmouth* (1938); D. J. Porrit, *The Duke of Monmouth* (1953).

Earl of Shaftesbury (1621–83) – *see* Anthony Ashley Cooper.

Robert Spencer, 2nd Earl of Sunderland (1641–1702)   Born in Paris; son of Henry Spencer, 1st Earl; educated Christ Church, Oxford; married Anne Digby

(1665); succeeded to the peerage (1643). Officer in Prince Rupert's regiment of horse (1667); member of embassy sent to Madrid (1671); ambassador extraordinary to Louis XIV (1672) and at Nimeguen peace negotiations (1678). Appointed Privy Councillor and Gentleman of the Bedchamber (1674); Secretary of State (North) and member of the inner cabinet with Essex, Halifax and Temple (1679); member of the triumvirate (with Godophin and Hyde) known as 'The Chits', who directed affairs during Charles II's illness (1679). An opportunist, followed public opinion by supporting the Exclusion Bill (1680), but struck off the Council (1681); opened negotiations with William of Orange through Henry Sidney, envoy at The Hague. Reconciled with Charles II through the efforts of the Duchess of Portsmouth (1682); readmitted to the Council and reappointed Secretary of State (North) in 1683; approved of the executions of Russell and Sydney. Signed the proclamation of James II (1685); agreed to support repeal of the Test Act; made Lord President (1685); urged severe treatment of the Monmouth rebels (1685); became member of the new ecclesiastical commission (1686) and Knight of the Garter (1687); schemed for the dismissal of Rochester as Treasurer (1687); signed committal of the seven bishops (1688); publicly renounced the Protestant religion and took Mass (1688). Dismissed on approach of the revolution; fled to Rotterdam (1688); excepted from the Act of Indemnity (1690). Returned to England (1691); declared himself a Protestant; took oath of loyalty to William III; attended Parliament and court (1692); advised the King to appoint a Whig ministry; helped to reconcile the King and Princess Anne (1695); appointed Lord Chamberlain and member of the regency, but resigned in the face of public opinion (1697). Died 28 September 1702.

BIOGRAPHY: J. P. Kenyon, *Robert Spencer, Earl of Sunderland, 1641–1702* (1958).

Earl of Strafford (1593–1641) – *see* Thomas Wentworth.

John Thurloe (1616–68)   Born June 1616; son of Thomas Thurloe, rector of Abbot's Roding, Essex; married (1) Miss Peyton and (2) Anne Lytcott; law student. Secretary to the Parliamentary commissioners at the Treaty of Uxbridge (1645), but played no part in the execution of the King (1649). Appointed secretary to Strickland and St John on mission to Holland (1651); secretary to the Council of State (1652); clerk to the Committee for Foreign Affairs (1652); member of the Council of State (1653); Controller of Intelligence (1653); bencher at Lincoln's Inn (1654); Controller of the Post (1655); Chancellor of Glasgow University (1658). MP for Ely (1654 and 1656) and for Cambridge University (1659). His network of intelligence agents kept him advised on the intentions of foreign states and internal conspirators; responsible for explaining government policy to Parliament, but exerted little influence on Cromwell's decisions; a loyal supporter of Cromwell, believing that he should accept the offer of kingship (1657). Supported the accession of Richard Cromwell; led his party of supporters in the 1659 parliament, where he came under personal attack for his espionage system; advised Richard against dissolution under pressure from the army. Reappointed Secretary of State by the restored Rump; opened negotiations with Hyde for a possible restoration, but suspected by the royalists. At the Restoration arrested and accused of high treason (1660), but released on condition that he should assist the new Secretaries of State as required. Retired to Great Milton; died 21 February 1668.

BIOGRAPHY: D. L. Hobman, *Cromwell's Master Spy: A Study of John Thurloe* (1961).

Sir Henry Vane (1613–62)   Baptised 26 May 1613 at Debden, Essex; son of Sir Henry Vane, Comptroller of the King's Household; educated Westminster School and Magdalen Hall, Oxford; married Francis Wray (1640); converted to Puritanism (1628). Emigrated to New England (with Hugh Peters and John Winthrop) to secure freedom of worship (1635); became freeman of Massachusetts and Governor (1636); but dismissed following policy of un-restricted religious freedom and returned to England (1637). Appointed Joint Treasurer of the Navy (1639); granted knighthood (1640); elected MP for Hull in the Long Parliament (1640); provided important evidence at the trial of Strafford (1641); partly responsible for the Root and Branch Bill (1641); led the Popular party in Parliament during the temporary absence of the Five Members (January 1642). Prominent in the 'war party'; sent as commissioner to negotiate the Scottish alliance (1643); responsible for the insertion, into the Solemn League and Covenant, of the phrase 'according to the word of God' (as applied to the reform of the Church). With St John took over the leadership within Parliament after the death of Pym (1643); proposed formation of the Committee of Both Kingdoms to organise the war (February 1644); seconded Tate's motion for the Self-Denying Ordinance (December 1644); supported army reorganisation and Fairfax's appointment as General of the New Model. Appointed commissioner for the Treaty of Uxbridge negotiations (January 1645). Supported the army in its quarrel with the Presbyterian majority in Parliament (1647), but opposed their vote of no further addresses to the King (January 1648). Voted for non-alteration of government by King, Lords and Commons (April 1648); appointed commissioner at the Treaty of Newport; supported proposal to continue negotiations with the King (December 1648). Absent from Commons after Pride's Purge (3 December 1648 to 7 February 1649); opposed the trial and execution of the King. Elected to the Council of State, but unwilling to take oath approving of execution (February 1648); loyally supported the Commonwealth; served on numerous committees; a close friend of Cromwell; appointed head of the commission governing the navy (1649), Treasurer of the Navy (1650). Disagreement with Cromwell over dissolution of the Long Parliament (1653); retired to Lincolnshire; wrote tract, *A Healing Question Propounded and Resolved* (1656), for which imprisoned for three months. MP for Whitchurch in Richard Cromwell's parliament (1659); opposed the government and supported Lambert's forcible dissolution of the restored Rump. Arrested after the

Restoration (1660); wholly excepted from pardon; imprisoned for two years, tried and executed (1662).

BIOGRAPHIES: J. H. Adamson, *Sir Harry Vane: His Life and Times* (1973); J. K. Hosmer, *The Life of Young Harry Vane* (1888); J. Foster, *Sir Henry Vane the Younger* (1838); V. Rowe, *Sir Henry Vane the Younger* (1970).

George Villiers, 1st Duke of Buckingham (1592–1628)   Born 28 August 1592; son of Sir George Villiers of Brooksby, Leics; educated Billesdon School; married Lady Katherine Manners (1620). Appointed Cupbearer to the King (1614), Gentleman of the Bedchamber and knight (1615); created Viscount Villiers (1616), Knight of the Garter (1616), Earl of Buckingham (1617), Marquis of Buckingham (1618), Duke of Buckingham (1623). Appointed Lord High Admiral (1617). Dominant at court and favourite of the King after the fall of Somerset (1615) and removal of the Howards. Supported James I's plans for a marriage alliance between Prince Charles and the Spanish Infanta; accompanied Charles on an unsuccessful visit to Spain (1623). Then favoured war against Spain to recover the Palatinate for the King's son-in-law. Supported the marriage of Charles to Henrietta Maria, daughter of Louis XIII of France, but angered Parliament by promise of concessions to English Catholics (1624). Strongly criticised by Charles I's first parliament for the failure of Mansfeld's expedition to the Palatinate, owing to lack of supplies (1625). Organised the alliances with Denmark and the United Provinces (1625); planned the abortive expedition to Cadiz (1625). Attacked and impeached by the 1626 parliament for mismanagement of the war but saved from demands for his dismissal by the King's order for dissolution. After the declaration of war against France, led the fleet in person to assist the Huguenots in La Rochelle; but, after landing on the Isle of Rhé, driven back with heavy losses (1627). Singled out as 'the cause of all our miseries' by Eliot and Coke in the 1628 parliament, which passed a remonstrance demanding his dismissal; saved again by its dissolution. Assassinated by John Felton, a disgruntled ex-army officer, at Portsmouth, where he was planning another expedition to La Rochelle (1628).

BIOGRAPHIES: P. Erlanger, *George Villiers, Duke of Buckingham* (1953); K. Thomson, *Life and Times of George Villiers, Duke of Buckingham* (1860).

Thomas Wentworth, 1st Earl of Strafford (1593–1641)   Born 13 April 1593; son of Sir William Wentworth; educated St John's College, Cambridge, and Inner Temple; married (1) Margaret Clifford (1611) and (2) Arabella Holles (1625). Knighted (1611); MP for Yorkshire (from 1614); appointed Custos Rotulorum in Yorkshire (1615) and Sheriff (1625). Favoured the Popular party in Parliament; opposed James I's assertion that Parliament's privileges were not 'the ancient and undoubted right' of the House (1621); imprisoned for non-payment of forced loan (1627); vigorously defended the liberties of the subject (1628); attempted to use his great influence in Parliament to bring about a settlement between King and Commons; opposed the growth of Puritanism and

Parliament's desire to seize executive power. Became a servant of the King – created Baron Wentworth and Viscount Wentworth (1628); appointed President of the Council of the North (1628), where he applied the law strictly, and Privy Councillor (1629). Made Lord Deputy of Ireland (1632); protected trade, established flax manufacture, reformed the administration and organised the army in his policy of Thorough; became unpopular with English colonists for his stern regime and with native Irish for his threatened replantation of Connaught. Recalled to England (1639) as head of commission to deal with the Scottish problem; became chief adviser to the King. Created Earl of Strafford, Lord Lieutenant of Ireland and Lieutenant-General of the army (1640). Recommended calling the Short Parliament (1640) and the use of various expedients to provide for the Scottish war (debasement of the coinage, use of an Irish army, loan from Spain, etc.). Planned to impeach popular leaders for treasonable correspondence with the Scots, but was himself impeached by Pym following the assembly of the Long Parliament (1640). Tried in Westminster Hall, but convicted by Bill of Attainder; fear of popular rising forced Charles I to give his assent; executed 12 May 1641.

BIOGRAPHY: C. V. Wedgwood, *Strafford* (1962 edn).

5 PARLIAMENT

COMPOSITION

GROWTH PRIOR TO 1603

When Henry VII became King in 1485, the House of Commons was already of considerable size. Some thirty-seven counties and 111 boroughs returned 296 members. Thus the Commons had gradually grown over the preceding years, as successive reigns had seen small additions to the numbers of constituencies.

Growth of Composition of the Commons 1307–1603

Year	Counties	Boroughs	Total
Death of Edward I (1307)	74	160	234
Death of Edward II (1327)	74	172	246
Death of Edward III (1377)	74	194	268
Death of Henry VI (1461)	74	210	284
Death of Edward IV (1483)	74	222	296
Death of Henry VII (1509)	74	222	296
Death of Henry VIII (1547)	90	251	341
Death of Edward VI (1553)	90	285	375
Death of Mary (1558)	90	308	398
Death of Elizabeth (1603)	90	370	460

The thirty-seven counties represented were the ancient counties of England, less Chester, Durham and Monmouth.

Under the Tudors, membership of the Commons had risen swiftly, from 296 in 1509 to 460 by 1603, a rise of 56 per cent. Whilst some of these additions were the result of the calling of MPs from such areas as Wales and Chester (and Calais for the brief period 1536–58), by far the most important factor had been the enfranchisement of new and restored English boroughs.

GROWTH DURING THE STUART PERIOD

Composition during the Stuart Period, 1603–88

Reign	Method of creation	Counties	Boroughs	Universities	Total
James I	Prerogative charters	–	11	4[a]	487
	Resolutions of the House of Commons	–	12		
Charles I	Resolutions of the House of Commons	–	20	–	507
	Long Parliament	90	413	4	507
Charles II	Act of Parliament	2[b]	2	–	513
	Prerogative charter	–	2		

[a] These were the Universities of Oxford and Cambridge.
[b] The county of Durham.

BOROUGHS ENFRANCHISED BY JAMES I AND CHARLES I

Boroughs Enfranchised under James I

Amersham (Bucks)	2	Ilchester (Somerset)	2
Bewdley (Worcs)	1	Marlow (Bucks)	2
Bury St Edmunds (Suffolk)	2	Pontefract (Yorks)	2
Evesham (Worcs)	2	Tewkesbury (Glos)	2
Harwich (Essex)	2	Tiverton (Devon)	2
Hertford (Herts)	2	Wendover (Bucks)	2
		Total in 1625	381

Boroughs Enfranchised under Charles I

Ashburton (Devon)	2	Northallerton (Yorks)	2
Cockermouth (Cumberland)	2	Okehampton (Devon)	2
Honiton (Devon)	2	Seaford (Sussex)	2
Milborne Port (Somerset)	2	Shaftesbury (Dorset)	2
New Milton (Yorks)	2	Weobley (Hereford)	2
		Total in 1640	401

PARLIAMENTARY REPRESENTATION OF ENGLAND BY COUNTY, 1603

County	Represented 1603
Bedfordshire	4
Berkshire	10
Buckinghamshire	8
Cambridgeshire	4
Cheshire	4
Cornwall	44
Cumberland	4
Derbyshire	4
Devon	18
Dorset	18
Durham	–
Essex	6
Gloucestershire	8
Hampshire	26
Herefordshire	6
Hertfordshire	4
Huntingdonshire	4
Kent	18
Lancashire	14
Leicestershire	4
Lincolnshire	12
Middlesex	8
Monmouthshire	4
Norfolk	12
Northamptonshire	10
Northumberland	8
Nottinghamshire	6
Oxfordshire	8
Rutland	2
Shropshire	12
Somerset	12
Staffordshire	10
Suffolk	14
Surrey	14
Sussex	26
Warwickshire	6
Westmorland	4
Wiltshire	34
Worcestershire	6
Yorkshire	26

FRANCHISE AND QUALIFICATIONS

COUNTY FRANCHISE

By a statute of 1430 (18 Hen. VI c. 7) the county franchise was restricted to persons resident in the county having freehold to the minimum value of 40s. per annum. Those eligible for election (according to a statute of 1445 (23 Hen. VI c. 14) were to be 'notable knights of the same counties for which they are to be chosen' or persons of similar substance. Effectively, only persons with land of the annual value of £20 were thus eligible.

BOROUGH FRANCHISE

Originally the borough franchise had probably rested with all those entitled to describe themselves as burgesses (i.e. those free inhabitants of the borough who paid the proper dues and were enrolled at the court leet). As early as 1485, however, the tendency had already extensively developed to limit the franchise to a more selective and oligarchic system. The new boroughs which were granted charters by the Tudors often vested the franchise in a very small body – the later the charter, the more oligarchic the borough constitution.

OFFICERS OF THE HOUSE

SPEAKERS OF THE HOUSE OF COMMONS, 1603–88

Date of election	Name	Constituency
27 Oct 1601	Sir John Croke (1553–1620)	City of London
19 Mar 1604	Sir Edward Phelips (1560–1614)	Somerset
5 Apr 1614	Sir Randolph Crewe (1558–1646)	Saltash
30 Jan 1621	Sir Thomas Richardson (1569–1635)	St Albans
19 Feb 1624	Sir Thomas Crewe (1565–1634)	Aylesbury
6 Feb 1626	Sir Heneage Finch (d. 1631)	City of London
17 Mar 1628	Sir John Finch (1584–1660)	Canterbury
13 Apr 1640	Sir John Glanville (1586–1661)	Bristol
3 Nov 1640	William Lenthall (1591–1662)	Woodstock
30 July 1647	Henry Pelham (n.a.)	Grantham
6 Aug 1647	William Lenthall (1591–1662)	Woodstock
5 July 1653	Francis Rous (1579–1659)	Devonshire
4 Sep 1654	William Lenthall (1591–1662)	Oxfordshire
17 Sep 1656	Sir Thomas Widdrington (d. 1664)	Northumberland
27 Jan 1657	Bulstrode Whitelocke (1605–75)	Buckinghamshire
27 Jan 1659	Chaloner Chute (d. 1659)	Middlesex
9 Mar 1659	Sir Lislebone Long (1613–59)	Wells
16 Mar 1659	Thomas Bampfylde (d. 1693)	Exeter
7 May 1659	William Lenthall (1591–1662)	Oxfordshire

Date of election	*Name*	*Constituency*
13 Jan 1660	William Sày (1604–65)	Camelford
21 Jan 1660	William Lenthall (1591–1662)	Oxfordshire
25 Apr 1660	Sir Harbottle Grimston (1603–85)	Colchester
8 May 1661	Sir Edward Turnour (1617–76)	Hertford
4 Feb 1673	Sir Job Charlton (1614–97)	Ludlow
18 Feb 1673	Sir Edward Seymour (1633–1708)	Totnes
11 Apr 1678	Sir Robert Sawyer (1633–92)	Wycombe
6 May 1678	Sir Edward Seymour (1633–1708)	Totnes
15 Mar 1679	Sir William Gregory (1624–96)	Weobley
21 Oct 1680	Sir William Williams (1634–1700)	Chester
19 May 1685	Sir John Trevor (1637–1717)	Denbigh
22 Jan 1689	Henry Powle (1630–92)	Windsor

CLERKS OF THE PARLIAMENTS

1597	Sir T. Smith	1638	J. Browne
1609	R. Bowyer	1644	E. Norgate (at Oxford)
1621	H. Elsynge	1649	H. Scobell
1635	T. Knyvett	1660	J. Browne
1637	D. Bedingfield		

CLERK ASSISTANTS

c.	1597	O. Reynolds	1664	J. Walker
c.	1614	H. Elsynge	1682	J. Walker
	1621	J. Throckmorton		

GENTLEMAN USHER OF THE BLACK ROD (FROM 1683)

1683   T. Duppa

YEOMAN USHER OF THE BLACK ROD (FROM 1660)

1660   J. Whynyard

SERJEANTS-AT-ARMS

1585	C. Hampden
1606	J. Tyler
1609	W. Leigh
By 1628	W. Leigh
	H. Leigh
1673	Sir G. Charnock
	R. Charnock

DATES OF PARLIAMENTS, 1604–90

Dates	Remarks
19 Mar 1604 – 9 Feb 1611	1st parliament of James I
5 Apr 1614 – 7 June 1614	2nd parliament of James I (Addled Parliament)
30 Jan 1621 – 6 Jan 1622	3rd parliament of James I
19 Feb 1624 – 27 Mar 1625	4th parliament of James I
18 Jun 1625 – 12 Aug 1625	1st parliament of Charles I
6 Feb 1626 – 15 Jun 1626	2nd parliament of Charles I
17 Mar 1628 – 10 Mar 1629	3rd parliament of Charles I
13 Apr 1640 – 5 May 1640	4th parliament of Charles I (Short Parliament)
3 Nov 1640 – 20 Apr 1653	5th parliament of Charles I (Long Parliament). Pride's Purge, 6 Dec 1648. During the Interregnum, the Long Parliament continued as the Purged parliament until 20 April 1653
4 July 1653 – 12 Dec 1653	Parliament of Saints, Barebones parliament, or Assembly of Nominees
3 Sep 1654 – 22 Jan 1655	1st parliament of the Protectorate
17 Sep 1656 – 4 Feb 1658	2nd parliament of the Protectorate
27 Jan 1659 – 22 Apr 1659	Richard Cromwell's parliament
7 May 1659 – 13 Oct 1659	Long Parliament restored. Members excluded by Pride's Purge restored on 21 February 1660
26 Dec 1659 – 16 Mar 1660	
25 Apr 1660 – 29 Dec 1660	Convention parliament of the Restoration
8 May 1661 – 24 Jan 1679	Pension parliament
6 Mar 1679 – 12 July 1679	Habeas Corpus Parliament (prorogued on 27 May 1679 and never met again)
7 Oct 1679 – 18 Jan 1681	Exclusion Bill Parliament (prorogued before it met, and did not sit until 21 October 1680)
21 Mar 1681 – 28 Mar 1681	Oxford Parliament
19 May 1685 – 2 July 1687	James II's parliament (prorogued 2: November 1685 and never met again)
22 Jan 1689 – 6 Feb 1690	Convention Parliament of the Revolution

ATTENDANCE AT PARLIAMENT, 1660–88

HOUSE OF LORDS

Dates	Average attendance of Lords		
	Temporal	Spiritual	Total
25 Apr 1660 – 13 Sep 1660	65	–	65
6 Nov 1660 – 29 Dec 1660	65	–	65
8 May 1661 – 30 July 1661	80	–	80
20 Nov 1661 – 19 May 1662	63	18	81

Dates	*Average attendance of*		
	Lords		
	Temporal	*Spiritual*	*Total*
18 Feb 1663 – 27 July 1663	59	14	73
16 Mar 1664 – 17 May 1664	72	18	90
24 Nov 1664 – 2 Mar 1665	52	15	67
9 Oct 1665 – 31 Oct 1665	23	9	32
18 Sep 1666 – 8 Feb 1667	59	11	70
10 Oct 1667 – 19 Dec 1667	67	18	85
6 Feb 1668 – 9 May 1668	60	12	72
19 Oct 1669 – 11 Dec 1669	65	12	77
14 Feb 1670 – 11 Apr 1670	66	14	80
24 Oct 1670 – 22 Apr 1671	56	11	67
4 Feb 1673 – 29 Mar 1673	71	12	83
7 Jan 1674 – 24 Feb 1674	74	15	89
13 Apr 1675 – 9 June 1675	80	15	95
13 Oct 1675 – 22 Nov 1675	67	15	82
15 Feb 1677 – 28 May 1677	72	14	86
28 Jan 1678 – 13 May 1678	67	14	81
23 May 1678 – 15 July 1678	57	10	67
21 Oct 1678 – 30 Dec 1678	63	11	74
18 Mar 1679 – 27 May 1679	70	12	82
21 Oct 1680 – 10 Jan 1681	68	11	79
21 Mar 1689 – 28 Mar 1681	53	13	66
19 May 1685 – 2 July 1685	70	18	88
9 Nov 1685 – 20 Nov 1685	64	17	81

SOURCE: *English Historical Documents*. The above table of figures is based on lists of those present in the respective Journals of the House of Lords and House of Commons.

COMPOSITION OF PARLIAMENT

HOUSE OF COMMONS

Year	Total no.	Lawyers	Merchants
1614	475	48	42
1640	507	75	45

SOURCES: Mary F. Keeler, *The Long Parliament 1640–41* (1954), and Thomas L. Moir *The Addled Parliament* (1958).

HOUSE OF LORDS

Year	Total no. (excluding bishops)
1603	55
1610	80
1628	126 (Buckingham's sale of peerages)

6 LOCAL GOVERNMENT

THE COUNTY

ADMINISTRATIVE DIVISIONS

COUNTY: since Henry VIII's statute of 1536, England had been clearly divided into forty counties and Wales into twelve.

COUNTY CORPORATE: by 1689 there were in addition nineteen cities and boroughs styled 'counties in themselves' by royal charter (viz. Bristol, Canterbury, Carmarthen, Chester, Coventry, Exeter, Gloucester, Haverfordwest, Hull, Lichfield, Lincoln, London, Newcastle, Norwich, Nottingham, Poole, Southampton, Worcester, York). Exempt from control by the county sheriff; but most within the military jurisdiction of the Lord Lieutenant (although London and Haverfordwest appointed their own).

COUNTY PALATINE: county in which the prerogative, normally exercised by the Crown, was claimed by a great earl or bishop. By the seventeenth century only four such areas effectively remained: Lancashire, Cheshire, Durham and the Isle of Ely. The Lord Palatine assumed responsibility for all major appointments (i.e. Lord Lieutenant, Sheriff, Coroner, justices of the peace, Custos Rotulorum, etc). The counties palatine had special judicial organisation, operated by their own chief justices, outside the normal Assize circuits.

HUNDRED (or WAPENTAKE, WARD, LATHE, RAPE): an administrative sub-division of the county under a group of justices and a High Constable for matters of law, order and rate collection.

PARISH (see also below): smallest administrative unit, into which hundreds were subdivided; under a Petty Constable for matters of law, order and rate collection.

COUNTY ADMINISTRATION

FUNCTION: designed to enable central government to extract from the county its service to the State – not to encourage establishment of local self-government; but a large proportion of adult males, all unpaid, were involved in the structure of local government as jurymen or officials at parish level.

90

CONTROLS EXERCISED BY CENTRAL GOVERNMENT:
(1) All major officers (except coroners) appointed and dismissed by the monarch.
(2) The Court of King's Bench could overrule the justices of the peace by taking cases out of their hands or quashing their verdicts if a mistake had been made.
(3) All civil officers required to present themselves at the Assizes before the King's judges to give an account of the maintenance of law and order within the county.
(4) The Privy Council could issue orders at any time for immediate implementation of statutes and common law.

SERVICES DEMANDED BY CENTRAL GOVERNMENT AND EXECUTED BY COUNTY OFFICIALS:
(1) Military service: either the *posse comitatus* (against internal rebellion) or the *militia* (for national defence).
(2) Taxes: aids, subsidies, land tax, ship money, etc.
(3) Maintenance of the peace.
(4) Upkeep of main bridges and gaols.

COUNTY OFFICERS

LORD LIEUTENANT: office dated from mid-sixteenth century; its holder was normally chosen from among the greatest noblemen and appointed for life; he presided over the whole county. One man could hold office for more than one county. From 1689 the office was often combined with that of Custos Rotulorum (Keeper of the Rolls of the Peace). Responsible for organising the county militia and nominating justices of the peace; frequently a member of Privy Council.

DEPUTY LIEUTENANTS: controlled the militia during absences of the Lord Lieutenant; normally nominated by the latter (subject to royal approval) from amongst the ranks of the lesser nobility or greater gentry.

CUSTOS ROTULORUM: a civil officer, keeper of the county records; from the sixteenth century normally a leading justice, appointed by the Crown. During the seventeenth century the office was increasingly combined with that of Lord Lieutenant.

HIGH SHERIFF: appointed for one year, normally from amongst the minor nobility; service was obligatory. The office had declined in importance since the Middle Ages. Responsible for the County Court, control of Parliamentary elections, nomination of jurymen and ceremonial duties for judges of Assize.

UNDER SHERIFF: a professional appointed for one year by the High Sheriff to undertake all but his ceremonial duties; responsible for execution of all writs and processes of law, for suppression of riots and rebellions, and for holding the County Court.

HIGH BAILIFF: appointed by the High Sheriff to execute his instructions in the hundred.

FOOT BAILIFF (or BOUND BAILIFF): appointed by the High Sheriff or Under Sheriff to carry messages or search out individuals for the execution of justice.

CLERK OF THE PEACE: a professional officer receiving fees for his services to individuals; appointed for life by the Custos Rotulorum. Duties: to draft formal resolutions of the justices at Quarter Sessions and to advise them on matters of law. Duties often performed by a Deputy Clerk (a leading solicitor in the county town).

CORONER: a professional officer earning fees from his service; between two and twelve elected for life by freeholders of the county from amongst their own number (in certain liberties the traditional right of appointment held by an individual or group – e.g. the Dean of York in the Liberty of St Peter, York; holders of office then known as FRANCHISE CORONERS). Duties: to hold inquests on (1) suspicious deaths, committing to trial anyone whom the Coroner's Jury find guilty of murder; (2) treasure trove, pronouncing on rightful ownership.

HIGH CONSTABLE: appointed normally for one year by Quarter Sessions; service was obligatory; assisted by petty constables in each parish. Duties: to execute instructions of the justices in the hundred; towards the end of the seventeenth century also responsible for collecting the county rate assessed at Quarter Sessions and for repair of bridges and gaols.

COMMISSION OF THE PEACE

JUSTICES OF THE PEACE: gradually, under the Tudors and Stuarts, took over from the great officers the government of the county, both judicial and administrative, executing statutes issued from central government. Qualifications for office: had to be a £20 freeholder resident in the county; to receive the sacraments in accordance with the Anglican rite; to have sworn the oaths of allegiance and supremacy; and to have (in theory) some knowledge of law and administration. Nominated by the Lord Lieutenant and appointed by the monarch, normally for life, from amongst the noblemen and gentry. Duties: 'to keep and cause to be kept all ordinance and statutes for the good of our peace' and 'to chastise and punish all persons that offend' against such statutes. Commission revised in 1590 to enable justices to act in three ways: individually; jointly, with colleagues in a division; collectively, as a General Sessions of the county.

COURT OF QUARTER SESSIONS: a General Sessions of the Peace for the whole county to be held four times a year; all justices of the peace summoned to attend under the theoretical chairmanship of the Custos Rotulorum; also summoned were the Sheriff, high bailiffs, high constables, coroners and petty constables, who were required to report offences from within their areas. Juries in attendance: one Jury of Inquiry from each hundred; a Grand Jury and petty juries from the county at large. Functions of the Court:

(1) to try private individuals for breaches of the law;
(2) to hear presentments against parishes or hundreds (or against individual officers) for failure to carry out their duties;
(3) to carry out routine administration – e.g. licensing of traders, maintenance of gaols and bridges, regulation of wages and prices, supervision of houses of correction, etc.; and
(4) to hear appeals against decisions by local justices.

PRIVATE OR SPECIAL SESSIONS: Divisional Sessions, usually based on the hundred and meeting in many cases at monthly intervals. Summoned to attend: justices from the division; local parish and hundred officials. Empowered by Privy Council Order (1605) to deal with all matters not requiring juries (e.g. vagrancy, poor relief, etc.).

PETTY SESSIONS: various legislation empowered any two justices sitting together to appoint local overseers of the poor and surveyors of the highways, to supervise accounts of parochial officials, to make rates, to license alehouses, to make orders for maintenance of illegitimate children and removal of paupers, to try and to punish certain categories of offenders (e.g. poachers, unlicensed ale-keepers, rioters, etc.), and to hear and commit to Quarter Sessions more serious cases (e.g. larceny, assault, etc.).

THE QUORUM CLAUSE: the Commission required that, where only two justices were sitting, one should be a justice who had been 'named' in the Commission (i.e. who possessed real knowledge of the law). By the end of the seventeenth century, this clause was scarcely valid, because all justices were named as of the quorum.

JUSTICES ACTING INDIVIDUALLY: each justice had the power

(1) to commit suspects to the county gaol to await trial;
(2) to require a person by summons to appear at the next Quarter Sessions;
(3) to punish by fine or stocks those guilty of profane oaths, drunkenness, non-attendance at church, breaking the Sabbath, rick-burning or vagrancy; and
(4) to present at Quarter Sessions any parishes or parish officers failing in their responsibilities for highway maintenance and poor relief.

COUNTY COURT: although by the seventeenth century most of its dealings had been taken over by Quarter Sessions, etc., it still met under the High Sheriff (or, in practice, the Under Sheriff). Functions:

(1) to recover civil debts under 40s.;
(2) to witness the High Sheriff's return to the writs requiring election of a Coroner and of two knights of the shire to represent the county in Parliament; and

(3) to assess, with the help of a jury, matters of compensation (for road-widening, etc.).

GRAND JURY (or GRAND INQUEST): composed of between twelve and twenty-four men, usually drawn from landowners, merchants, manufacturers, clergy and other professional people; summoned by the High Sheriff to attend for one or two days at Quarter Sessions or Assizes; verdicts and presentments valid if at least twelve members agreed. Functions:

(1) to consider criminal bills of indictment; then as 'true bills' (if a *prima facie* case had been established) or to reject them with the endorsement 'ignoramus';
(2) to consider presentments of parishes and hundreds (or individual officers) for neglect of their duty, and to return a 'truebill' (as above) if case established;
(3) to make a formal presentment for repair of the county gaol, county hall, bridges or houses of correction before county funds were released for these purposes by the justices; and
(4) to express county opinion on matters of common concern in petitions to Parliament or presentments at Quarter Sessions or Assizes (e.g. over unlawful assemblies, vagrancy, etc.).

HUNDRED JURY (or PETTY JURY OF INQUIRY): each hundred and borough would have its own Petty Jury, composed of between twelve and twenty-four men and summoned by the High Sheriff through the high bailiffs. Unanimity not required in verdicts or presentments, if at least twelve members agreed. Functions: to make a presentment at Quarter Sessions of any public nuisances (especially concerning rivers, bridges, roads) or any local officials neglectful of duties. By the end of the seventeenth century these juries were falling into disuse; tasks taken over by high constables and petty constables.

TRAVERSE OR FELONS' JURIES: formed from a panel of petty jurymen summoned by the High Sheriff from the county as a whole; used to decide issues of fact in criminal trials.

THE PARISH

ADMINISTRATIVE FUNCTION

By the seventeenth century the parish was both the ecclesiastical division (in which a priest performed his duties to the inhabitants) and a unit of local government within the larger area of a hundred. By employing unpaid amateurs as parish officers, supervised by justices of the peace, the central government succeeded in collecting its dues and enforcing its statutes even at the remotest local level. Parishes varied considerably in size and population, a few spanning the boundaries of two counties.

NATURE OF PARISH OFFICE

TERMS OF OFFICE: service unpaid, compulsory, one year's duration (or until a replacement appointed).

QUALIFICATION FOR OFFICE: no property or religious qualification; in some parishes all males served in rotation, in others holders of certain units of land served in rotation.

EXEMPTIONS FROM OFFICE: peers, clergy, members of Parliament, barristers, justices of the peace, revenue officers, members of the Royal College of Physicians, aldermen of the City of London; exemption could also be gained by paying a fine or finding a substitute.

RESPONSIBILITIES: officer personally responsible to the justices or to the Bishop (in the case of churchwardens), not to the parish; duties were arduous, time-consuming and often unpopular.

PARISH OFFICERS

CHURCHWARDENS: usually between two and four appointed annually. Method of appointment varied considerably: by methods described above, by election at an open or close meeting of the Vestry, by nomination of retiring churchwardens, by appointment by the incumbent – or by a combination of these. Sworn in by the Archdeacon. Responsible for

(1) maintenance and repair of church fabric;
(2) provision of materials required for services;
(3) allocation of seats in church;
(4) maintenance of churchyard;
(5) annual report to the Bishop on the progress of the incumbent, condition of the fabric and moral state of the parish;
(6) assistance to the Constable and surveyors of highways in civil duties within the parish;
(7) assistance to overseers of the poor in relief of poverty, lodging of the impotent poor, apprenticing of children; and
(8) levying a church rate on all parishoners when required for poor-law purposes, and maintaining proper accounts.

CONSTABLE: established in office by two justices (or, occasionally, by surviving manorial Court Leet); responsible to justices of the peace, working under High Constable for the hundred; expenses paid by a 'constable's rate' on the parish or by fees for specific duties. Duties:

(1) to deal with vagrants according to the law;
(2) to supervise alehouses;
(3) to call parish meetings as required;
(4) to apprehend felons;

    (5) to place minor trouble-makers in the stocks;

    (6) to attend the justices in Petty and Quarter Sessions, making presentments on law-breakers, etc.; and

    (7) to levy the county rate in the parish.

SURVEYOR OF THE HIGHWAYS: established by statute in 1555; formally appointed by the Constable and churchwardens after consultation with other parishoners; responsible to the justices of the peace for giving a regular report on state of the roads, for receiving instructions on work to be done and for rendering his accounts. Duties:

    (1) to direct 'statute labour' as required on local roads (wealthier inhabitants to send men, oxen and horses; ordinary parishoners to offer six days' personal labour);

    (2) to collect fines from defaulters and commutation fee from those who bought exemption;

    (3) to order the removal of obstructions from the highways (e.g. overgrown hedges and trees, undrained ditches, etc.); and

    (4) to collect a highway rate, if authorised at Quarter Sessions, and any fines imposed on the parish for failure to maintain its highways.

OVERSEERS OF THE POOR: established by statute in 1597; between two and four appointed for each parish by the justices to whom they were responsible. Duties (in co-operation with churchwardens):

    (1) to relieve destitute people;

    (2) to remove paupers without settlement rights to their former parish;

    (3) to make provision for illegitimate children;

    (4) to apprentice destitute children;

    (5) to assess and collect the poor rate;

    (6) to prepare accounts for the justices.

MINOR PAID OFFICES:

Parish Clerk	Hogwarden
Sexton	Pinder
Bellringer	Beadle
Scavenger	Dog Whipper
Town Crier (or Bellman)	Vestry Clerk
Hayward	

PARISH VESTRY: a parish meeting held in church at Easter, and at other times if necessary. Functions:

    (1) to elect usually one churchwarden;

    (2) to decide on a church rate to defray the churchwardens' expenses and to cover repairs to the fabric;

    (3) to make any new by-laws for the parish; and

    (4) to administer the pound and common pasture.

MUNICIPAL CORPORATIONS

By 1689 there were approximately 200 boroughs in England and Wales which had received the privilege of incorporation through royal charter. These possessed some or all of the powers listed below.

POWERS OF THE CORPORATION

(1) To own, administer and sell property in land.
(2) To administer the common meadow and wasteland.
(3) To control trade; to hold markets and fairs.
(4) To return burgesses to sit in Parliament.
(5) To create a magistracy for the purpose of holding borough Petty Sessions and borough Quarter Sessions.
(6) To formulate by-laws.
(7) To levy local taxes and tolls.

OBLIGATIONS OF THE CORPORATION

(1) To collect the King's revenue and to execute his writs.
(2) To maintain the King's peace; to enforce his laws; to organise the nightly watch.
(3) To support financially the borough's burgesses in Parliament.
(4) To repair walls, bridges and streets.
(5) To administer charitable trusts for schools, hospitals, poor people, etc.

MEMBERSHIP OF THE CORPORATION

Method of gaining membership, seldom stipulated in the Charter, varied considerably. Qualifications required for gaining 'freedom' included at least one of the following:

(1) ownership of freehold within the borough (in some cases only the owners of certain specified burgages would qualify);
(2) working an apprenticeship under a freeman of the borough (usually for seven years);
(3) birth (i.e. sons of freeman) or marriage (i.e. husbands of freeman's widow or daughter);
(4) membership of local guilds or trade companies;
(5) co-option by gift, redemption or purchase;
(6) membership of the Governing Council (i.e. no freemen outside). Freemen were normally admitted to membership by formal presentment of a local jury or court. Freemen could also be disfranchised for breach of duty, misdemeanour, etc.

MINOR OFFICIALS OF THE CORPORATION

Responsible to the chief officers; often salaried or collecting fees; usually possessing uniform or staff of office.

AGRICULTURAL OFFICIALS: haymakers, pound-keepers, woodwards, pasture-masters, common-keepers, mole-catchers, swineherds, etc.

MARKET OFFICIALS: bread-weighers, butter-searchers, ale-tasters, searchers and sealers of leather, searchers of the market, fish and flesh searchers, coalmeters, cornprizers, etc.

ORDER AND MAINTENANCE OFFICIALS: water bailiffs, bridge-keepers, Serjeant-at-Mace or Beadle, Town Crier or Bellman, Scavenger or Street Warden, Cleaner of the Castle Walks, Cleaner of Water Grates, Sweeper of Streets, Weeder of Footpaths, etc.

CHIEF OFFICERS OF THE CORPORATION

MAYOR (OR BAILIFF, PORTREEVE, ALDERMAN, WARDEN): named in the charter as head of the Corporation; with wide powers. Presided at all meetings of the Council; responsible for the management of Corporate estates; always a justice of the peace, presided at the borough Quarter Sessions; responsible for courts under the Corporation's jurisdictions; usually acted as Coroner and Clerk of Market; sometimes acted as Keeper of Borough Gaol and Examiner of Weights and Measures; appointed minor officials.

BAILIFFS: status varied considerably – in forty boroughs they were heads of the Corporation, in about 100 they were minor officials, in about thirty they were chief officers. Normally two bailiffs. As chief officers, responsible for summoning juries, accounting for fines, collection of rents, etc.; sometimes acted also as Treasurer, Coroner, Keeper of Borough Gaol, Clerk of Market; often, as justices of the peace, sat as judges on borough courts; occasionally undertook duties of the Sheriff within the borough. Usually elected by the Council.

RECORDER: a lawyer; legal adviser to the Corporation. Presided at some of the borough courts; administered oath of office to Mayor; as a justice of the peace, sat at the Borough Court of Quarter Sessions; usually received an attendance fee or nominal stipend.

CHAMBERLAIN (or TREASURER, RECEIVER): the treasurer of the Corporation, usually appointed by the Council.

TOWN CLERK: usually appointed by the Council, but not a member of it. Responsible for a wide range of administration: often Clerk of the Peace, Clerk to the Magistrates and clerk of all the borough courts; sometimes Coroner, Keeper of the Records, Deputy Recorder, president of the borough courts; usually a justice of the peace.

ALDERMEN

Known usually as the Mayor's Brethren; sometimes responsible for ensuring that by-laws were enforced in a particular ward of the borough; but principally a permanent and select consultative council (always part of the Common Council). Also collectively performed some judicial functions (licensing alehouses, making rates, appointing constables, etc.); tenure was normally for life.

COUNCILLORS

Usually twelve, twenty-four or forty-eight in number; had no specific functions other than to form the Court of Common Council (together with the aldermen and chief officers).

COURTS OF THE CORPORATION

COURT OF RECORD (or THREE WEEKS' COURT, COURT OF PLEAS or MAYOR'S COURT): a court of civil jurisdiction consisting of one or more of the specified judges (usually, Mayor, Bailiff, Recorder, Town Clerk, aldermen, etc.); often met every three weeks. Jurisdiction limited to suits arising within the borough: usually personal actions for debt or concerning land.

COURT LEET: right to hold court normally granted in the Charter; responsible for minor criminal jurisdiction, making of by-laws, control of commons and wastes, appointment of officers and admission of new tenants and freeholders. Administrative functions gradually taken over by the administrative courts during the latter part of the seventeenth century.

BOROUGH COURT OF QUARTER SESSIONS: gradually took over criminal jurisdiction from the Court Leet; normally only six Justices of the Peace, all of whom held particular positions (e.g. Mayor, Recorder, High Steward, Common Clerk, Coroner, etc.); often sat monthly or even weekly to hear a great variety of offences and complaints and to pass administrative orders.

COURT OF PIE POWDER: held by Mayor or deputy to deal summarily with offenders at the market or fair.

COURT OF ORPHANS: held by Mayor or deputy to administer estates of minors.

COURT OF CONSERVANCY: held by Mayor or deputy to enforce rules concerning the river.

COURT OF ADMIRALTY: held by Mayor or deputy to deal with matters concerning harbours fishing or shipping.

COURT OF COMMON COUNCIL: an administrative court consisting of aldermen, councillors and chief officers; members fined for absence, sworn to secrecy and obliged to wear their gowns of office; committees appointed to deal with particular functions; by the seventeenth century had acquired wide powers of imposing taxes, passing by-laws, controlling revenue, etc.

7 THE CHURCH

THE ESTABLISHED CHURCH

The history of the established Church during the seventeenth century is centred round its attempt to secure an ecclesiastical monopoly. In 1689 its failure to identify Church and State was acknowledged by the legislation of the Toleration Act. Throughout the preceding period it worked to achieve this by appeasing dissident elements within the Church and eliminating opposition from outside.

In appeasing dissident elements within the Church, there was a constant tension between the aims of uniformity and comprehension. Uniformity was ultimately seen to be preferable, which meant forgoing the Church's claim to an ecclesiastical monopoly. The elimination of opposition from outside the Church proved impossible, with the result that efforts were instead directed towards making it impotent.

The problems faced by James I revolved around Parliament's claims to intervene in religious matters, James having demonstrated at the Hampton Court Conference that he was unwilling to depart from the Elizabethan settlement. He emphatically reaffirmed the authority of bishops, and refused to allow any of the more substantial changes demanded by Puritans. On the other hand, he was deeply opposed to Arminianism. Under Charles I the Arminians, who had hitherto been only a faction at court, gained sway. Through the exercise of patronage they were able to secure a number of important ecclesiastical posts. This caused the whole Church to polarise between them and those who adhered to the traditional Calvinistic theology. The more that the Laudians emphasised ceremony, the position of the priest, the sacraments and introduced changes in church furnishings, the stronger grew the Puritan opposition. The combination of this opposition with the political opposition to Charles I's arbitrary government led ultimately to the overthrow of both the episcopacy and the monarchy. One of the strongest fears aroused by the religious policies of the 1630s was that the Laudians were trying to re-establish Roman Catholicism. Although there was little truth in this, it was a powerful factor in consolidating the opposition to the Established Church.

In 1640 Charles I summoned Parliament after eleven years without its meeting. It had little time to discuss religious questions, but the Convocation which met at the same time was given special permission to continue sitting after the dissolution of Parliament. It drew up new canons for the Church. The parliament which met in November 1640 at once challenged the legality of the canons. In the months following it attacked episcopacy, the church courts and Laud's innovations. The attack on the bishops was directed against their involvement in Charles I's government and against their exercise of secular jurisdiction (e.g. sitting in the House of Lords). Charles was prepared to exclude bishops from the government and to deprive them of their powers in the church and prerogative courts, but he held out until February 1642 against excluding them from the House of Lords. Gradually the Commons attack turned to the very existence of the episcopacy. This had the effect of reversing some opinion in Charles's favour. But bishops were abolished in 1646, and cathedral clergy in 1649. During this period parliament arrogated to itself the power not just to criticise the Church, but also to direct it.

Technically the episcopal church was disestablished and replaced by a Presbyterian church during the period 1646–60. In fact there was a high degree of continuity in the parishes. Possibly a quarter of parish clergy were replaced during this period for reasons other than death or promotion. The basic system of tithes for supporting the parish clergy remained the same, and lay patronage continued. Both bishops and church courts continued to function in some areas until the late 1640s. By the mid 1650s, however, the number of surviving bishops was so small as to endanger the apostolic succession and to make ordination a problem. Many ordinations were performed secretly by itinerant Irish bishops. The church courts disappeared completely. Their work was taken over by the civil magistrate, who, even before the Civil War, had taken over many of their functions. The one church court to survive was the Probate Court, which was not replaced until 1653.

That episcopacy would be restored in 1660 was not in doubt, but the doctrinal position of the Church was a matter for debate. Charles II seemed to favour either a considerable degree of toleration or a loosely comprehensive settlement, certainly including Presbyterians. Ejected clergy were restored and Presbyterians and Anglicans met at the Savoy to discuss an accommodation. The desires of the clergy were frustrated by Parliament, who were the real architects of the settlement. In the Clarendon Code they asserted their refusal to allow any sort of comprehension or toleration. Church membership was defined by willingness to receive the Anglican sacraments and penalties for those who refused them were enacted. Little of the later religious legislation of the reign affected the established Church, although the clergy were shaken to discover how many Protestant nonconformists registered under the 1672 Declaration of Indulgence. The Exclusion struggle and the successive Exclusion Bills pressed the claim for a Protestant monarch, but less for love of the Anglican settlement than for fear of the consequences of having a Roman Catholic monarch. Thus, during Charles II's reign Parliament finally established its control over the established Church and associated Anglicanism with loyalty.

James II's intentions towards the established Church were uncertain, although many churchmen, disturbed by the disruptions of the Popish Plot, the Exclusion crisis, and Monmouth's rebellion, were prepared to trust him. They were soon to discover that he wanted to secure for Roman Catholics the same rights as Anglicans possessed. His desire for toleration as far as was consonant with political stability was quite out of step with Parliament's ideas of what was tolerable. Parliament reflected the views of many Anglicans that the established Church was seriously under threat from James's policies. The open practice of Roman Catholicism finally created such fears that seven bishops, led by the Archbishop of Canterbury, Sancroft, were moved to protest. Their subsequent imprisonment, trial and acquittal asserted Parliament's control of religion, and its refusal to allow the church settlement to be threatened. The political overtones of allowing the toleration of Roman Catholicism were, in part, responsible for the Revolution of 1688.

The Bill of Rights confirmed William III's assumption of the throne and limited the terms under which he was to rule. Certain of the Anglican clergy, however, felt unable to acknowledge his right to the throne, and, refusing to take the Oath of Allegiance, were deprived of their benefices.

PURITANISM AND NONCONFORMITY

At James I's accession there was a sizeable body of Puritan opinion in the established Church. Their views were embodied in the Millennary Petition. Many of them were disappointed at the outcome of the Hampton Court Conference and their cause suffered a setback in the ejections of 1604. James was not ill disposed to their demands for a more Protestant settlement, but refused to allow his right to dictate religious questions to be impaired. Puritans had a considerable amount of support in Parliament and during James I's reign made more extensive demands to discuss religious questions. Parliament also sought stricter observance of the Sabbath than the King wanted.

During the later years of James's reign and under Charles I, Puritans found that conformity was being more narrowly interpreted and more stringently enforced. They thus began increasingly to use lectureships as a vehicle for disseminating their views within the Church. It is important to remember, however, that lectureships were also used extensively by the more orthodox members of the established Church. It was not until the 1620s that Puritans began to see the possibilities that they afforded. Archbishop Laud, too, saw these possibilities, and mounted a vigorous campaign to enforce a higher degree of orthodoxy amongst lecturers.

Under James I Puritans became more politically oriented. This was, in part, a consequence of his inability to prevent Parliament from discussing religious questions. Elizabeth had successfully quashed Parliament's claims in this area, but had had actively to combat them. James found himself unable to do this. The war in the Palatinate and Bohemia and the Spanish marriage scheme strengthened Parliament's demands for a Protestant foreign policy. Under Charles I, Puritans in Parliament pressed their claims for church reform and for a voice in religious questions even more vociferously. Charles, however, backed by Laud, was less willing than his father to allow them. He tried to suppress theological controversy, while Laud worked to control clerical appointments and enforce censorship. As a result of these policies, and the means by which they were enforced in the prerogative courts, many Puritans were forced into opposition. From criticising Laud's policies, they turned to criticising the institutions that were capable of allowing such policies to be enforced. The demands of the Short and Long Parliaments were for a basic reconsideration of the church settlement. This polarisation of opinion created many problems for Puritans, for not all opposed the King. Indeed, at the outbreak of war, many of those who had led the opposition to the King's policies and his ministers found themselves unable to rebel against the lawful ruler.

Once war had broken out, Parliament shelved its consideration of religious questions until June 1643, when it set up the Westminster Assembly, the synod of divines called for in the Grand Remonstrance. Its debates made concrete the latent tension between English and Scottish Presbyterianism, the former being erastian, and between Presbyterianism and Independency, a State church against gathered congregations. These tensions made the enforcement of a universal church settlement in England impossible. Despite the legislation passed by Parliament on the advice of the Westminster Assembly to establish a State Presbyterian church, Parliament's most effective ecclesiastical legislation during the Civil War and Interregnum concerned clerical salaries and appointments, and the enforcement of the Covenant and the Directory of Worship, which were used as political tests.

During the early 1640s there began to emerge a number of groups of people who challenged the basic precept of a national church. Some of these were Independents, who principally differed from the Presbyterians in the matter of church organisation. During the 1640s their political influence increased, partly as a result of the prevalence of Independency in the New Model Army. Pride's Purge, in 1648, secured an Independent majority in Parliament, and they continued to dominate the government until 1659. During this period there were several serious attempts to establish religious toleration, a principal held in general by most Independents. Owing to the lax enforcement of such persecuting legislation as remained in force, toleration existed in fact, although it was rarely extended to Roman Catholics and episcopalians, usually for political reasons.

The other religious groups to challenge the Presbyterians are covered by the blanket term 'sectaries'. In the main they denied that the authority, civil or ecclesiastical, had the power to coerce in religious questions. Before the Civil War these views were expressed by the separatists. Although there is little continuity between the separatists of the early seventeenth century and the separatists and sectaries of the Civil War period, they represented the same ecclesiastical tradition. In the early 1640s separatist sects usually professed a belief in the gathered congregation and a Calvinist theology. The General and Particular Baptists already existed as distinct formations. During the later 1640s and 1650s, however, many more sects developed distinctive characteristics. Thus, there was a proliferation of types of sect and a hardening of the divisions between them. Ranters, Quakers and Fifth Monarchists are three of the groups to emerge in this period as distinct formations. The extremist beliefs and behaviour of some sectaries caused a reaction against religious toleration, reflected in the terms of the Humble Petition and Advice of 1657 and the legislation against blasphemy. Antinomianism, millennarianism and the beliefs of the Quakers were discredited because they were seen to lead to socially disruptive behaviour.

When the Long Parliament was restored with its excluded members in 1660 the Presbyterians returned briefly to power and were closely involved in the Restoration. The Savoy Conference met to discuss the possibility of the comprehension of Presbyterians into the State Church. The election to Parliament of the Cavalier Parliament, which wanted a strongly and exclusively Anglican church settlement, ended all possibility of comprehension for the Presbyterians. The Independents and sectaries could hope for little more than toleration at the Restoration. In the event, neither they nor the Presbyterians secured even that. Only the Quakers, however, were singled out amongst the nonconformists for particular opprobrium. All those Presbyterians, Independents and sectaries who had held benefices were ejected during the period 1660–2. In the main, nonconformist groups continued to operate, despite the penal legislation. Many of them registered under the terms of the 1672 Declaration of Indulgence, and were subsequently persecuted as a result of the information with which they had provided the authorities. Some nonconformists refused on principle to register, on the grounds that toleration is an inalienable right. After the Restoration many of the sects that had sprung up in the 1640s and 1650s died out, especially those which depended on a charismatic leader. The groups which survived most successfully were the Presbyterians, the Independents or Congregationalists, the Baptists and the Quakers.

The violent antipathy to those who became nonconformists, reflected in the Cavalier Parliament's legislation in the Clarendon Code, proved to be fairly short-lived. Although there was no possibility of nonconformists, being tolerated and being given full civil rights, there were a number of attempts during Charles II's reign to alleviate their condition. It proved difficult to draft legislation against Roman Catholics which did not also apply to Protestant nonconformists. On the other hand, the Declarations of Indulgence of 1672, 1687 and 1688 benefited them, although intended primarily for Roman Catholics. Many nonconformists were, however, very unhappy at being granted toleration by James II. They found an advocate in William III, but it proved impossible to pass the Comprehension Bill, which had been intended to modify the Toleration Act in favour of nonconformists.

ROMAN CATHOLICS

Throughout the period 1603–88, Roman Catholicism provided a source of fear quite unrelated to the number of Roman Catholics in England. Catholics were seen as presenting a political threat. In addition to their allegiance to the monarch, they owed allegiance to the Pope, who claimed the power to excommunicate and depose Christian monarchs. There was a real distinction to contemporaries between Catholic and Papist, and a number of attempts were made to distinguish between loyal and disloyal Catholics. The use of English Catholicism by foreign powers also aroused distrust. Except in the early years of James I's reign, the Catholic powers felt little interest in or concern for the fate of English Catholics, nor did the Catholic Counter-Reformation make much headway in England.

Persecution was spasmodic and was usually intensified in response to specific incidents or threats: the efforts of a very small minority of Catholic activists, or of unpopular pro-Catholic policies of the government. Persecution was also localised because of the regional distribution of Catholics. The survival of Roman Catholicism in England depended almost entirely upon the gentry, for it was only they who could afford to pay the fines for non-attendance at their parish church, towards the ministrations of a priest, and for Catholic tutors or education abroad for their children. There was also a certain reluctance on the part of their gentry neighbours to upset the local status quo by enforcing the penal laws too stringently. Thus gentry families suffered less from persecution than lower-class Catholics, and were able to recover from its effects more easily.

The organisation of English Catholics was a major source of debate. In the early years of James I's reign, the English Catholic community was deeply divided by the Archpriest controversy. This was finally resolved in 1623 by the appointment, after thirty years of petitioning, of a bishop to take charge of the secular clergy. To forestall the political problems which might ensue from the revival or creation of an English see, he was nominated Bishop of Chalcedon. Disputes continued about the extent of his powers: whether he had the same powers as a bishop in a Catholic country, or whether they were more limited. Owing both to the controversy surrounding his jurisdiction and to the government's attempts to arrest him, Richard Smith, Bishop from 1624, went abroad in 1631 and died there in 1655. After 1660 vicars apostolic were appointed to administer the Catholic church in England, which they did until the revival of the hierarchy in 1850.

The Archpriest controversy concerned both jurisdiction over English Catholics and the conditions under which their existence in England was tolerated. Attempts were made to tender the Oath of Allegiance to Catholics on the assumption that loyal Catholics were tolerable. Increasingly it became clear that toleration of Roman Catholicism was not possible, but that the King might occasionally dispense individual Catholics from the operation of the penal laws. In any case, the presence of foreign Catholics was unavoidable, both in foreign embassies and in the households of successive Catholic queens.

Catholics greeted James I optimistically, but the Catholic plots of the early years of his reign and Parliament's implacable opposition to toleration of Catholics brought them no relief. The Gunpowder Plot, in particular, led to the execution of several prominent Catholics for whose involvement in the plot there is no evidence, to renewed persecution and to legislation intended to distinguish between loyal and disloyal Catholics. James I's Catholic foreign policy likewise led to demands in Parliament for the stricter enforcement of the penal laws.

Despite Charles I's marriage to a French princess, on his accession he initiated a number of anti-Catholic measures. However, his later leniency towards a number of Catholics and his association with the Laudian innovations became confused in the minds of his opponents. Demands for more Protestant reforms in the Established Church united with anti-Catholic sentiment, with opposition to Laud's religious policies and with opposition to the government's political activities. The penalties meted out on Catholics were seen to be less savage than those suffered by Puritans such as Prynne, Burton and Bastwick. Laud's disapproval of concessions to Catholics passed unnoticed, especially when Charles I appealed to Catholics for funds for the First Bishops' War.

The event which turned Parliament's attention to the Catholics and away from their attack on those seen to be responsible for the pro-Catholic policy of the government, was the outbreak of the rebellion in Ireland in 1641. Parliament's fear of Catholic plotting was reflected in many of its declarations. During the period 1640–2 there were a number of anti-Catholic riots, apparently motivated by fear of what the Catholics were supposed to be plotting. The laws against Catholics were not, however, altered. There is little evidence to support the fears of the anti-Catholics, for there was no significant increase in Catholic activity. In fact, their cause suffered more as a result of the support of an unpopular Anglican government than from any of their own activities.

During the Civil War many Catholics fought for the King, although there were some in the Parliamentary army. The King gave his cause much bad publicity by enlisting Irish Catholics into his army. Their presence in England was short-lived, for they were routed soon after their arrival, but legends were built up around the atrocities they were supposed to have committed. Many Catholics' estates were sequestered, or compounded. Penal laws against Catholics remained in force, but were seldom enforced. They benefited from the repeal of the law enforcing church attendance and the substitution of the Engagement for the oaths of Supremacy. Allegiance and Obedience. All the proposals to legislate for religious toleration excluded the Catholics, although the Baptists and Quakers believed that they should be tolerated. Cromwell himself wanted to extirpate Roman Catholicism in Ireland, but seemed prepared to tolerate it in England, if Parliament were to agree. In practice, Catholics during the period 1642–60 may have suffered less persecution than before or after this period. Nevertheless, they were still subject to the penal laws and had no civil rights. They were still objects of hatred as the embodiment of the myths which associated despotism, foreign interference and plotting with Roman Catholicism, especially as much of the royalist plotting of the Interregnum took place in Catholic courts on the Continent.

At the Restoration many exiled royalists returned to England with Charles II. Some of them had always been Catholic, some had been converted whilst in exile. Charles II hoped to afford them toleration and raised their hopes by his declarations. The provisions of the Clarendon Code were originally intended to operate against Puritans, but there were few regrets that they also operated against Catholics. Once the Puritans had been restrained, Parliament ceased to consider them a serious threat, but their old fears of Roman Catholics were soon revived, partly as a result of Louis XIV's policies, and as a result of the favour shown to Catholics at court. It was during Charles II's reign that the distinction between court and country Catholics became very marked, especially as court Catholics were strongly influenced by continental Catholicism.

The penal laws were not strictly enforced during the 1660s. The great anti-Catholic backlash occured in the 1670s. The activities of the Cabal and the Declaration of Indulgence led to the Test Act, which disqualified Catholics, including the Duke of York, who announced his conversion in 1672, from holding office. The prospect of a Catholic king produced the atmosphere in which the Popish Plot was taken seriously. The Popish Plot led to the imprisonment of many Catholics and the execution of a few. The fear of Catholicism led to the hysteria surrounding the Exclusion crisis, although Charles II steadfastly refused to alter the legitimate line of succession to the throne. By the early 1680s the authors of the Popish Plot had been discredited and the Rye House Plot diverted attention to the nonconformists as a possible party of sedition.

James II succeeded to the throne peacefully but for Monmouth's rebellion. Initially he behaved discreetly in dispensing only a few people from the Test Act. Soon however, the large number of Catholics in the government, the army and the universities aroused fears of arbitrary rule marching hand in hand with Catholicism. In 1687 James issued a Declaration of Indulgence intended, in part, to conciliate the nonconformists. There was also evidence of attempts to restore the Catholic hierarchy, in the appointment in 1685 of John Leyburne as Bishop of Andrumetum, with the powers of a vicar apostolic, and in 1688 of three further vicars apostolic. The event which, more than any other, consolidated the opposition to James II was the birth of a son. James's reign had shown how few in numbers were the Roman Catholics, but it had confirmed in the minds of many Englishmen the association of Popery with arbitrary rule. A Catholic heir now meant that there was no foreseeable end to this. That such moderate men as Archbishop Sancroft could become popular heroes demonstrates how great was the reaction to James's government.

William III made use of anti-Catholic sentiment to take power in England. The Toleration Act did not extend to Catholics, who were still subject to the penal laws and to civil disabilities. The chief effect of the Revolution for Catholics was to extend the operation of the Test Act to the King. The penal laws were not normally invoked and there was no resumption of the periods of savage persecution to which Catholics had been subject in periods of anti-Catholic fear.

BIOGRAPHIES AND GLOSSARY OF TERMS

GEORGE ABBOT(1562–1633):   Archbishop of Canterbury 1611–33. Abbot was chosen to succeed Bancroft, on his death, after considerable indecision by James I. He had won a reputation as an administrator in Scotland, working to re-establish Scottish episcopacy. His theology was firmly Calvinist. He worked hard to defend the ecclesiastical courts, especially the High Commission, against the encroachments of the common lawyers. He favoured a Protestant foreign policy and opposed the Spanish marriage, despite his friendship with Buckingham, and worked hard to secure aid for Elizabeth of Bohemia. He forfeited James's trust by his opposition, in 1613, to the Earl of Essex's divorce, and to the issuing of the Book of Sports, and never regained it. In 1621, whilst hunting, he accidentally killed a man. He was temporarily suspended from his duties, and was eventually restored, but he had lost the confidence of many of those who were most influential at court and in the Church. He shared James I's abhorrence of Arminianism, but was unable to combat its influence, especially after Charles I's accession. He was again suspended in 1627–8, but although he recovered his jurisdiction he had, after Buckingham's assassination, no support amongst the King's councillors. Laud in practice governed the Church, and Abbot played no part in working to realise his ideal of a Catholic Apostolic church.

ANTINOMIANISM: Antinomianism was the belief that those who were saved were therefore exempted from the operation of God's ordinances, and were free to behave in any way they chose. It was usually an extreme Calvinist position. Its principal exponents were the Ranters, although it was commonly used as a term of abuse for most sectaries.

APPELLANT OR ARCHPRIEST CONTROVERSY: In 1598 the Pope created the office of Archpriest to provide an ecclesiastical superior for the secular priests (i.e. not members of religious orders) working in England. George Blackwell was appointed the first Archpriest, with no jurisdiction over the Jesuits or over the laity. The controversy centred round whether he had the right to consult with and work with members of the regular religious orders, with whom the secular clergy were on very bad terms. Spain generally supported the regulars and France the seculars. Other matters of dispute were whether Blackwell should work with the Jesuits and whether he should seek some sort of accommodation with the government. The government tried to exploit these divisions. Negotiations finally broke down in 1605 and Blackwell was removed from office for taking the Oath of Allegiance in 1607. The office of Archpriest lapsed in 1621 and in 1623 a bishop was appointed to supervise the secular clergy. The Jesuits, Benedictines and Franciscans each had their own superior in England.

The Appellants were those who opposed Blackwell's association with the members of the regular orders, and wanted a bishop chosen by the secular clergy as their leader. They directed an appeal to Rome to this effect.

ARMINIANISM: The doctrine named after the Dutch theologian Jacob Arminius, which rejected the Calvinist doctrine of predestination in favour of a belief in salvation by works. This had previously been a characteristically Roman Catholic doctrine.

RICHARD BANCROFT(1544–1610): Bishop of London 1597–1604. Archbishop of Canterbury 1604–10. Bancroft succeeded Whitgift to the see of Canterbury, having during the latter months of Whitgift's life done much of his work. Bancroft worked tirelessly at church administration. He worked indefatigably to implement the resolutions of the Hampton Court Conference to improve the standard of the clergy, by improving their education and by augmenting their incomes. By this he hoped to eradicate such abuses as pluralism and non-residence, which sometimes resulted from clerical poverty. He believed strongly in government by bishops, and it was in his generation of churchmen that the earliest notions of the apostolic succession of the episcopacy began to emerge, although he was theologically a Calvinist. He also encouraged James I in his belief that kings were God's vassals on earth.

GILBERT BURNET (1643–1715): Bishop of Salisbury after 1689. He devised the theory of providential delivery, i.e. that divine providence had caused James II to leave the country and had brought William over to England. James had abused the divine trust placed in him, consequently providence had deposed him and installed William peacefully. In effect this allowed many people to believe that William did not have significantly less moral right to the throne than James. This was one of the theories which created the position known as Broad Church.

CALVINISM: Calvinism is the theology derived from the work of John Calvin. Its most characteristic doctrine is predestination: that some are foreordained by God to salvation and that others are foreordained to damnation. The elect (those who are saved) are visible by their observance of God's ordinances, and by their godly behaviour. The established Church in England was predominantly Calvinist under Elizabeth. Hooker and Bancroft started the reaction against Calvinism in the established Church, and this movement culminated in Laud's work.

CLARENDON CODE: The name given to the legislation of the early years of Charles II's reign which effected the religious settlement. Church courts, except for the High Commission, and episcopal jurisdictions were restored. Between 1660 and 1662 about 1760 Puritan clergy were ejected from their livings, of whom 171 subsequently conformed. The Act of Uniformity ended the possibility of a church settlement which comprehended those who were now to become nonconformists. Bishops were restored to Parliament. Parliament refused to legislate for the King to dispense from any of the acts, although his power to dispense individuals from their operation was not challenged. They quashed Charles II's attempt in 1662 to issue a Declaration of Indulgence and established their decisive voice in legislating on religious matters.

The terms of the Clarendon Code were intended to prevent Puritans from holding any political power and from worshipping freely. In the years following a number of its provisions were not renewed, as those who, by its terms, had become nonconformists were seen not to present any political threat. It did, however, make the practice of nonconformity liable to severe penalties. The only sect to be specifically legislated against in the Code was the Quakers, who were considered to be socially disruptive. Once the anti-Puritan fervour of the Cavalier Parliament had subsided, many of the provisions of the Code were invoked more frequently against Roman Catholics than against nonconformists, although their original intention was more anti-Puritan than anti-Catholic.

COMPREHENSION: The term used to describe the policy by which the established Church would act as an umbrella for a wide variety of opinion, where unity was more important than uniformity of belief and practice.

COURT OF HIGH COMMISSION: The Court of High Commission was the chief church court. It was a prerogative court, summoned at the sovereign's discretion and able to administer severe penalties outside the common law. Its use was revived by Whitgift to enforce uniformity. It was particularly concerned with censorship. It was one of the institutions attacked most fiercely by the Long Parliament. It was seen as an institution in which the Church exercised a secular power to which it was not entitled, and also as the means by which Laud's religious policy was arbitrarily implemented. It was abolished in 1641, but revived by James II, under the name of the Commissioners for Ecclesiastical Causes, despite the confirmation of the Court's abolition in 1661. Safeguards were built into the Revolution settlement to prevent such a court from ever existing again.

EX OFFICIO OATH: An oath used especially in the prerogative courts by which a man could be required to indict himself on his own evidence, thus infringing a basic principle in common law.

FIFTH MONARCHISTS: The Fifth Monarchists were millennarian activists. They believed in taking political action to assist the imminent arrival of Christ on earth. They were involved in various attempted risings, in particular in 1657 and in 1661.

GENERAL BAPTISTS: The General Baptists originated with John Smyth's separatist congregation in the Netherlands, which in 1608 or 1609 introduced baptism of adult believers. They subsequently sought union with the Dutch Mennonites (an Anabaptist group), but did not derive their ideas from continental Anabaptism. In 1612 some members of this congregation came to England with Thomas Helwys and established the first congregation of General Baptists. By this time they had absorbed many of Arminius's ideas of free grace and salvation by works. By 1626 there were congregations in such towns as Lincoln, Coventry, Salisbury and Tiverton, as well as London. There is no sign of these congregations in the 1630s, but they could have formed the nucleus of proselytising General Baptists who appeared in the Home Counties in the 1640s. Like the Particular Baptists, the General Baptists developed an organisation during the 1650s, and had links with a number of radical groups. They, too, were proponents of toleration. The General Baptists were divided on the question of oath-taking. Some, like the Quakers, believed it to be wrong to swear oaths. By 1660 the General Baptists were losing ground to the Particualr Baptists. Some were disabled from taking the Oath of Allegiance, because they refused to take any oath. All remained politically passive after the Restoration. The General Baptists tried, on several occasions, to come to an accommodation with the Particular Baptists, but the latter expressed little interest in such an arrangement. They gained no civil rights through the Toleration Act, although they were allowed to make a public declaration instead of taking an oath, where this was required.

RICHARD HOOKER(1554–1600):   Author of *Of the Laws of Ecclesiastical Polity*. This work was a landmark in the development of a distinctively Anglican theology, and marks the reaction to Calvinism which began at the end of Elizabeth's reign, and developed during the seventeenth century.

IMPROPRIATION: A benefice whose tithes are in the hands of a layman, who then appoints a cleric to fulfil the ecclesiastical functions at a salary paid by him.

INDEPENDENTS: Independents believed in a Calvinist theology and in a church based on gathered congregations to which the minister was called by the members. They rejected the idea of a parochial state church, of tithes and of religious uniformity imposed by the civil magistrate. Some of the separatist congregations of the early seventeenth century can best be described as Independents; they are also known as Congregationalists. As a group, they first started to emerge in the Westminster Assembly, when the dissenting brethren opposed the plans to institute Presbyterianism. They won an increasing amount of support, especially in the army. By 1647 the army had taken the political initiative, with the result that Independency had greater political weight than Presbyterianism. Independents dominated the government during the period 1649–59. Whilst they did little to implement a distinctively Independent settlement, they did try to establish toleration for all except Catholics and episcopalians. For much of the period, toleration existed *de facto*, but there was a reaction against it after what were regarded as the excesses of the sectaries and the Barebones Parliament.

Most of the legislation of the period 1649–59 for the conduct of religious matters related to the maintenance of ministers and to the organisation of the universities. When, by 1650, it became plain that the Presbyterian organisation had never taken root, a system of committees was set up to examine the fitness of the beneficed clergy. Many Independents in the government did not approve of a state church based on parishes and supported by tithes, but every effort seems to have been made to maintain this system. There was repeated legislation to enforce payment of tithes, to prevent unlicensed persons from preaching and to confirm the rights of those clergy who had taken over benefices from ejected royalist clergy. Only during the Barebones Parliament was the existence of a state church questioned, but the proposed legislation against tithes and lay patronage failed. The Humble Petition and Advice went so far as to propose a Confession of Faith, subscription to which would be a condition for holding public office. Like the Presbyterians, the Independents who held power during the Interregnum merely offered an alternative form of state church to the episcopalian church. Theirs was more flexible and comprehensive, but they did not achieve any really substantial reforms.

At the Restoration the Independents could hope for little more than toleration. In the event they did not achieve even that. They continued to exist as gathered congregations, meeting in secret. The Declaration of Indulgence of 1672 afforded them temporary relief, but the information which it provided the government formed the basis of a number of subsequent prosecutions. They also benefited from James II's Declaration of Indulgence and from the Toleration Act, although they were not able to secure civil rights. Survival in opposition during the period 1660–99 consolidated Independents' views, and made them less comprehensive than they had been in the period 1645–60.

WILLIAM JUXON (1582–1663): Bishop of London 1633–60. Archbishop of Canterbury 1660–63. Juxon rose because of his favour with Laud and in 1636 was made Lord Treasurer, from which post he was removed in the Parliamentary attack on the secular power of bishops. He was, however, the only bishop to be allowed to enjoy his revenues until 1649, and was accorded a number of marks of respect by Cromwell.

WILLIAM LAUD (1573–1645): Bishop of London 1628–33. Archbishop of Canterbury 1633–45. (*See also* Laudianism.) Under James I Laud had won little influence, despite the favour in which he was held by Prince Charles. James I disliked Arminianism, and was wise enough to see that the assertion in public of the divine right of Kings and of the apostolic succession of episcopacy would encourage opposition. On Charles I's accession the position changed. Laud became the most potent force in the Church, partly through the suspension and subsequent loss of influence of Archbishop Abbot. Laud's religious ideas appalled an increasingly large section of the population. Despite Laud's belief in the continuing apostolic tradition of the English church, many of his innovations were seen as marking a return to Rome. His attempts to realise his ideal of a church at one with the State through his co-operation with Wentworth in the policy of Thorough fused the opposition to his religious policies and his political activities. His efforts to secure a better paid and educated clergy and to prevent bishops' non-residence were ignored when he attacked lectureships in the interests of uniformity and when he used the Court of High Commission to enforce his policies. His use of the coercive powers of the Church during the King's rule without Parliament identified him and his policies with arbitrary government.

When Parliament met in 1640, attacks were made not just on Laud's policies, but also on its executors and on the means by which it was enforced. It vociferously opposed the exercise of secular power by bishops, and in particular the involvement of bishops in the government. Laud was impeached primarily for being an evil counsellor to the King. More than anything else, Laud's involvement in the government during the eleven years' personal rule, his identification with arbitrary government and with press censorship and the suppression of lectureships led to parliament's attack on episcopacy, and to Laud's impeachment and execution.

LAUDIANISM: The set of beliefs named after Archbishop Laud, their most powerful and forceful exponent. They combined Arminius's belief in salvation by works with Laud's ideas of the beauty of holiness, which resulted in a greater emphasis on ceremonial, on the sacraments and on the priesthood. Laud combined this with the conviction that the English Church had a continuing tradition from the earliest days of Christianity and that the Reformation had revived the catholic apostolic tradition. For Laud, this tradition was exemplified by episcopacy, which he believed to be divinely ordained. He also believed in the divine right of Kings.

LECTURESHIPS: Lectureships had existed in the established Church since the Reformation as a means of augmenting the preaching of the beneficed clergy. During Elizabeth's reign there was a considerable increase in their number. The emphasis on preaching resulted partly through the Puritan belief in salvation through the word, although most lectureships were held by orthodox clergy. It was not until the 1620s that lectureships were particularly exploited by Puritans, whether individuals, municipal corporations or groups like the feoffees for impropriations. The possibilities for exploitation existed because there was less episcopal vigilance over appointments to lectureships than to benefices, and the oaths required of beneficed clergy by the 1604 Canons were not a condition of tenure. Thus, many man who were not prepared to take these oaths because they disagreed with the doctrines of the established Church, were able to preach to congregations legitimately, for a licence was required for anyone to preach in public. Laud recognised that lectureships were being used by Puritans who actively opposed him, and imposed the same tests on lecturers as were required from the beneficed clergy. In limiting the freedom of lecturers he saw himself as remedying an anomaly which allowed too great a degree of comprehension in the Church.

MILLENNARIANISM: The term derives from the belief that Christ's second coming would be followed by his reign on earth for a thousand years. For some this millennium was to be a spiritual reign, for others a literal resurrection with precise and concrete features. Thus in many instances millennarianism was a passive belief. A minority of activists were working for the second coming which they believed to be imminent. Many of those who supported the Barebones Parliament believed that rule by godly men was the prelude to it. Fifth

Monarchists chose other ways of implementing, or at least anticipating, Christ's rule on earth. Ranters, too, had a practical attitude to Christ's rule.

PARTICULAR BAPTISTS: Particular or Calvinistic Baptists believed in the Baptism of adult believers and in the Calvinist idea of predestination. They developed from the Calvinistic Independent congregations stemming from Henry Jacob's Independent church. The first Particular Baptist congregation did not appear in England until the 1630s. During the late 1640s and 1650s the Particular Baptists began to establish an organisation, and grew in numbers. Many Baptists were involved with radical groups, having links with Levellers, Diggers, Quakers and Fifth Monarchists. They were amongst the most consistent proponents of toleration. By 1660 the Particular Baptists were more numerous and better led than the General Baptists. They were not significantly affected by the ejections of beneficed clergy in 1662, for, as a matter of principle, few Baptists held benefices. The number of congregations remained fairly stable during the reign of Charles II, despite persecution. They were politically passive during this period. The Particular Baptists refused to co-operate with the General Baptists. The freedom which they gained under James II's Declaration of Independence was reduced under the Toleration Act, as the civil disabilities imposed by the Clarendon Code were not removed.

PRESBYTERIANS: Used to describe those who believed in a Calvinist theology and a Presbyterian church government based on assemblies of clergy and elected lay elders at the level of parish (*presbytery*) and district (*classis*), over which sat provincial and national synods. Some Presbyterians saw no room at all for bishops, some saw them as executive officers; all rejected the idea of a divinely ordained episcopacy.

The Presbyterian movement of Elizabeth's reign had effectively been dispersed, but the idea of a Presbyterian system remained alive and was advocated by many Puritans. James I made it quite clear at the Hampton Court Conference that he would not consider it. But when church reform was proposed by Parliament in the Grand Remonstrance (1641) and the Nineteen Propositions (1642), there was an implicit assumption that some sort of Presbyterian system should be considered. The conclusion of the Solemn League and Covenant changed matters. Instead of an erastian Presbyterianism (in which the civil government had the final voice) the Scots tried to impose their own model upon the English, and met with considerable opposition. This conflict can be seen in the debates of the Westminster Assembly and Parliament. Parliament brought in legislation to establish Presbyterianism in the period 1644–8, but relied for its enforcement upon the county authorities. Consequently it was very unevenly implemented. The ordinances concerning the Covenant and the Directory of Worship were best enforced, as they were used as tests of political affiliation, but the system of presbyteries, classes, provincial and national synods was never realised.

The terms offered to the King at Uxbridge (1644) and Newcastle (1646) by

Parliament included guaranteeing to introduce Presbyterianism within a specified period. Subsequent negotiations did not contain this provision, reflecting the
loss of power by Parliament (predominantly in favour of a Presbyterian
settlement) to the army (predominantly in favour of religious toleration, with a
bias towards Independency). With the loss of political advocates,
Presbyterianism lost its chance of becoming the state church, although many
individuals remained committed to it. The refusal of many Presbyterians to
consider allowing any form of religious toleration excluded them from finding a
satisfactory settlement during the 1650s. The restored Long Parliament raised
the hopes of many Presbyterians, but they were soon dashed, for the instability of
the political situation made consideration of a firm religious settlement
impossible.

The part that Presbyterians played in the Restoration led them to anticipate
that they would be comprehended in the church settlement. The King's
declarations encouraged them in this, and the temper of the Convention was
favourable. But the Savoy conference showed that differences over ceremonies
were too great to overcome, and ended any hopes of toleration. The Anglican
backlash, embodied in the Clarendon Code, showed that they were not even to
be tolerated. This precipitated a crisis of conscience from which they never
recovered. The basis of the Presbyterian system was that it should be a state
church based on parishes. Without even a remote possibility of this being
realised, it became a church whose membership was voluntary, which was quite
antithetical to its basic principles. Presbyterians were severely demoralised by
the ejections of 1662. Considerable numbers survived in 1672, but their existence
in opposition was precarious. Many Presbyterians subsequently conformed,
some joined other nonconformist churches, but by the eighteenth century they
chiefly survived in the Unitarian Church.

(NB. Presbyterians as a political formation are not considered here.)

PURITAN: This term is often used generally to refer to all those, inside and
outside the established Church, who believed in further reform in a Protestant
direction. It is used here specifically to denote those inside the established
Church who wanted such reforms. The substance of the changes they demanded
altered during the period 1603–40. In 1603 the changes that they wanted were
outlined in the Millennary Petition. Their desire for more preaching in the
Church led them to use lectureships, especially when Arminianism began to
become more influential in the established Church. Under Archbishop Laud
they were increasingly forced into a position of opposition: he encouraged
doctrines and practices which they deprecated, and they retaliated by developing
new methods of sustaining what they believed to be important in the Church.
The unification of ecclesiastical opposition with political opposition gave
Parliamentary support to many Puritan demands, and changed the tenor of their
grievances. Instead of attacking the doctrines and practices current in the
Church, they turned to more structural criticisms. They refuted the claims made
for episcopacy as divinely ordained and began to demand its abolition.

During the Civil War and Interregnum they diversified into a multiplicity of sects, many of whose features were very similar. As time went on, however, the sects became more distinct and more exclusive. By the time of the Restoration it is hard to identify Puritanism as anything other than a political interest. In religious terms it had been replaced by Presbyterians, Independents, Baptists, Quakers, etc., and Low Churchmen. Nonconformity to the Act of Uniformity gave them the name of nonconformists. The passing of the Toleration Act changed nonconformity to the Act of Uniformity to dissent to the established Church.

QUAKERS: The Quaker movement began in the early 1650s. From its very earliest days it incited opposition. Often this was because Quakers, or Friends, as they called themselves, broke up church services and interrupted preaching by the clergy. They opposed all manifestations of an organised church: set prayers, the clergy, especially if it was paid, church buildings. They believed that God manifested himself in man through an inner light which each man had to find for himself. Ultimately they regarded this inner light as more authoritative than either the Scriptures or any human law or institution. They were persecuted continuously through the Commonwealth and Protectorate, although Cromwell himself was sympathetic to them and no special legislation was passed against them. They seem to have been persecuted as much because they were misunderstood as for causing disturbances. Their reputation was damaged by the claims of James Naylor, who rode into Bristol on an ass and was hailed by his followers as Christ. They also suffered from being associated with the Ranters. Their refusal to use titles, remove their hats, take oaths, their mysticism and their belief in the inner light aroused antagonism, because of their strangeness and apparently anarchic implications. They were the only sect to be legislated against by name in the Clarendon Code. Few Quakers registered in 1672, on the grounds that toleration was an inalienable right. Nevertheless, the Quakers and the Baptists were the two sects that most successfully survived the Restoration. The Quakers were dominated by the personality of their leader, George Fox. There was active persecution under Charles II, and many Quakers spent long periods in prison. A number of Quakers were involved in plots and uprisings, including Monmouth's rebellion. They were eventually forced to set up a form of organisation, with regular monthly, quarterly and annual meetings, but only after considerable debate, for many Quakers saw this as compromising with worldliness. They secured some amelioration of the persecution in the 1690s.

RANTERS: The Ranters were never a sect in the proper sense, rather a movement which emerged during the early 1650s in the aftermath of the political radicalism of the war. They were Antinomians and believed that God was present in every man. They thought that people should demonstrate their salvation by flaunting God's ordinances. Some did this by blaspheming, others by sexual licence. The Blasphemy Act was passed in 1650 to curb their activities.

WILLIAM SANCROFT, (1617–93): Archbishop of Canterbury 1677, suspended 1689, deprived 1691. Sancroft was led, with six other bishops, in 1688, to protest to James II at his policies, especially in allowing the open practice of Roman Catholicism, and in admitting Roman Catholics to civil offices, to the army and to Magdalen College, Oxford. The bishops' subsequent imprisonment, trial, and acquittal was in part a confirmation of the nation's refusal to let the King exercise the suspending power. It was also an assertion of Parliament's control of religion. After William III's arrival in England, Sancroft found it impossible to acknowledge him as King, and was one of the non-juring bishops. He was suspended and later deprived of his see.

SECTARIES: This term is usually used to refer to those whose Protestantism was more radical than that of the Independents or Presbyterians. It covers Baptists, Quakers, Seekers, Ranters, Fifth Monarchists and others of the host of groups that proliferated during the Civil War and Interregnum and whose beliefs encompassed every extreme and every variety of theology, including some traditionally regarded as heretical. The only feature common to the sectaries was their rejection of a national parochial church structure. In general they favoured independent congregations, with an elected minister. Some did not believe that there should be a paid ministry; some, like the Quakers, did not believe that there should be a ministry at all. The two sects most successfully to survive the Interregnum and the Restoration settlement were the Baptists and the Quakers.

SEPARATISTS: The name given to those who separated from the established Church primarily because they believed that the purest form of church organisation was the gathered congregation, and who thus rejected a national church based on a parochial system. The first separatists appeared under Elizabeth, but a number survived into James I's reign, some in England and some in the Netherlands. These congregational separatists had strong links with continental reformed churches, especially in the Netherlands, and with reformers in England. Some of these congregations began to adopt the practice of baptism of adult believers; some adopted Arminius's ideas on free grace. Few of the separatist congregations of the early seventeenth century recognisably survived into the 1640s, but there is a strong continuity in the beliefs and practices of the early separatists and of the Civil War Independents and sectaries. Separatist ideas were also preserved in the foreign congregations which settled in England, often to escape persecution elsewhere. They were granted privileges to worship freely, until Laud, seeing them as a source of encouragement to English Puritans, limited them.

WESTMINSTER ASSEMBLY: After the outbreak of the Civil War, Parliament temporarily shelved its consideration of religious questions until June 1643, when the Westminster Assembly was summoned to meet. The Grand Remonstrance had called for a synod of divines to consider church reforms. The Assembly's main task was to establish Presbyterianism in England on the

Scottish model. It was never fully implemented, for a number of reasons. Many Englishmen wanted a Presbyterian system, but did not want to import the Scottish system wholesale. There was a vociferous and articulate minority in the assembly who, as Independents, challenged the concept of a parochial state church. These people won more and more support, especially in the army. By 1647 there was little chance of a Presbyterian system being able to succeed, because of lack of support. The Assembly's plan was legislated between 1644 and 1648 and relied for its implementation upon the co-operation of the county authorities, many of whom were unable or unwilling to do anything. The imposition from above of a new system of church government at the parish level proved impossible. Of the ordinances passed at the instigation of the Assembly, those concerning the Covenant and the Directory of Worship were the best enforced. These were used as tests of political as well as of religious affiliation, and as a means of ejecting royalist clergy. The system of parish, classical and provincial assemblies and of church discipline was never fully implemented, partly because the legislation was passed too late.

JOHN WHITGIFT (1530?–1604):   Archbishop of Canterbury 1583–1604. By the time of James I's accession Whitgift was too frail to execute his archiepiscopal functions, and he died within a year. During this period much of his work was done by Bancroft, then Bishop of London. Whitgift had been a tireless exponent of Elizabeth's *via media*. He was, perhaps, best known for his attack on Puritanism, but made strenuous efforts to reform the Church in his attempts to secure outward conformity. He did, for example, succeed in improving the education of the clergy, and went some way towards remedying abuses in the church courts.

CHRONOLOGY, 1602–89

1602   The Papal Brief. The Archpriest, superior of the secular Roman Catholic Clergy in England, was forbidden to treat with the Jesuits on any matter concerning the English Catholics.

1603   Accession of James I to the throne of England (24 March).
   The Millennary Petition was presented by a large number of ministers of the established Church (supposedly a thousand) to James I on his journey southwards. It asked for minor changes in ceremonial and practice to bring the Church of England more into line with the continental reformed churches. The main items of the Petition were that clergy should be required to subscribe not to the Prayer Book but only to the Thirty Nine Articles, that the wearing of surplices should be optional, that the use of the sign of the cross in baptism and the ring in marriage should be abolished, that there should be no more bowing at the name of Jesus, that pluralism and non-residence should be discouraged, that excommunication should be pronounced only for serious offences and never by laymen, and that preaching should be encouraged.

The Bye and Main Plots. Three priests and a number of Catholic gentry were involved in a scheme to seize the King and force him to grant toleration to Roman Catholics.

Archpriest George Blackwell tried to get the Papal Brief of 1602 reversed.

1604 The Hampton Court Conference (14, 16 and 18 January). The Conference was summoned as a result of the Millennary Petition. It consisted of members of the Church hierarchy and the Privy Council and influential Puritans, led by Dr Rainolds of Corpus Christi College, Oxford. In calling the conference, James caused a certain amount of ill feeling, since he had, by inviting various influential Puritans to represent themselves, implied that their opinions were as authoritative as those of the bishops. James was not as strongly opposed to the Puritans as used to be thought, but he did not care sufficiently about the changes in the Prayer Book and the modifications in the organisation of the church courts proposed as a result of the conference to ensure that the bishops actually responsible for implementing them did so.

New Prayer Book Proclaimed (5 March) which embodied minor changes proposed at the Hampton Court Conference, but none that were of any significance to the Puritans, who wanted to make the English Church a fully reformed church with no Catholic remnants.

Apology of the House of Commons (June). The Apology was never actually presented to the King, although he evidently knew of its contents. It was the result of the Commons' discussion of those religious reforms which they felt still needed to be implemented, and it demonstrated the wide measure of support which there was in Parliament for church Puritanism. James prorogued Parliament soon after, because he denied its right to discuss religious questions and believed that it so doing was an infringement of his prerogative, especially as it denied his right to alter any laws concerning religion without its consent.

In the same month Whitgift died and was succeeded as Archbishop of Canterbury by Bancroft.

The Bill for the due execution of the statutes against Jesuits, seminary priests and recusants received the royal assent (8 July). Parliament re-enacted the Elizabethan penal laws against Roman Catholics as a result of the Bye and Main Plots.

A proclamation enjoining conformity was issued (16 July). In the aftermath of Parliament's discussion of religious questions and their consequent prorogation, James issued a proclamation to enforce conformity to the new Prayer Book by November 1604.

The Canons of 1604 (September). The Canons defined orthodoxy and required the subscription of ordained clergy to the assertion that the Prayer Book contained nothing contrary to the Word of God and that all the Thirty Nine Articles were agreeable to the Word of God. These canons were unacceptable to a considerable number of Puritans within the Church; consequently between eighty and ninety clergy were deprived for non-subscription, although a number were subsequently restored.

1605   The Gunpowder Plot (5 November). A scheme for blowing up the King and Parliament was conceived by Robert Catesby, to be followed by a national Catholic uprising. The Jesuits knew of and disapproved of the Plot. Several of the conspirators were killed on the spot when they were caught at Holbeche House, Staffs. Many Catholics were rounded up on very slender evidence of involvement and in 1606 Guy Fawkes and the Jesuit superior, Henry Garnet, were executed.

1606   The Penal Laws. As a result of the Gunpowder Plot, and in an attempt to distinguish between loyal and disloyal Catholics, Catholics were required to take the Oath of Allegiance renouncing the doctrine that the Pope could depose kings. To receive the sacraments in accordance with the Anglican rite at least once a year, rather than merely to attend church, became the test of conformity.

1607   Archpriest Blackwell was deposed for his approval of the Oath of Allegiance. He was succeeded by Birkhead, who, like Blackwell, was an associate of the Jesuits, but was of a more conciliatory temper. He appointed the principal Appellants as his assistants and supported the demand of the secular clergy for a bishop. The Pope reaffirmed the Brief of 1602.

1610   Bill to abolish pluralities. Bancroft pleaded with James I to stop this Bill, because otherwise the shortage of clergy would mean that many benefices held in plural would no longer have a minister.
    Commons Petition on Religion (July). The Petition took up the demands of the Millennary Petition and denied the King's right to alter laws concerning religion without Parliament's consent. In addition the Petition opposed the deprivations for nonconformity of 1604 and demanded that subscription be required only for articles of faith and not for ceremonies. It also demanded that the recusancy laws be more strictly enforced.

1611   The Authorised Version of the Bible was published. The new translation had been ordered at the Hampton Court Conference.
    George Abbot was translated to the see of Canterbury after the death of Bancroft in 1610.
    The Court of High Commission. After challenges to its powers by the common lawyers and the issuing of writs of prohibition to delay its proceedings, the King issued new letters patent for the Court. These defined the crimes which the Court could adjudicate and gave it power to imprison and power to use the *ex officio* oath.

1612   Thomas Helwys's General Baptist congregation came to England from the Netherlands.

1618   The Book of Sports was issued by the King in response to growing Sabbatarianism. It contained a list of games and pastimes permitted on Sundays. James ordered it to be read throughout the country, but, seeing the opposition to it, led by Archbishop Abbot, did not press the point.

1618–23   The Spanish marriage scheme.

1621   A Bill for Stricter Sabbath Observance was discussed in Parliament in response to the Book of Sports.

Commons petition (3 December): 'finding how ill your Majesty's goodness hath been requited by princes of different religion, who even in time of treaty have taken opportunity to advance their own ends, tending to the subversion of religion and disadvantage of your affairs and estate of your children, by reason whereof your ill affected subjects at home, the Popish recusants, have taken too much encouragement and are dangerously increased in their number and in their insolencies'. This petition was presented partly because of the Commons' dislike and distrust of the Spanish marriage proposals, and partly because of their consciousness of James's reluctance to support the Protestant cause of the Elector Palatine in Europe. They opposed the King's pro-Spanish, pro-Catholic policy and the influence at court of Gondomar, the Spanish ambassador.

The Commons Protestation. The House of Commons asserted its right to discuss any matter, religious or otherwise, which concerned the security of the realm. It was partly sparked off by James's efforts to obstruct the Bill for stricter Sabbath observance.

1622   Directions to preachers (August). As a result of the preaching on behalf of the Elector Palatine and a Protestant foreign policy in opposition to the Spanish match, James issued instructions to bishops to take greater care in licensing preachers and limited the subjects on which they might preach.

1623   William Bishop was appointed Bishop of Chalcedon by the Pope, with jurisdiction over the secular clergy in England and Wales but without the powers of an ordinary (i.e. of a bishop with a diocese).

1624   Richard Montague published *A New Gag for an Old Goose*, which asserted the continuous tradition of the Church of England with the Early Christian Church, and other non-Calvinist doctrines. It was attacked in the Commons as Popish but Archbishop Abbot was powerless to do anything more than deliver a mild admonition, because of the strong support for Montague at court.

1625   Charles I succeeded James I (March), married Henrietta Maria and concluded an alliance with France (May). Even so, the same year saw the issue of the Instructions on Papists, by which Charles ordered that Papists should be sought out and repressed.

Montague published *Appello Caesarum*, which was a more definite statement of the Arminian position. The House of Commons summoned him to the bar in June, but Charles I appointed him a royal chaplain and ordered the Commons not to attack one of his personal servants. The following Parliament, of 1626, proposed to impeach him for drawing people into Popery, but this was not proceeded with, because of the attack on Buckingham and the consequent dissolution of Parliament. In 1628 Montague was made Bishop of Chichester.

The Feoffees for Impropriations. A number of Puritan clergy and laity started the following scheme: twelve feoffees (four lawyers, four clergy and four citizens of London) were to buy vacant lay impropriations, the existence of which in any case constituted a Puritan grievance, and would fill the benefices with Puritan ministers and pay them salaries. Lectureships were to be set up with any proceeds.

1626   Declaration against Controversy (16 June). The Declaration was issued after the dissolution of the Parliament of 1626 to try to silence the debate on Arminianism provoked by Montague.

Charles I expelled from England all the French priests in Henrietta Maria's entourage.

1627   Dr Sibthorpe delivered a sermon asserting royal supremacy in Church and State, the King's power to make laws and the subject's necessary obedience to them as a religious duty, with special reference to forced loans. Buckingham was anxious to publish the sermon, which Archbishop Abbot refused to license, because of its inflammatory nature. Eventually Mountain, Bishop of London, licensed it and Abbot was suspended until 1628 and his jurisdiction put into commission, headed by Laud.

1628   Parliament censured Dr Manwaring for two sermons he had preached and printed maintaining that the subject was bound to obey his sovereign however dubious the legality of his commands. He was sentenced to suspension, a fine and imprisonment despite his proof before the House of Lords that his doctrine was derived from Calvin. Most of his sentence was remitted on his humble submission. He was given the living vacated by Dr Montague on his translation to the see of Chichester.

The Commons Remonstrance (11 June) called for the strict enforcement of the penal laws and the suppression of Arminian doctrines.

The King's Declaration against Controversy (November) was published as a preface to a new edition of the Thirty Nine Articles and stated that the articles were to be taken in their literal and grammatical sense and were not to be debated. It was issued partly as a result of the attacks on Manwaring and Sibthorpe.

1629   The Commons sub-committee on religion reported (24 February) that the laws against Papists should be enforced, that there should be suitable penalties for holding Popish or Arminian doctrines, that the sense of the Thirty Nine Articles was the Calvinistic sense expounded in the Lambeth Articles of 1595.

Three Resolutions were passed by the Commons (2 March) shortly before its dissolution. One stated that whoever introduced any innovation in religion to bring in Popery or Arminianism should be accounted a capital enemy of King and kingdom. The other two related to illegal taxation.

Laud's Instructions to Bishops. Bishops were to live permanently in their dioceses unless they had court appointments and were forbidden to alienate episcopal property. In addition, they were not to allow anyone to take up a lectureship who would not undertake to accept a benefice with cure of souls when one in the vicinity became vacant. In earnest of this they were to establish their orthodoxy by reading divine service from the Prayer Book in hood and surplice at least once a year. Afternoon sermons were to be replaced by catechising.

1633 Archbishop Abbot died, having been suspended in 1621 and 1627–8, and was succeeded by Laud.

The Feoffees for Impropriations were disbanded. So successful had they been in increasing the amount of Puritan preaching that Laud initiated long and involved legal proceedings against them to disband them. When he succeeded in doing so, their impropriations passed to the King.

Laud's Instructions. Bishops were instructed not to ordain anyone without a benefice to go to; otherwise they would have to be personally responsible for their maintenance. Further restrictions were placed on the alienation of church lands, and a survey and inventory of church property was ordered.

The Book of Sports of 1618 was reissued.

1637 Prynne, Burton and Bastwick had their ears clipped and were sentenced to perpetual imprisonment and heavy fines, and Prynne to branding as well, by the Star Chamber. All three had written attacking the church hierarchy and Laud's ecclesiastical policy.

Royal proclamation against withdrawing the King's subjects from the Church of England (December). It was published as a result of Laud's complaints against the growth of the Roman Catholic party, especially at court.

Charles I ordered the universal adoption in Scotland of a Prayer Book based on the English Book of Common Prayer.

1637–8 The Scots entered a Covenant for the defence of their religion.

1639 The First Bishop's War, which was concluded in June by the Treaty of Berwick. Henrietta Maria asked Catholics for financial support for the King's troops and Laud asked for a clerical subsidy.

1640 From June, the Second Bishops' War, which was concluded in October by the Treaty of Ripon.

The Canons of 1640 were published (June). They were, in effect, a codification of Laud's innovations (for example, the communion table to be placed as an altar and surrounded by rails) and made a defence of the divine right of Kings and of the unlawfulness of resistance. The canon which caused most controversy was the 'et cetera oath', by which all ordained clergy were required to swear not to alter the government of the Church 'by archbishops' bishops, deans and archdeacons, etc., as it stands now established', and that the doctrine and discipline of the Church of England contained all things necessary to salvation.

The Root and Branch Petition (11 December) was supposedly subscribed by 15,000 Londoners petitioning for the complete abolition of episcopacy.

Parliament declared that the 1640 Canons bound neither clergy nor laity because they had not been confirmed by Parliament (15 December).

The Canons were declared illegal (16 December).

Archbishop Laud was impeached in the Commons and imprisoned in the Tower (18 December).

1641 Charles agreed (23 January) that bishops should lose any power injurious to the State, but he would not deprive them of their seats in the House of Lords.

The Root and Branch Bill was debated in the House of Commons (18 February), but made little progress before the end of the session and was not revived.

The Commons Protestation (3 May) was an attempt to rally support by reviving the Elizabethan Oath of Association, which amounted, in effect, to a national agreement to support the true reformed Protestant religion against Popery and Popish doctrines.

The prerogative courts of Star Chamber and High Commission were abolished (5 July).

The Commons Resolution on ecclesiastical innovations (1 September) ordered the suppression of Laudian innovations and the due observance of the Sabbath.

News arrived (1 November) of the outbreak of rebellion in Ireland.

The Grand Remonstrance (1 December) demanded the removal of bishops' temporal powers and of the oppressions which they were responsible for introducing. It advocated the uniting against Popery of all those who believed in the same fundamental truths and that all church questions should be referred to a synod of divines.

The Bishops' Protestation was signed by twelve bishops (29 December) as a protest against the mobs in Westminster who obstructed them. They further asserted that everything done in Parliament in their absence was illegal, whereupon the Commons impeached them.

1642 The Clerical Disabilities Act (13 February) disenabled all persons in holy orders from exercising any temporal jurisdiction or authority, thus depriving bishops of their temporal jurisdiction and their seats in the House of Lords.

The Nineteen Propositions (1 June) were offered as the terms of a dictated peace by Parliament. They included the proposal that the King should accept the reformation of the Church by a synod and should surrender his rights of appointment in every sphere of government. Charles naturally refused to accept such terms.

An order for sequestering notorious delinquents' estates (27 March). Royalist clergy and laity had their estates sequestered. Later they were allowed to compound for their property.

An alliance, the Solemn League and Covenant, was concluded with the Scots (9 June). In exchange for Scottish military support Parliament undertook to introduce Presbyterian church government in England on the Scottish model.

Parliament set up (12 June) the Assembly of Learned and Godly Divines for the Settling of the Government of the Church. The membership consisted mainly of Church Puritans, although some supporters of the established Church were invited but did not attend. The majority of members were in favour of some sort of Presbyterian church settlement. After the conclusion of the alliance with the Scots, the Assembly turned from considering whether to have a Presbyterian system, or what kind of Presbyterianism to have, to considering how to implement the Scottish system. The small but vociferous group of Independents, the 'Dissenting Brethren', were the only people consistently opposed to Presbyterianism.

In accordance with this all members of Parliament and the army had to take the Solemn League and Covenant (September).

All members of the Common Council in London or office-holders there had to take the Solemn League and Covenant (December).

1644   Ordinance enjoining taking the Covenant by everyone else was passed (5 February).

The Uxbridge Peace Propositions (24 November) included the following clause on religion: the posts of all ьishops and cathedral clergy to be abolished and religion to be reformed according to the advice of the Assembly of Divines, based on the Covenant.

1645   Ordinance (4 January) for abolishing the Book of Common Prayer, imposing penalties on those who used it, and putting into execution the Directory for the Public Worship of God, compiled by the Westminster Assembly. This was the first major step in establishing Presbyterianism.

Archbishop Laud was executed (10 January).

Ordinance (26 April) for none to preach but ordained ministers.

The Newcastle Propositions for peace (13 July) included the following religious provisions: that all bishops and cathedral clergy be abolished and that religion be reformed according to the advice of the Assembly of Divines in consultation with Parliament and based on the covenant.

Ordinance (19 August) regulating the election of elders for setting up the Presbyterian system at the parish level.

1646   Ordinance (9 October) for abolishing bishops and archbishops. Their lands and possessions were settled on trustees for the use of the Commonwealth, and all courts which had operated under their jurisdiction were abolished.

1647   The Heads of Proposals (1 August). Bishops and all other ecclesiastical officers should be deprived of any coercive powers. All the laws which enabled the civil magistrate to administer civil penalties for ecclesiastical censures should be repealed. All acts enjoining the use of the Prayer Book and imposing penalties for neglecting them should be repealed, as also the acts imposing penalties for not attending church. Roman Catholics should be disabled and Jesuits and Roman priests prevented from disturbing the State. The Covenant should not be forced on anyone. There should be religious toleration for all but Roman Catholics.

1648   Ordinance (29 January) for settling counties into classical Presbyterian and Congregational elderships.

Ordinance (29 August) for the form of church government to be used in England and Ireland. The final ordinance for establishing a fully Presbyterian. system throughout the country. By the terms of the ordinance a committee of Lords and Commons was set up to judge scandalous offences.

1648–9   The Whitehall Debates (December–January) were debates between the Council of Officers of the New Model Army and other individuals on the Agreement of the People, especially on its religious terms.

1649   Repeal (9 February) of the Oaths of Obedience, Allegiance and Supremacy.

The Trustees for the Maintenance of Preaching Ministers were appointed (5 April).

Act for Abolishing Deans, Deans and Chapters, Canons, Prebends and Other Offices and Titles of, or Belonging to, Any Cathedral Church or Collegiate Church or Chapel within England and Wales (30 April). Trustees were set up to administer their possessions for the benefit of creditors of the Commonwealth. All archidiaconal courts and similar jurisdictions were abolished, although the last records of one actually operating are for 1646.

1650   The Blasphemy Act was passed against the Ranters (9 August), because of the political threat implied by their extreme Antinomianism.

Repeal (27 September) of the laws imposing penalties for not attending church.

1653   A Bill to abolish lay patronage was read in the Barebones Parliament (November). It was stopped by the dissolution of Parliament and not subsequently revived.

A central probate court was established and the Prerogative Court of Canterbury abolished, thus removing the final remnants of the old ecclesiastical jurisdiction.

The Instrument of Government (16 December) proposed some sort of State church and toleration except to 'Popery nor Prelacy, nor to such as, under the profession of Christ, hold forth and practice licenciousness'. It acknowledged the principle of toleration a little uneasily.

1654   The Commissioners for the Approbation of Public Preachers, or 'Triers' were appointed (20 March).
   Commissioners for ejecting scandalous, ignorant and insufficient ministers, or 'ejectors', were appointed (22 August).

1655   The Jews were readmitted to England.

1657   The Humble Petition and Advice (25 May). This document proposed that a confession of faith be drawn up. It contained the idea that it was possible to agree on the essentials of religion while differing on matters of detail. Subscription to the confession was to be a qualification for office-holding. One clause about disturbing assemblies was directed against the Quakers. It marks a definite reaction against toleration.

THE ADMINISTRATION OF THE CHURCH, 1642–60

ORDINATION

1644   Arrangements were made (4 October) by the Westminster Assembly for the ordination of ministers *pro tempore* provided that certain presbyters, to be appointed, should perform the service.

1645   The second ordinance for ordination (8 November) provided that various classical presbyteries should approve and ordain ministers.

1646   Ordinance (28 August) for the ordination of ministers by classical presbyteries.

APPROBATION OF PREACHERS

1644   The Committee for Plundered Ministers was ordered (September) to consider the institution of ministers.

1648   The House of Commons ordered (July) that Presbyterian classes should be able to institute ministers.
   In the succeeding years various schemes for approving preachers were mooted, but none was ever put into practice until –

1654   The Act establishing the Commissioners for the Approbation of Public Preachers (20 March) which was given the power to appoint ministers to benefices and thus, by implication, to examine their credentials and fitness to hold a benefice. They were not allowed to grant benefices to sequestered or delinquent ministers except with the approval of the Protector and the Council. They had no power of ordination, but their certification was required for a minister to obtain an augmentation.

1660   The Rump allowed the commissioners in London to appoint commissioners in the counties with the same powers plus the power of ordination (14 March).

MAINTENANCE AND AUGMENTATION OF BENEFICES

1642   The Committee for Plundered Ministers was set up (31 December) for the relief of ministers plundered by the royalists and to consider the sequestration of malignant clergy. Gradually its powers grew to absorb those of several of the Parliamentary committees set up to administer the Church.

1643   The ordinance for the sequestration of delinquents' estates (31 March). This ordinance did not treat lay and clerical estates differently; therefore any money granted for ecclesiastical purposes was granted by Parliament from its general funds, although by the end of the year it had begun to allocate clerical revenues for the maintenance of ministers or for augmenting benefices.

1646   Ordinance abolishing episcopacy (9 October). The revenues from benefices, tithes and specifically clerical sources of income were reserved for the maintenance of the clergy and were administered by the Trustees for the Sale of Bishops' Lands, who were empowered to use any other income, either from the sale or rental of land, for secular purposes.

1649   Ordinance (30 April) for the sale of the lands of deans and chapters. Contained the same provisions as for the administration of bishops' lands.
   The Trustees for the Maintenance of Ministers were set up (8 June). They were to administer the appropriate tithes of bishops and of deans and chapters and to pay salaries or augmentations to ministers or schoolmasters. In 1650 they in effect took over the powers of the trustees for the sale of bishops' and deans and chapters' lands and were given a larger fund to draw on. The trustees had to act on the advice of the Committee for Plundered Ministers or the Committee for the Reformation of the Universities (which existed between 1650 and 1653).

1654   The powers of the old Committee for the Reformation of the Universities and the Committee for Plundered Ministers were transferred to the Trustees for Maintenance (2 September).

1659   The reassembled Rump revived the Committee for Plundered Ministers (22 June) and proposed to restore to it the administration of augmentations, but never actually did so.

SCANDALOUS MINISTERS

1640 The Committee for Scandalous Ministers was set up (December) by the Long Parliament specifically to deal with the opinions of the clergy. It was not concerned with clerical appointments or incomes.

1643 Sequestration of royalists' estates commenced; thus, under this legislation royalist clergy were deprived. Scandal in life or Popery in doctrine were now dealt with by the Committee for Plundered Ministers.

1653 When the Committee for Plundered Ministers lapsed, its functions in respect of scandalous ministers were taken over by Cromwell and the Council of State.

1654 Separate bodies of commissioners were appointed (22 August) for each county of England and Wales and were assisted by nominated divines to eject, after trial, all scandalous, ignorant, insufficient or negligent clergymen and schoolmasters, and to consider the relief of the ejected and the appointment of a successor.

PRESBYTERIAN CHURCH DISCIPLINE

The intention of Presbyterian discipline was that by means of the elders' vigilance the unworthy should be prevented from receiving sacraments.

1645–6 Ordinances concerning the exclusion of people from the sacraments (20 October 1645, 14 March and 9 June 1646). Although the ordinances were not stringent enough to satisfy many of the Presbyterian clergy, they were vigorously opposed by many other ministers. They enumerated offences for which individuals might be excluded from the sacraments and set up a committee of Lords and Commons to which elders were to certify offences.

CONFIRMATION OF THE RIGHTS OF INTRUDED CLERGY

Acts confirming the rights of possession of clergy intruded into benefices sequestered from delinquent clergy, or from which clergy had been ejected for scandal (23 August 1647 and 26 June 1657).

TITHES

1644–60 Acts and ordinances enforcing payment of tithes to parochial incumbents (8 November 1644, 9 August 1647, 27 October 1648 and 16 March 1660).

1648 Act for enforcing the payment of tithes to London ministers (4 August).

BLASPHEMY

1645   Ordinance for None to Preach but Ordained Ministers (26 April).

1647   Ordinance Concerning the Growth and Spreading of Errors, Heresies and Blasphemies, and for Setting Apart a Day of Public Humiliation, to Seek God's Assistance for the Suppressing and Preventing of the Same (4 February).

1648   Ordinance for the Punishing of Blasphemies and Heresies (2 May).

1650   Act for the Better Preventing of Profane Swearing and Cursing (28 June).
   Act against Several Atheistical, Blasphemous and Execrable Opinions, Derogatory to the Honour of God, and Destructive to Human Society (9 August). This act was intended to quell the Ranters, and to some extent succeeded.

FESTIVALS

1644   Ordinance (19 December) that Christmas be celebrated as a fast.

1647   Act (8 June) for abolishing festivals.

PRESS CENSORSHIP

Acts to enforce the licensing of printed books and the regulation of printing (14 June 1643, 30 September 1647, 20 September 1649 and 7 January 1653).

ROMAN CATHOLICS

1646   Act (1 April) excluding Papists and others from the Cities of London and Westminster.

1648   The same, though now including delinquents, ministers, officers and soldiers of fortune that adhered to the enemy (23 May).
   The same (16 June).

1650   The same and for encouraging such as discover priests and Jesuits, their receivers and abettors (26 February).

1651   Act for convicting, discovering and repressing popish recusants.

1660   Act and declaration (12 March) for putting the laws against priests and Jesuits in speedy and effectual execution.

1660   The Declaration of Breda (4 April). Charles II offered to give his assent to any legislation which offered a measure of religious toleration.

Act (13 September) for settling and restoring ministers. Restored ejected ministers to their livings. About 695 intruded clergy were ejected, although many left their benefices before the Act came into force.

Charles II's declaration on ecclesiastical affairs (the Worcester House Declaration, 23 October), which was rejected by the Convention, contained the following: Charles's resolution to support the Church of England, to call a synod and appoint various divines to review the Prayer Book. Charles agreed to waive minor points of ceremony and excuse subscription to canonical obedience as a condition of ordination. The Declaration resulted in the calling of the Savoy Conference.

1661 Venner's rising (January). Thomas Venner, a wine bottler, led a band of fifty men to set up the Fifth Monarchy of King Jesus. Despite the failure of the plot, it jeopardised the cause of nonconformity in the Restoration settlement.

The Savoy Conference was called (April), as a result of the Worcester House Declaration. Anglicans and Presbyterians were summoned to the Savoy to try to work out a church settlement. The Presbyterians, led by Richard Baxter, were prepared to accept a modified episcopacy along the lines proposed by James Ussher, but were absolutely immovable in their refusal to allow anything that smelt, however faintly, of Popery. The reforms they demanded were similar to those of the Millennary Petition of 1603. The Anglicans behaved towards the Presbyterians as if they were already rulers of the Church and were strengthened in their resolve by the meeting of the Cavalier Parliament (May) and the speed with which it became apparent that they would not give way at all to the Presbyterians. At the time, differences over Popish ceremonies loomed larger than similarities on such subjects as limited episcopacy and a state church based on parishes and supported by tithes, on both of which issues the Presbyterians were in accord with the Anglicans and opposed to the sectaries.

Bishops were restored to the House of Lords (30 June). The church courts, except for the Court of High Commission, were restored, as part of the bishops' recovery of their jurisdiction.

The Corporation Act (November) excluded from the government or from borough corporations those who would not take the oaths of allegiance and supremacy, receive the sacraments in accordance with the Anglican rite, abjure the Solemn League and Covenant and declare the illegality of taking up arms against the King.

1662 Act against Quakers aimed at those who refused to take oaths or encouraged others to refuse. Often they were charged with offences and asked to swear on oath of loyalty, the refusal to do so was sufficient to secure their conviction.

A new Prayer Book was drawn up as a result of recommendations made by the Savoy Conference, although the chief Puritan objections were ignored.

The Act of Uniformity (May). Authorised the use of the Prayer Book as revised by Convocation after the Savoy Conference and restricted the holding of benefices to episcopally ordained clergy. As a result some 900 clergy were ejected on St Bartholomew's Day. The Commons quashed a Lords amendment to allow the King to dispense from the Act. Immediately after it was passed, Charles II tried to suspend its operation for three months, but was frustrated by the opposition of the bishops and constitutional lawyers.

Royal declaration (December) in favour of toleration. Charles undertook, if Parliament agreed, to exercise the dispensing power on behalf of dissenters.

1663   The Commons protested (February) against any scheme for establishing schism by law.

The Farnley Wood Plot (October). A plot conceived by various former Cromwellian officers which provided the immediate excuse for the Conventicle Act.

1664   The Conventicle Act forbade meetings of five or more people not members of the same household. In effect the act acknowledged the existence of a separate Protestant community. It expired in 1668.

Archbishop Sheldon surrendered the clergy's right to tax themselves and thus rendered Convocation impotent.

1665   The Five Mile Act. Ministers ejected by the Act of Uniformity and other unlicensed preachers were forbidden to come within five miles of the parish where they had been incumbent, or of any city or town.

1666   The Great Fire of London.

1670   The Treaty of Dover (May). With at least the Cabal's partial approval Charles II concluded a treaty with Louis XIV. In its secret clause he agreed to declare war on Holland and grant toleration to Roman Catholics.

The Conventicle Act of 1664 was renewed as a result of the revival of Quaker activity.

1672   The Declaration of Indulgence (March). Charles declared the suspension of the penal laws against nonconformists and recusants. It was a great source of relief for Protestant nonconformists, despite actually being intended for Roman Catholics by the secret terms of the Treaty of Dover. A scheme was introduced whereby nonconformist ministers, teachers and meeting houses could be registered and were thus exempt from the penal laws. The categories for registration were Independent, Congregational, Presbyterian and Baptist. The Quakers and some Baptists did not register, chiefly on the grounds that toleration was an inalienable right.

1673   The king was forced (March) to repeal the Declaration, since Parliament was withholding supply. The information provided by the register of nonconformists was used to enforce the renewed persecution which ensued.

The Test Act. Those holding public office were forced to deny transubstanti-ation, and take the oaths of supremacy and allegiance. Thus many Church Papists were excluded from holding office. Clifford of the Cabal and James, Duke of York were both disqualified from office. The publication of the terms of the Treaty of Dover exacerbated anti-Catholic feeling.

The Bill for the Ease of Protestant Dissention was passed (March) by the Commons in the wake of anti-Catholicism following the Declaration of Indulgence, but was stopped in the Lords. Subscription to the Prayer Book and abjuration of the Solemn League and Covenant were no longer to be required, provided that the oaths of supremacy and obedience were taken and assent given to those of the Thirty Nine Articles concerned with doctrine.

1678   The second Test Act reinforced and extended the provisions of the 1673 Act as a result of the Popish Plot (see below). It enforced on members of both Houses of Parliament an oath stricter than that demanded of Crown office-holders in 1673, thus excluding Catholics from Parliament until the nineteenth century.

The government issued (November) a proclamation which implied that all priests arrested should be tried on the spot, although in practice they were usually sent to London.

1678–81   The Popish Plot. A scheme to murder Charles II, put James on the throne and forcibly restore England to Roman Catholicism was revealed (September 1678) by Titus Oates, Israel Tonge and their associates. The revelation that Danby had been negotiating a secret treaty with France increased alarm, as did the murder of Sir Edmund Berry Godfrey, the magistrate before whom Oates had deposed his evidence. As a result of the plot the exclusion of James from the succession was proposed. By 1680 Oates's credibility was beginning to suffer; even so, Lord Stafford was executed and, the following year, the Archbishop of Dublin. The panic over the Plot helped the Whigs to stay in power and consequently they to some extent encouraged it. The persecution resulting from the Plot fell heaviest on the Jesuits, who in the early days were blamed for it. The organisation of the secular clergy was so nebulous that it is difficult to know whether it was at all affected by the Plot. The government was reluctant to proceed against members of the Catholic landed classes except under the penal laws. Even the judges at the various treason trials made a clear distinction between the priesthood and the laity. The expense and upheaval of fleeing abroad was probably the most severe burden imposed by the Plot on the Catholic lay community. Magistrates were never ordered to tender the anti-Papal test to suspected Catholics, but were only required to exact the oaths of Supremacy and Allegiance. Most Catholics would take the second, and many the first. Parliament hoped to eliminate Catholicism, but saw the means of doing so as the better enforcement of the existing laws. Catholics were to be coerced into political conformity by taking oaths and by the enforcement of the penal laws, especially in 1681, when the penal laws were ordered to be enforced against dissenters as well. The resulting persecution was severe but erratic.

1679   The First Exclusion Bill (May).

The Meal Tub Plot (October). A spurious Presbyterian plot which was produced by various Catholics in an attempt to counter the Popish Plot, but the discovery of which merely discredited Catholics further. The investigations which followed revealed the continued existence of a large and unsubdued Catholic community in London, despite numerous proclamations against Catholics remaining there.

1680   The Second Exclusion Bill (November).

A Bill to distinguish Protestant dissenters from Popish recusants was cut short by the dissolution of Parliament (December). It was intended to liberate dissenters from the Elizabethan statutes intended against Catholics, but which actually operated against dissenters as well. The Commons also passed a bill to annul the Elizabethan statute requiring dissenters to abjure the kingdom, but this never received the royal assent. A measure aimed at comprehension was also considered, but did not get anywhere.

Impeachment (7 December) of Viscount Stafford, one of the Catholic Lords imprisoned as a result of Titus Oates's deposition.

1681   Third Exclusion Bill (March).

1683   The Rye House Plot (April) released all the dormant fears that dissent was the prime cause of sedition. As a result there was renewed persecution of Protestant nonconformists. The intention of the plot was to assassinate Charles II and put Monmouth on the throne to save the Protestant cause.

1685   Death of Charles II, accession of James II (6 February).

The Revocation of the Edict on Nantes meant the end of toleration for Protestants in France.

Monmouth's rebellion (June).

The Pope appointed John Leyburne Bishop of Andrumetum to supervise the Roman Catholic secular clergy in England, but without the powers of an ordinary.

James II extended to England the practice of dispensing army officers from the terms of the Test Act, which already existed in Ireland.

1686   Catholics were admitted to the commissions of the peace and other positions in the county administration, after being dispensed from the terms of the Test Act by James II.

The Court of Ecclesiastical Commission was established illegally (August) by James II, since the law abolishing the earlier Court of High Commission had forbidden the setting up of any similar court. James II established it as part of his attempt to keep the Church of England in order, as it was becoming increasingly unco-operative towards his pro-Catholic policy. Archbishop Sancroft refused to serve on the Court, partly because its chairman was a layman (Lord Chancellor Jeffreys).

Godden v. *Hales*. This was a test case as to whether James II might exercise the dispensing power, particularly in respect of the Test Act. The judges decided in favour of the King.

1687   Roman Catholics were admitted to government offices by dispensation from the Test Act by James.

In the spring James II tried to force the Fellows of Magdalen College, Oxford, to elect a Roman Catholic President, in contravention of their statutes. The Fellows resisted and tried to elect their own candidate. They were then expelled and their places filled with nominees of the Ecclesiastical Commission. In October 1688 the Fellows and their President were restored. Having been the principal proponent of the doctrine of passive obedience, Oxford now led the lawful resistance to the King's illegal acts.

The Declaration of Indulgence (4 April) suspended the operation of the penal laws and of the church courts on both Roman Catholics and dissenters.

The Papal Nuncio was received in state by James (3 July).

Announcement of the Queen's pregnancy.

1688   England and Wales were divided into four provinces for the administration of the Roman Catholic secular clergy. Three vicars apostolic were appointed to take charge of them, in addition to the Bishop of Andrumetum.

The Declaration of Indulgence of 25 April repeated the terms of the 1687 Declaration, which had suspended the penal laws against Roman Catholics and dissenters.

James issued (4 May) an order-in-council requiring the bishops to have the Declaration read in all churches and chapels in their dioceses. Seven bishops (William Sancroft, Archbishop of Canterbury; Thomas Ken, Bishop of Bath and Wells; John Trelawney, Bishop of Bristol; William Lloyd, Bishop of St Asaph; John Lake, Bishop of Chichester; Francis Turner, Bishop of Ely; and Thomas White, Bishop of Peterborough) presented a petition to the King announcing their refusal to order the reading of the Declaration, because of the illegality of the suspending power.

The seven bishops were summoned before the Privy Council (8 June) for publishing seditious libel. They were committed to the Tower for pleading their privilege as peers for not having to enter into recognisances to appear when summoned to the Court of King's Bench.

The seven bishops were brought to trial (29 June) and were found not guilty of conspiring to diminish royal power.

The birth of a son to James II (10 June).

Sancroft and five other bishops presented to James (3 October) a set of ten propositions for reforms in the Church of England. James complied with some of them too late and showed no inclination to agree to the rest.

William III landed (5 November).

James II escaped from England (10 December).

1689   William and Mary were declared King and Queen (6 February).

The Bill of Rights (February–December) confirmed William's assumption of the throne. It included a simplified Oath of Allegiance, abolished the suspending power and the prerogative courts and condemned the dispensing power. It included the sovereign under the terms of the Test Act.

Nine English bishops (the Archbishop of Canterbury, the bishops of Bath and Wells, Chichester, Ely, Chester, Peterborough, Gloucester, Worcester and Norwich), one Irish bishop, all the Scottish bishops and many of the Scottish clergy and about 400 English clergy refused to swear allegiance to William III, believing that James II was still King *de jure*. Those who failed to take the Oath of Allegiance by 1 August 1689 were to be suspended and, if still obdurate by 1 February 1690, to be deprived. Bishop Cartwright of Chester and Bishop Thomas of Worcester died before they could be deprived. Some of the non-juring bishops continued to consecrate clergy, to ensure the continuance of the apostolic succession. The non-jurors hoped for some sort of rapprochement with Queen Anne, but in vain.

The Presbyterians in Scotland expelled the episcopalian clergy, whereupon William (in July) recognised the Presbyterian Church as the Established Church in Scotland and consented to the abolition of the Scottish episcopacy.

The Toleration Act (24 May) was intended to operate with the Comprehension Bill and thus to apply only to the most intransigent nonconformists. Its terms were that nonconformists who took the oaths of supremacy and allegiance and made a declaration against transsubstantiation might worship separately in their own meeting houses, which had to be registered by a bishop. Ministers had to subscribe to those of the Thirty Nine Articles which did not concern church government, with further exceptions for Baptists. Catholics and Unitarians were not included. The Test and Corporation Acts remained in force.

The Comprehension Bill (February–March) aimed at comprehending the majority of nonconformists by allowing limited subscription to the doctrines of the Church of England and of restoring the right to hold civil offices to such nonconformists as were comprehended. It failed because of William's precipitate proposal to abolish the Test and Corporation Acts, which thoroughly alarmed Parliament. A second attempt to introduce the bill (in the autumn) was defeated by the intransigence of convocation.

LIST OF ARCHBISHOPS AND BISHOPS, 1603–89

PROVINCE OF CANTERBURY

CANTERBURY

1583	John Whitgift	1660	William Juxon
1604	Richard Bancroft	1663	Gilbert Sheldon
1610	George Abbot	1677	William Sancroft
1633	William Laud		

LONDON

1597	Richard Bancroft	1628	William Laud
1604	Richard Vaughan	1633	William Juxon
1607	Thomas Ravis	1660	Gilbert Sheldon
1610	George Abbot	1663	Humfrey Henchman
1611	John King	1675	Henry Compton
1621	George Monteigne		

WINCHESTER

1597	Thomas Bilson	1632	Walter Curie
1616	James Montague	1660	Brian Duppa
1619	Lancelot Andrewes	1662	George Morley
1628	Richard Neale	1684	Peter Mewes

BATH AND WELLS

1593	John Still	1629	Walter Curl
1608	James Montague	1632	William Piers
1616	Arthur Lake	1670	Robert Creighton
1626	William Laud	1672	Peter Mewes
1628	Leonard Mawe	1685	Thomas Ken

BRISTOL

1589	Richard Fletcher	1644	Thomas Howell
1603	John Thornborough	1661	Gilbert Ironside
1617	Nicholas Felton	1672	Guy Carleton
1619	Rowland Searchfield	1679	William Gulston
1623	Robert Wright	1684	John Lake
1633	George Coke	1685	Sir Jonathan Trelawney
1637	Robert Skinner	1689	Gilbert Ironside
1642	Thomas Westfield		

CHICHESTER

1596	Anthony Watson	1619	George Carleton
1605	Lancelot Andrewes	1628	Richard Mountague
1609	Samuel Harsnet	1638	Brian Duppa

1641	Henry King	1679	Guy Carleton
1669	Peter Gunning	1685	John Lake
1675	Ralph Brideoke	1689	Simon Patrick

ELY

1600	Martin Heton	1638	Matthew Wren
1609	Lancelot Andrewes	1667	Benjamin Laney
1619	Nicholas Felton	1675	Peter Gunning
1628	John Buckeridge	1684	Francis Turner
1631	Francis White		

EXETER

1598	William Cotton	1662	Seth Ward
1621	Valentine Carey	1667	Anthony Sparrow
1627	Joseph Hall	1676	Thomas Lamplugh
1642	Ralph Brownrigg	1689	Sir Jonathan Trelawney
1660	John Gauden		

GLOUCESTER

1598	Godfrey Goldsborough	1624	Godfrey Goodman
1604	Thomas Ravis	1660	William Nicholson
1607	Henry Parry	1672	John Pricket
1611	Giles Tomson	1681	Robert Frampton
1612	Miles Smith		

HEREFORD

1586	Herbert Westfaling	1636	Theophilus Field
1603	Robert Bennet	1636	George Coke
1617	Francis Godwin	1661	Nicholas Moncke
1634	Augustine Lindsell	1662	Herbert Croft
1635	Matthew Wren		

LICHFIELD

1580	William Overton	1622	Robert Wright
1609	George Abbot	1644	Accepted Frewen
1610	Richard Neile	1661	John Hacket
1614	John Overall	1671	Thomas Wood
1619	Thomas Morton		

LINCOLN

1595	William Chaderton	1642	Thomas Winniffe
1608	William Barlow	1660	Robert Sanderson
1614	Richard Neile	1663	Benjamin Laney
1617	George Monteigne	1667	William Fuller
1621	John Williams	1675	Thomas Barlow

NORWICH

1595	William Redman
1603	John Jegon
1618	John Overall
1619	Samuel Harsnet
1629	Francis White
1632	Richard Corbet

1635	Matthew Wren
1638	Richard Mountague
1641	Joseph Hall
1661	Edward Reynolds
1676	Anthony Sparrow
1685	William Lloyd

OXFORD

1589	John Underhill
1604	John Bridges
1619	John Howson
1628	Richard Corbet
1632	John Bancroft
1641	Robert Skinner
1663	William Paul

1665	Walter Blandford
1671	Nathaniel, Lord Crewe
1674	Henry Compton
1676	John Fell
1686	Samuel Parker
1688	Timothy Hall

PETERBOROUGH

1584	Richard Howland
1601	Thomas Dove
1630	William Piers
1633	Augustine Lindsell
1634	Francis Dee

1639	John Towers
1660	Benjamin Laney
1663	Joseph Henshaw
1679	Willaim Lloyd
1685	Thomas White

ROCHESTER

1578	John Yong
1605	William Barlowe
1608	Richard Neile
1611	John Buckeridge
1628	Walter Curie

1630	John Bowle
1638	John Warner
1666	John Dolben
1683	Francis Turner
1684	Thomas Spratt

SALISBURY

1598	Henry Cotton
1615	Robert Abbot
1618	Martin Fotherby
1620	Robert Townson
1621	John Davenant
1641	Brian Duppa

1660	Humphrey Henchman
1663	John Earle
1665	Alexander Hyde
1667	Seth Ward
1689	Gilbert Burnet

WORCESTER

1597	Gervase Babington
1610	Henry Parry
1617	John Thornborough
1641	John Prideaux
1660	George Morley
1662	John Gauden

1662	John Earle
1663	Robert Skinner
1671	Walter Blandford
1675	James Fleetwood
1683	William Thomas
1689	Edward Stillingfleet

PROVINCE OF YORK

YORK

1595	Matthew Hutton	1642	John Williams
1606	Tobias Matthew	1660	Accepted Frewen
1628	George Monteigne	1664	Richard Sterne
1629	Samuel Harsnet	1683	John Dolben
1632	Richard Neile	1688	Thomas Lamplugh

DURHAM

1595	Tobias Matthew	1628	John Howson
1606	William James	1632	Thomas Morton
1617	Richard Neile	1660	John Cosin
1628	George Monteigne	1674	Nathaniel, Lord Crewe

CARLISLE

1598	Henry Robinson	1629	Barnabas Potter
1616	Robert Snowden	1642	James Usher
1621	Richard Milbourne	1660	Richard Sterne
1624	Richard Senhouse	1664	Edward Rainbow
1626	Francis White	1684	Thomas Smith

CHESTER

1597	Richard Vaughan	1662	George Hall
1604	George Lloyd	1668	John Wilkins
1616	Thomas Morton	1673	John Pearson
1619	John Bridgeman	1686	Thomas Cartwright
1660	Brian Walton	1689	Nicholas Stratford
1662	Henry Ferne		

SODOR AND MAN

1599	George Lloyd	1663	Isaac Barrow
1604	John Phillips	1671	Henry Bridgman
1634	William Forster	1682	John Lake
1635	Richard Parr	1685	Baptis Leving
1661	Samuel Butter		

8 THE ARMED FORCES

PARLIAMENT AND THE ARMY

PETITION OF RIGHT, 1628

This was a Parliamentary protest against arbitrary imprisonment, arbitrary taxation, the imposition of martial law in peacetime and the billeting of troops in private homes.

CONTROL OF THE MILITIA, 1641–2

Sir Arthur Haselrig introduced a Militia Bill in Parliament on 7 December 1641, giving supreme command of all trained bands in England to a general appointed by Parliament; it was passed as the Militia Ordinance on 5 March 1642. One of the Nineteen Propositions passed by Parliament on 1 June 1642 and laid before the King at York was that he should hand over custody of fortified places and command of the militia to Parliament, which he refused to do. On 11 June 1642 Charles issued a Commission of Array to raise the trained bands on his behalf.

NEW MODEL ARMY, 1645

On 6 January 1645 the Committee of both Kingdoms recommended the establishment of a permanent army, to consist of twelve regiments of foot, comprising 14,000 men; eleven regiments of horse, comprising 6600 men; and one regiment of dragoons, comprising 1000 men. It was to be brought up to strength by impressment, and supported by regularised taxation.

The New Model Army was officially formed on 4 April 1645. Sir Thomas Fairfax held the chief command, with Philip Skippon as Major-General of the Foot. Cromwell was granted a dispensation from the provisions of the Self-Denying Ordinance of 3 April, by which MPs had to give up their commands, and became Lieutenant-General, involving command of the Horse.

PARLIAMENT VERSUS THE ARMY, 1647–53

On 27 May 1647 Parliament ordered the New Model Army to disband without its arrears of pay. On 31 May Cromwell sent Cornet Joyce to safeguard a train of artillery at Oxford, and then to Holmby House, where the King was in custody, to secure him from removal to London by Parliamentary agents. The Declaration of the Army on 14 June set out the army's case for opposing Parliament. On 6 August the army occupied London, and eleven Parliamentary leaders were expelled from their seats.

When the Second Civil War ended, in August 1648, Parliament continued negotiations with the King. On 1 December the army again marched on London, and moved the King from the Isle of Wight to Hurst Castle. On 2 December Parliament passed a Militia Bill in an attempt to take control of the militia as a bulwark against the army. However, Colonel Pride carried out his 'purge' of the Commons on 6 December. The remaining members, the Rump, set up a High Court of Justice, which tried and condemned the King.

The Rump sat until 1653. When it tried to increase its powers, Cromwell went to the Commons on 20 April with a body of musketeers, and dissolved it.

RULE OF THE MAJOR-GENERALS, 1655–7

After a royalist rising led by Colonel Penruddock in March 1655, by an order of 9 August the country was divided into ten – later eleven – military districts. Each was governed by a major-general, with between 1000 and 1500 men, mainly cavalry, at his disposal. The system was financed by the decimation tax, which took 10 per cent of the property of all royalists.

The second Protectorate parliament met on 17 September 1656, and Major-General Disbrowe brought in a Bill on 25 December to continue the decimation tax. It was rejected on 28 January 1657, and the rule of the Major-Generals was abandoned.

RESTORATION OF THE MONARCHY, 1659–60

Cromwell died on 3 September 1658, and was succeeded as Protector by his son Richard. The army demanded that his brother-in-law, Fleetwood, should be independent Commander-in-Chief. Parliament passed two resolutions, stating that during Parliamentary sessions there should be no general council or meeting of officers of the army without permission of the Protector and both Houses, and that no officer should retain his post unless he promised not to disturb the meeting of Parliament. But on 22 April 1659 Fleetwood forced Richard to dissolve Parliament by a show of strength, and on 7 May the Council of Officers recalled the Rump. It appointed Fleetwood as General, but withheld from him the power to name officers; all commissions had to be signed by the Speaker. Richard Cromwell resigned on 25 May.

Friction increased between Parliament and the army. Following the suppression of a royalist rising in August 1659, the army made new demands in a petition presented to Parliament. The organisers of the petition, Lambert, Disbrowe and seven other officers, were cashiered, and command of the army was entrusted to seven commissioners. In response Lambert marched to Westminster on 13

October 1659, and blocked the entrance to the House with musketeers. However, riots forced Fleetwood to reinstate the Rump on 26 December.

In January 1660 General Monck marched from Scotland to London with 7000 men. On 21 February he readmitted to the Commons the members excluded by Colonel Pride in 1648. The Long Parliament dissolved itself on 16 March, and a new Parliament met on 25 April. Negotiations with Charles resulted in his being proclaimed King on 8 May, and landing at Dover on 25 May.

MILITIA AND STANDING ARMY, 1660–89

1660   The Disbanding Act of 13 September dissolved the Cromwellian army.

1661   An insurrection by Fifth Monarchy Men on 4 January led to the King's being allowed to retain some royal guards. Standing forces were also needed to garrison Tangiers, which was part of the dowry of Catherine of Braganza, whom Charles II married in 1662.

1661–3   By three Militia Acts, control of the militia was placed in the hands of the King and his lord lieutenant in each county. Obligations to serve in the militia were redistributed, and it was stated that punishment of soldiers was reserved to the civil authorities as martial law was still unknown to the constitution.

1667   The first article against Clarendon on his impeachment was that he had advised the King to govern by a standing army.

1679   On 1 April the Commons resolved that the continuation of any standing force other than the militia was illegal and a grievance and vexation to the people.

1685   After Monmouth's rebellion, James II said in his speech from the throne when Parliament met on 9 November that he required 'a good force of well-disciplined troops in constant pay', in which Catholics might hold commissions, contrary to the Test Act of 1673. A motion introduced on 12 November that a supply be granted 'for the army' was rejected. The House then voted £700,000, instead of the £1,200,000 wanted by the court, and agreed to bring in a Bill for remodelling the militia. James prorogued Parliament on 20 November.

1689   The Convention Parliament drew up the Declaration of Right, which received the royal assent as the Bill of Rights on 16 December, including the statement that there could be no standing army in peacetime without the consent of Parliament. On 28 March 1689 the Mutiny Act was passed. The immediate reason for this was the mutiny at Ipswich of Scottish soldiers being sent to Holland. By the Act, from 12 April to 10 November anyone who stirred up mutiny would suffer the penalty imposed by a court martial (this did not apply to the militia). This was the first of a succession of Mutiny Acts, which renewed for short periods Parliament's permission granted to the Crown to keep a standing army and discipline it.

CHRONOLOGY OF THE CIVIL WARS

1639
June 18   First Bishops' War ended by the Pacification of Berwick.

1640
Apr 13   Short Parliament met, and demanded redress of grievances before granting supplies.

May 5   Short Parliament dissolved.

Aug 20   Second Bishops' War: Scottish army crossed the border.

28   King's army defeated at Newburn.

29   Scots entered Newcastle; agreement reached in November after negotiations at Ripon.

Nov 3   Long Parliament met.

1641
May 12   Earl of Strafford executed.

Oct 23   Outbreak of rebellion in Ireland.

Nov 22   Grand Remonstrance passed by 159 votes to 148.

1642
Jan 4   Charles I arrived at the House of Commons with 300 armed men to arrest the Five Members – John Pym, Denzil Holles, William Strode, John Hampden and Sir Arthur Haslerig. They had been warned and were sheltered by the City of London.

6   The citizens of London took to arms and closed the gates.

10   The King and his family left London, moving from Whitehall to Hampton Court.

31   Parliament ordered Sir John Hotham to take control of Hull.

Feb 23   Queen Henrietta Maria sailed for Holland to raise men and money for the King.

Mar 2   The King left for York with Prince Charles.

5   Parliament passed the Militia Ordinance, giving control of the militia to the lord lieutenants of the counties.

Apr 23   The King denied entry into Hull by Sir John Hotham.

June 1   Parliament passed the Nineteen Propositions, which were sent to the King.

10   Parliament issued an ordinance for 'the bringing in of money or plate to maintain horsemen, and arms, for the preservation of the public peace, and for the defence of the King and both Houses of Parliament'.

11   The King issued Commissions of Array to raise the trained bands on his behalf.

July 2   The navy declared for Parliament, and the Earl of Warwick appointed Admiral.

12	Marquis of Hertford left York with a commission as 'Lieutenant-General of all the western parts of the Kingdom'.
15	Earl of Essex appointed Captain-General of Parliament's forces.
20	Parliament appointed county committees to co-ordinate the work of raising men and money.
Aug 2	Governor of Portsmouth, George Goring, declared for the King.
5	12,000 Parliamentarians mustered at Chewton Mendip, Somerset.
6	Shots fired at Hertford's royalist forces in Wells; Hertford fled to Sherborne Castle.
21	Dover Castle fell to Parliamentarian forces.
21	Prince Rupert and Prince Maurice arrived from the United Provinces to join their uncle, the King, at Nottingham.
22	The King raised his standard at Nottingham.
Sep 2	Earl of Bedford besieged Sherborne castle with 7000 men.
7	Sir William Waller captured Portsmouth for Parliament.
7	Skirmish at Babylon Hill, near Yeovil; Sir Ralph Hopton driven back into Sherborne.
10	Earl of Essex reached Northampton with 20,000 men.
19	Hertford evacuated Sherborne.
20	The King arrived at Shrewsbury to make contact with his Welsh recruits.
20	Lord Fairfax appointed General of Parliament's northern forces, and began to raise an army in the West Riding.
23	Skirmish at Powick Bridge, near Worcester; Prince Rupert routed Parliamentarian forces under Colonel John Brown.
23	Hertford left Minehead for South Wales; Hopton left for Cornwall.
24	Essex captured Worcester.
Oct 12	The King left Shrewsbury to march on London.
19	Essex left Worcester to head off the King's advance on London.
23	Battle of Edgehill – indecisive.
25	Essex withdrew to Warwick.
27	The King took Banbury as he resumed his march on London.
29	Royalist forces arrived in Oxford.
Nov 4	The King reached Reading.
8	Essex returned to London with his army.
12	Rupert took Brentford by storm.
13	The London Trained Bands, under Major-Gen. Philip Skippon, joined Essex at Turnham Green to block the royalists' advance on London. The King withdrew without conflict, first to Reading, on 19 November, and then to Oxford, on 29 November, where winter quarters were established.
30	Earl of Newcastle succeeded the Earl of Cumberland as Lieutenant-General of the King's Northern forces.
Dec 1	Earl of Newcastle, with 8000 royalists, crossed the Tees at Piercebridge, *en route* for York.

5   Henry Wilmot stormed Marlborough for the King.
6   Newcastle attacked Tadcaster, held by Fairfax's Parliamentarian forces; Fairfax withdrew to Selby on 7 December.
13 Waller captured Winchester for Parliament.
15 Parliament established a Midland Association under Lord Grey of Groby to organise the war in the counties of Nottingham, Rutland, Bedford, Derby, Leicester, Northampton and Huntingdon.
20 Parliament established an Eastern Association under Lord Grey of Wark to organise the war in the counties of Norfolk, Suffolk, Cambridge, Essex and Hertford.
27 Waller captured Chichester for Parliament.

1643

Jan 17 Sir Ralph Hopton invited to become Commander-in-Chief of Cornish army of royalists.
19 Sir Ralph Hopton and Sir Bevil Grenvile defeated General Ruthin at Braddock Down, securing Cornwall for the King.
23 Sir Thomas Fairfax stormed Leeds; Wakefield and Pontefract also fell to the Parliamentarians. The Earl of Newcastle withdrew into York.
Feb 2   Prince Rupert stormed Cirencester.
11 Parliament established a Western Association under Sir William Waller to organise the war in the counties of Somerset, Wiltshire, Gloucester, Shropshire and Worcester.
22 The Queen landed at Bridlington with arms from the Netherlands; she moved on to York.
Mar 2   Prince Maurice commissioned to protect Gloucestershire against Waller's advance.
15 Waller gained control of Bristol, where he established his headquarters.
19 Earl of Northampton defeated the Parliamentarian forces under Sir John Gell and Sir William Brereton at Hopton Heath, near Stafford.
23 Charles Cavendish stormed Grantham for the King.
24 Waller defeated Lord Herbert's newly-raised Welsh forces at Highnam, near Gloucester.
26 Waller took Malmesbury, Wilts, after a short siege.
Apr 3   Rupert seized Birmingham.
4   Waller took Monmouth.
6   Waller took Chepstow.
11 Parliamentarians under Lord Willoughby defeated by Cavendish at Ancaster Heath.
12 Lt Col. Massey, Parliamentarian Governor of Gloucester, seized Tewkesbury.
13 Prince Maurice defeated Waller at Ripple Field, near Tewkesbury.

21 Rupert took Lichfield.

23 Hopton defeated Parliamentarians under James Chudleigh at Launceston, Cornwall.

25 Royalist forces attempting to relieve Reading defeated at Caversham Bridge.

25 Chudleigh defeated Hopton at Sourton Down, near Okehampton, following a night ambush.

25 Waller took Hereford.

27 Essex captured Reading, opening the route to Oxford.

May 13 Oliver Cromwell's cavalry defeated Cavendish at Grantham.

16 Hopton defeated the Earl of Stamford at Stratton in Devon.

19 Marquis of Hertford and Prince Maurice left Oxford to strengthen Hopton's army advancing from the West.

21 Sir Thomas Fairfax stormed Wakefield and defeated General Goring.

June 4 The Queen left York with 4500 men to join the King.

4 Hertford and Maurice joined forces with Hopton at Chard in Somerset.

8 Waller began to concentrate his Western forces around Bath.

10 Hopton's forces harried Alexander Popham's Parliamentarians near Chewton Mendip, Somerset.

18 Rupert defeated a Parliamentarian force at Chalgrove Field; John Hampden mortally wounded.

29 Newcastle inflicted a heavy defeat on Lord Fairfax and Sir Thomas Fairfax at Adwalton Moor, near Bradford; they retreated to Hull.

July 2 Cavendish stormed Burton-on-Trent.

5 Hopton and Waller fought a stiff battle on Lansdown, near Bath; royalist cavalry fled to Oxford; Sir Bevil Grenvile killed.

10 Hertford and Maurice broke out from Waller's siege of Devizes to bring relief from Oxford.

13 Maurice and Wilmot routed Waller's army at Roundway Down, near Devizes.

13 The Queen rejoined the King in Oxford.

15 Rupert left Oxford to join the King's Western army.

19 Parliament sent a delegation to Edinburgh to negotiate for a Scottish army.

20 Willoughby captured Gainsborough, but was besieged by Cavendish.

22 Lord Fairfax appointed Governor of Hull.

26 Rupert and Maurice stormed Bristol after a short siege; the Governor, Nathaniel Fiennes, surrendered.

28 Cromwell's cavalry defeated Cavendish, who was killed, and relieved Gainsborough.

Aug 4 Maurice, Lieutenant-General of the King's Western army, took Dorchester, gaining control of Dorset.

10 The King began the siege of Gloucester, held for Parliament by Colonel Massey.

24 Essex marched with the London Trained Bands to relieve Gloucester.

Sep 2 Newcastle began the siege of Hull.

4 Maurice took Exeter.

5 The King ended his siege of Gloucester on the approach of Essex.

8 Essex relieved Gloucester.

15 Marquis of Ormonde arranged a truce (or Cessation) with the Catholic Confederates in Ireland, hoping to free the King's forces for use in England.

16 Earl of Manchester, newly appointed Commander of Parliament's Eastern Association, took Lynn after a siege.

18 Rupert checked Essex at Aldbourne Chase, near Swindon.

20 The King failed to halt Essex's return to London and was defeated at the First Battle of Newbury; he withdrew to Oxford.

25 Parliament signed the Solemn League and Covenant, securing military help from Scotland.

Oct 6 Maurice took Dartmouth.

11 Manchester, Cromwell and Fairfax defeated Sir John Henderson and Sir William Widrington at Winceby.

11 Newcastle abandoned his siege of Hull.

Nov 4 Parliament appointed Waller to command the new South-Eastern Association of Surrey, Sussex, Kent and Hampshire.

23 Scots agreed to send an army of 20,000 to assist Parliament.

Dec 9 Hopton captured Arundel Castle.

13 Waller took Alton by storm.

13 Lord Byron besieged Sir William Brereton at Nantwich.

1644

Jan 6 Waller succeeded in retaking Arundel Castle.

19 Scottish army crossed the Tweed under Lord Leven.

25 Sir Thomas Fairfax ended the siege of Nantwich by defeating Byron after a long march.

Feb 6 Rupert left Oxford to establish a headquarters at Shrewsbury.

16 The Committee of Both Kingdoms established by Parliament to control the war.

Mar 21 Rupert relieved Newark, under siege by Sir John Meldrum, whose army surrendered.

29 Waller convincingly defeated Hopton and Forth at Cheriton, near Alresford, Hants.

Apr 11 Fairfax stormed Selby and opened the road to York.

17 The Queen left Oxford for Exeter.

18 Newcastle entered York with the royalist army, having abandoned Durham.

22	Fairfax and Leven commenced the siege of York.
May 6	Manchester took Lincoln by storm.
16	Rupert set out from Shrewsbury with 8000 men to relieve York.
18	Royalist forces abandoned Reading.
23	Earl of Warwick's ships ferried in supplies to the garrison at Lyme, besieged by Maurice.
24	Massey took Malmesbury.
25	Rupert took Stockport by storm.
26	Earl of Essex entered Abingdon, closing in on the King at Oxford.
27	Rupert took Bolton by storm.
30	Rupert's relief force joined by Goring and Lucas with 6000 men.
June 3	The King left Oxford with 7500 men, chased by Essex and Waller.
6	The King entered Worcester. Essex decided to march to the relief of Lyme, leaving Waller to pursue the King.
10	Waller took Sudeley Castle.
11	Rupert captured Liverpool after four days' fighting.
14	Maurice abandoned the siege of Lyme on the approach of Essex.
16	The Queen gave birth to a daughter at Exeter.
29	The King defeated Waller at Cropredy Bridge, near Banbury.
July 1	Rupert relieved Newcastle at York.
2	Parliamentarian forces under Leven, Manchester and Fairfax decisively defeated the combined royalist armies under Rupert and Newcastle at the Battle of Marston Moor, ending the King's control of the North.
2	Alasdair MacDonald arrived in Scotland with 1600 of his supporters from Ireland to join the Marquis of Montrose and fight for the King.
12	The King's army left Evesham for the south-west to protect the Queen at Exeter.
16	York surrendered to Parliament.
23	Essex occupied Tavistock on his way to relieve Plymouth.
26	Waller returned to London, after desertions had seriously reduced his forces; he pleaded with Parliament for the establishment of a professional army.
26	Essex entered Cornwall. The King arrived at Exeter.
Aug 21	The King defeated Essex at Beacon Hill, near Lostwithiel.
31	The King defeated Essex at Castle Dore, near Fowey; Essex escaped by sea.
Sep 1	Montrose defeated the Covenanter army of Lord Elgin at Tippermuir.
2	Skippon, with 6000 infantry from Essex's army, surrendered to the King.
11	Plymouth garrison refused the King's summons.
13	Montrose defeated the Covenanter army of Lord Balfour at Aberdeen.
Oct 15	The King occupied Salisbury.

20 Scottish army under Leven captured city of Newcastle for Parliament.

27 The King, seemingly trapped by the superior forces of Manchester, Waller and Cromwell, escaped by night after the Second Battle of Newbury.

Nov 1 The King returned to Oxford. Liverpool retaken for Parliament by Meldrum and Brereton.

6 The King restructured the royalist command: the Prince of Wales was made Commander-in-Chief, and Rupert Lieutenant-General of all the King's armies.

9 Rupert relieved Donnington Castle, Berks.

19 Colonel Gage relieved Basing House for the King.

23 The King went into winter quarters at Oxford.

Dec 19 The Self-Denying Ordinance, proposed by Zouch Tate, was passed by the Commons to exclude all members from holding military command.

1645

Jan 6 The Committee of Both Kingdoms recommended the establishment of a permanent army of 22,000 – the New Model Army.

11 Rupert failed to retake Abingdon.

13 House of Lords rejected the Self-Denying Ordinance.

Feb 2 Montrose and the MacDonalds defeated the Marquis of Argyll and the Campbells at Inverlochy.

19 Maurice relieved Chester, besieged by Brereton.

22 Colonel Thomas Mytton stormed Shrewsbury; the royalist Governor, Sir Michael Ernle, was killed.

Mar 1 Langdale relieved Pontefract for the King.

4 The Prince of Wales left Oxford with Culpeper, Richmond and Southampton, to set up a court in Bristol.

12 Waller defeated Colonel Long near Trowbridge and moved towards Bristol.

Apr 3 House of Lords passed an amended Self-Denying Ordinance.

4 New Model Army officially formed under Sir Thomas Fairfax; Manchester, Essex and Waller resigned their commands.

4 Montrose captured Dundee.

22 Rupert defeated Massey at Ledbury.

24 Cromwell defeated Northampton at Islip, Oxon, and took Bletchingdon House.

29 Cromwell failed to take Faringdon Castle by storm.

30 Fairfax left Windsor with the New Model Army with the aim of relieving Taunton.

May 8 Rendezvous of Royalist forces at Stow-on-the-Wold to plan policy. Goring returned to the west to check Fairfax; the King's main forces moved north against the Scots.

9 Montrose defeated the Covenanter army of Sir John Urry at Auldearn, Nairn.

9 Fairfax ordered to bring the New Model Army north to Oxford, leaving Colonel Weldon to relieve Taunton.

11 Taunton relieved by Weldon.

19 The King's Army reached Market Drayton.

26 Massey stormed Evesham.

30 Rupert took Leicester by storm.

June 4 The King's forces began to move south, aiming to relieve Oxford.

5 Fairfax moved north from Oxford to Newport Pagnell.

10 Cromwell officially appointed Lieutenant-General of Horse in the New Model Army.

14 Fairfax, Cromwell and the New Model Army decisively beat the King at Naseby.

18 Fairfax recaptured Leicester.

28 Fairfax left Marlborough with the aim of relieving Taunton, garrisoned by Blake; Goring abandoned the siege on his approach.

July 2 Montrose defeated a Covenanter army under Baillie at Alford, Aberdeenshire.

10 Fairfax defeated Goring at Langport, Somerset.

23 Fairfax captured Bridgwater.

30 Bath, garrisoned by Sir Thomas Bridges, surrendered to a detachment of the New Model Army under Colonels Rich and Okey.

Aug 1 Admiral Batten, newly appointed commander of Parliament's navy, combined with Major-Gen. Langharne to defeat Sir Edward Stradling at Colby Moor in Wales.

5 The King marched north from Cardiff in the hope of joining forces with Montrose.

14 Sherborne Castle captured by the New Model Army after a short siege.

15 Montrose defeated Baillie at Kilsyth.

18 The King reached Doncaster, but withdrew to Huntingdon when threatened by Leslie's Scottish forces.

Sep 4 The King arrived at Hereford.

10 Rupert surrendered Bristol to Fairfax.

13 Leslie defeated Montrose at Philiphaugh, Selkirkshire.

18 The King marched north from Raglan to join Montrose.

23 Cromwell captured Devizes Castle.

24 Col.-Gen. Poyntz defeated Langdale at Rowton Heath, near Chester, which was garrisoned by Byron with the King himself in residence; Charles withdrew to Newark.

Oct 5 Cromwell captured Winchester.

14 Cromwell took Basing House by storm.

15 Digby, newly-appointed Lieutenant-General of the King's forces

north of the Trent, defeated at Sherburn-in-Elmet, Yorks, and fled to Scotland.

Nov 3   The King marched from Newark to Oxford.

1646

Jan 9   Cromwell defeated Lord Wentworth's cavalry at Bovey Tracey, Devon.

15   The Prince of Wales appointed Hopton to command the Western forces.

19   Fairfax stormed Dartmouth.

Feb 3   Byron surrendered Chester to Parliament.

16   Fairfax defeated Hopton at Torrington.

Mar 2   The Prince of Wales and his Court set sail for the Scilly Islands.

12   Hopton surrendered to Fairfax at Falmouth.

21   Lord Astley surrendered the last Royalist field army at Stow-on-the-Wold.

Apr 9   Sir John Berkeley surrendered Exeter to Parliament.

27   The King left Oxford in disguise for Newark.

May 5   The King surrendered to the Scots at Southwell, Notts.

8   Lord John Belasye surrendered Newark on the King's instructions.

June 24   Colonel-General Sir Thomas Glemhan surrendered Oxford to Parliament.

Aug 16   Lord Arundel surrendered Pendennis Castle.

19   Marquis of Worcester surrendered Raglan Castle.

1647

Jan 30   The King handed over to Parliament by the Scots, and taken to Holmby House, Northants.

Mar 16   Harlech Castle, the last royalist stronghold, surrendered.

May 27   Parliament ordered the New Model Army to disband without its arrears of pay.

31   Cromwell sent Cornet Joyce to safeguard a train of artillery at Oxford, and then to Holmby House to secure the King from removal to London by Parliamentary agents.

June 4   Joyce removed the King to Newmarket.

14   Declaration of the Army set out the army's case for opposing Parliament in defence of its rights.

Aug 6   The army entered London.

Oct 28   General Council of the army met at Putney church to debate constitutional problems.

Nov 11   General Council broke up.

11   The King escaped from Hampton Court, and fled to Carisbrooke Castle, Isle of Wight.

Dec 26   The King signed the Engagement with the Scots.

1648

Mar 23	Colonel Poyer, Governor of Pembroke Castle, declared for the King.
Apr 28	Sir Marmaduke Langdale captured Berwick.
29	Sir Philip Musgrave took Carlisle.
May 21	Royalists seized Rochester as the revolt spread to Kent.
25	Colonel Ewer stormed Chepstow Castle for Parliament.
26	Dartford and Deptford captured by royalists.
27	The fleet in the Downs mutinied.
June 1	Fairfax took Maidstone, defended by the Earl of Norwich.
3	Norwich reached Blackheath and seized Bow Bridge, but Skippon closed the City gates against him; Norwich marched into Essex.
4	Rising by royalists in Colchester, led by Colonel Henry Farr.
11	Fairfax crossed the Thames at Tilbury.
13	Fairfax's attempt to storm into Colchester checked by Sir Charles Lucas.
14	Fairfax began siege of Colchester.
July 8	Duke of Hamilton crossed the border into England with a Scottish army of 9000.
11	Pembroke Castle surrendered to Cromwell.
Aug 12	Cromwell joined Lambert at Wetherby.
17–19	Cromwell defeated Scots at Battle of Preston.
28	Colchester surrendered.
Nov 30	New Model Army moved the King to Hurst Castle.
Dec 6	Colonel Pride's Purge of MPs favouring continued negotiations with the King.

1649

Jan 6	The Rump set up a 'High Court of Justice' to try the King.
30	Charles I beheaded in Whitehall.
Feb 5	Charles II proclaimed King in Edinburgh.
Mar 15	Council of State nominated Cromwell Lord Lieutenant and Commander-in-Chief in Ireland.
May 14	Cromwell suppressed Leveller mutinies in the army at Burford.
Aug 2	In Ireland the Royalists under Ormonde were defeated at the Battle of Rathmines.
Aug 15	Cromwell arrived in Dublin.
Sep 12	Cromwell took Drogheda by storm.
Oct 16	Cromwell stormed Wexford.

1650

Mar 23	Montrose landed at Kirkwall in the Orkneys.
Apr 27	Colonel Strachan defeated Montrose at Carbisdale.
May 21	Montrose hanged in Edinburgh.
Jun 1	Cromwell returned from Ireland.

12 Fairfax and Cromwell voted to command an army for war with Scotland, as General and Lieutenant-General.

20 Parliament declared its intention of invading Scotland.

23 Charles II accepted the Covenant.

26 Fairfax laid down his commission and Cromwell was appointed General in his place.

Jul 19 Parliamentarian army concentrated around Berwick.

22 Cromwell crossed the border into Scotland.

26 Supplies for the army landed at Dunbar from the fleet.

29 Cromwell found Leslie's position between Leith and Edinburgh too strong to assault.

Aug 31 After unsuccessful attempts to bring Leslie to battle, Cromwell began to withdraw to Dunbar.

Sep 1 Cromwell's army entered Dunbar.

3 Cromwell attacked and defeated Leslie in the Battle of Dunbar; Leslie took refuge in Stirling.

Dec 24 Edinburgh Castle surrendered.

1651

Jan 1 Charles II crowned at Scone.

Jul 17 Colonel Overton led Parliamentarian forces across the Forth.

20 Lambert attacked Major-General Browne near Inverkeithing, and killed nearly 2000 Scots.

30 Cromwell crossed the Forth.

31 Cromwell invested Perth.

Aug 2 Perth surrendered.

6 Charles crossed the border into England.

14 Stirling Castle surrendered.

22 Charles occupied Worcester.

25 Colonel Robert Lilburne routed the Earl of Derby at Wigan.

28 Lambert secured the bridge across the Severn at Upton.

Sep 1 Dundee taken by storm.

3 Cromwell defeated Charles at the Battle of Worcester.

Oct 13 Charles escaped to France.

OUTLINE OF PRINCIPAL CAMPAIGNS

EARLY STUARTS, 1603–30

1603 James I issued (23 June) a proclamation that the war with Spain had ended on his accession. A treaty of peace was signed in August 1604.

1618 Revolt in Bohemia began the Thirty Years' War. On the death of the Emperor Matthias, in March 1619, the Bohemians elected as their king the son-in-law of James I, Frederick, the Elector Palatine.

1620 The Bohemians were defeated at the Battle of the White Mountain (8 November).

1624 James I attempted to aid his son-in-law: an army of 12,000 men led by a German, Ernst Mansfeld, was landed in Holland to march to the Palatinate, but it quickly disintegrated through sickness and lack of supplies.

1625 Death of James I (27 March). Charles I decided to conduct a maritime war against Spain, but an expedition to seize Cadiz in October was a complete failure.

1626 A shipping dispute (April) precipitated war with France.

1627 Duke of Buckingham led an expedition of 7000 men to capture the Isle of Rhé, to support the Huguenots in La Rochelle. The force failed to take the island's citadel and had to be evacuated, with heavy losses.

1628 Further expeditions failed to relieve La Rochelle. Buckingham was assassinated at Portsmouth on 23 August.

1629 Peace with France (April).

1630 Peace with Spain (November).

FIRST ANGLO-DUTCH WAR, 1652-4

1651 The Navigation Act (9 October) struck a blow at the Dutch carrying trade.

1652 The English claim to the right of salute in the Channel led to an action off Dover (19 May) between fleets under Blake and Martin Tromp; the Dutch retired after losing two ships.
Engagement (16 August) between Sir George Ayscue and Michael de Ruyter off Plymouth.
The Battle of Kentish Knock (28 September): Blake, with sixty-eight ships, defeated a Dutch fleet of fifty-seven ships led by Tromp and Cornelis de Witt.
The Battle of Dungeness (30 November): after being ordered to send reinforcements to the Mediterranean, Blake had only forty-two ships when he was attacked by Tromp with eighty-five, and was forced to retreat to the Thames.

1653 The Three Days' Battle (18–20 February): a running battle in the Channel as Tromp with seventy-five ships tried to protect a convoy of 150 merchantmen against an English fleet of sixty ships. The English broke through, and Tromp lost eleven warships and fifty merchantmen.
The Battle of Gabbard Bank (2–3 June): an English fleet of 100 vessels under Deane and Monck engaged a Dutch fleet of similar size under

Tromp. When Blake arrived with reinforcements, Tromp withdrew after losing twenty ships and the English fleet blockaded the Dutch coast. Tromp put to sea, and De Witt escaped from Texel to join him (23 July). The Battle of Scheveningen (31 July): a twelve-hour battle between fleets of 130 vessels ended in the complete defeat of the Dutch, who lost thirty ships. Tromp was killed and the Dutch fleet took refuge in Texel.

1654   The Treaty of Westminster (5 April): the Dutch paid compensation for the Amboyna Massacre of 1623, and agreed to make annual payment to fish in English waters and to respect the Navigation Act and the English right of salute.

SPANISH WAR, 1655–9

1655   Cromwell sent an expedition of thirty-eight ships and 6000 men to the West Indies to capture Hispaniola. The force was unable to take the capital, San Domingo, so in May it sailed to Jamaica and successfully occupied the island.

1656   Spain declared war on England (February).
An English squadron under Captain Stayner captured part of the Spanish Plate fleet with its treasure off Cadiz (9 September).

1657   Treaty with France (23 March): England agreed to provide 6000 men, in French pay, and a fleet, and France an army of 20,000 for operations in Flanders. Mardyck was captured from the Spanish in the autumn.
Blake destroyed eleven Spanish ships in an attack on Santa Cruz (20 April).

1658   The Battle of the Dunes (14 June): French and English forces defeated the Spanish army. Dunkirk surrendered and was ceded to England (Charles II sold it to Louis XIV in 1662).

1659   The Peace of the Pyrenees (7 November) ended the war between France and Spain.

SECOND ANGLO-DUTCH WAR, 1665–7

1664   Sir Robert Holmes attacked the Dutch West African trading stations, and seized the Dutch colony of New Amsterdam, which was renamed New York. De Ruyter then recaptured the West African ports, but failed to retake New York.

1665   Charles II declared war on the Dutch (4 March).
The Battle of Lowestoft (3 June): a Dutch fleet of 100 ships led by Jacob Opdam attacked the English blockading fleet when it withdrew for supplies. Dutch were defeated, and took refuge in Texel after losing seventeen ships.

The Battle of Bergen (1 August): Earl of Sandwich detached Sir Thomas Teddiman with thirty ships to attack Dutch merchant ships sheltering in Bergen. Despite earlier negotiations, the Dutch batteries opened fire, and after three hours the English withdrew.

1666   In January France entered the war against England, in accordance with her treaty with the Dutch of 1662.

The Four Days' Battle (1–4 June): After Prince Rupert had been sent with twenty ships to intercept the French Toulon squadron, Albermarle was left with only fifty-six to oppose De Ruyter when he put to sea with eight-four ships. Nevertheless he attacked, but after fierce fighting he was forced to withdraw. Rupert returned on the third day of the battle, and after further fighting both sides returned to harbour.

The Battle of the North Foreland (25 July): in a battle between fleets of about ninety ships each, the English captured or destroyed twenty ships for the loss of one. In August Holmes followed up this victory by entering the Zuyder Zee and destroying 150 merchantmen. Charles II then decided to lay up the main fleet, and peace negotiations opened at Breda.

1667   De Ruyter led eighty ships in a surprise raid into the Thames estuary (June). He advanced to Chatham, devastating shipping, and then blockaded the mouth of the river.

The Peace of Breda (21 July): commercial concessions were made to the Dutch. Acadia was surrendered to the French and Surinam to the Dutch, who accepted, however, English possession of the North American colonies.

THIRD ANGLO-DUTCH WAR, 1672–4

1670   The secret Treaty of Dover (22 May): Charles II agreed to support French operations against Holland in return for a large subsidy.

1672   Sir Robert Holmes attacked the Dutch Smyrna convoy in the Channel (13 March), but allowed it to escape.

England declared war on the Dutch (17 March).

The Battle of Solebay (28 May): De Ruyter attacked the French and English fleets, and at nightfall, when he withdrew, the Allies had to retire to refit.

1673   The Dutch failed in an attempt to use blockships to close the Thames estuary channels (2 May).

The Battle of Schoonveldt Channel (28 May): the Allied fleet was·driven off when it attacked the Dutch coastal anchorage.

De Ruyter attacked the Allies (4 June), forcing them to retire to the Nore.

The Battle of Texel (11 August): De Ruyter successfully escorted an East Indies convoy; the Allies were unable to carry out their plans for a descent on Holland.

1674 The Treaty of Westminster (19 February): Dutch paid an indemnity, conceded the right of salute, and there was a mutual restoration of colonies.

COVENANTER REBELLION, 1679

1679 Scottish rebels defeated the royalists under John Graham, Viscount Dundee, at Drumclog (1 June).
The Duke of Monmouth led a royalist army which crushed the revolt at Bothwell Bridge (22 June).

MONMOUTH'S REBELLION, 1685

1685 The Duke of Monmouth landed at Lyme Regis (11 June), and was proclaimed King at Taunton. He established his headquarters at Bridgwater, and made an unsuccessful advance on Bristol.
Monmouth attempted a night attack on the royal army at Sedgemoor (5–6 July). He was defeated, captured and executed. Over 300 peasants were hanged by Judge Jeffreys in the Bloody Assize in September.

BATTLES

Aberdeen	13 Sep 1644	First Civil War
Adwalton Moor	29 June 1643	First Civil War
Aldbourne Chase	18 Sep 1643	First Civil War
Alford	2 July 1645	First Civil War
Ancaster Heath	11 Apr 1643	First Civil War
Auldearn	9 May 1645	First Civil War
Beacon Hill	21 Aug 1644	First Civil War
Bergen	1 Aug 1665	Second Anglo-Dutch War
Bothwell Bridge	22 June 1679	Covenanter Rebellion
Bovey Tracey	9 Jan 1646	First Civil War
Braddock Down	19 Jan 1643	First Civil War
Carbisdale	27 Apr 1650	Third Civil War
Castle Dore	31 Aug 1644	First Civil War
Caversham Bridge	25 Apr 1643	First Civil War
Chalgrove Field	18 June 1643	First Civil War
Cheriton	29 Mar 1644	First Civil War
Colby Moor	1 Aug 1645	First Civil War
Cropredy Bridge	29 June 1644	First Civil War
Dover	19 May 1652	First Anglo-Dutch War
Drumclog	1 June 1679	Covenanter Rebellion
Dunbar	3 Sep 1650	Third Civil War
Dunes	14 June 1658	Anglo-Spanish War
Edgehill	23 Oct 1642	First Civil War

Four Days' Battle	1–4 June 1666	Second Anglo-Dutch War
Gabbard Bank	2–3 June 1653	First Anglo-Dutch War
Grantham	13 May 1643	First Civil War
Highnam	24 Mar 1643	First Civil War
Hopton Heath	19 Mar 1643	First Civil War
Islip	24 Apr 1645	First Civil War
Inverkeithing	20 July 1651	Third Civil War
Inverlochy	2 Feb 1645	First Civil War
Kentish Knock	28 Sep 1652	First Anglo-Dutch War
Kilsyth	15 Aug 1645	First Civil War
Langport	10 July 1645	First Civil War
Lansdown	2 July 1643	First Civil War
Launceston	23 Apr 1643	First Civil War
Ledbury	22 Apr 1645	First Civil War
Lowestoft	3 June 1665	Second Anglo-Dutch War
Marston Moor	2 July 1644	First Civil War
Naseby	14 June 1645	First Civil War
Newburn	28 Aug 1640	Second Bishops' War
Newbury (1st)	20 Sep 1643	First Civil War
Newbury (2nd)	27 Oct 1644	First Civil War
North Foreland	25 July 1666	Second Anglo-Dutch War
Philiphaugh	13 Sep 1645	First Civil War
Preston	17–19 Aug 1648	Second Civil War
Rathmines	2 Aug 1649	Irish campaign
Ripple Field	13 Apr 1643	First Civil War
Roundway Down	13 July 1643	First Civil War
Rowton Heath	24 Sep 1645	First Civil War
Scheveningen	31 July 1653	First Anglo-Dutch War
Schoonveldt Channel	28 May 1673	Third Anglo-Dutch War
Sedgemoor	6 July 1685	Monmouth's Rebellion
Selby	11 Apr 1644	First Civil War
Sherburn-in-Elmet	15 Oct 1645	First Civil War
Solebay	28 May 1672	Third Anglo-Dutch War
Sourton Down	25 Apr 1643	First Civil War
Stratton	16 May 1643	First Civil War
Texel	11 Aug 1673	Third Anglo-Dutch War
Three Days' Battle	18–20 Feb 1653	First Anglo-Dutch War
Tippermuir	1 Sep 1644	First Civil War
Wigan	25 Aug 1651	Third Civil War
Winceby	11 Oct 1643	First Civil War
Worcester	3 Sep 1651	Third Civil War

BRITISH TREATIES

Date signed		Place signed
19/30 July 1603	Treaty with France for defence of the Netherlands	Villiers Cotterêts/Hampton Court
18 Aug 1604	Treaty of perpetual peace and alliance with Spain and Burgundy	London
24 Feb 1606	Treaty with France for security and freedom of commerce	Paris
26 June 1608	Treaty with the Netherlands guaranteeing treaty between the Netherlands and Archduke and Archduchess Albert and Isabella	The Hague
26 June 1608	Treaty with the Netherlands on debts and privileges	The Hague
24 Apr 1609	Treaty with France	–
17 June 1609	Agreement with France and the Netherlands guaranteeing truce with Spain	–
29 Aug 1610	Treaty of confederacy and alliance with King of France	London
28 Mar 1612	Treaty with the Electors of Germany (renewed 1619)	Wesel
29 Apr 1621	Hereditary treaty with Denmark and Norway	London
1 May 1623	Treaty of a general cessation of arms in the Empire with the Infanta the Archduchess of Austria	London
16 June 1623	Treaty for mercantile intercourse with Russia	Westminster
20 July 1623	Matrimonial contract between Charles, Prince of Wales, and Mary, Infanta of Spain	Westminster
5 June 1624	Treaty for continuing defensive league with the Netherlands (with a Secret Article)	London
20 Nov 1624	Treaty with France for marriage of Charles, Prince of Wales, and Princess Henrietta Maria	Paris
3 May 1625	Contract of marriage between Charles I and Henrietta Maria	Paris
17 Sep 1625	Treaty of a league, offensive and defensive, with the Netherlands	Southampton
9 Dec 1625	Treaty of alliance with Denmark and the Netherlands	The Hague
28 Jan 1628	Treaty with the town of La Rochelle	–

Date signed		*Place signed*
24 Apr 1629	Treaty of peace and confederacy with France	Susa
31 May 1630	Treaty between Gustavus Adolphus, King of Sweden, and James, Marquis of Hamilton	Stockholm
15 Nov 1630	Treaty of peace and alliance with Spain	Madrid
29 Mar 1632	Treaty with France for restitution of New France, Arcadia and Canada, and the ships and merchandises taken on both sides	–
29 Mar 1632	Treaty with France for the re-establishment of commerce	St Germain-en-Laye
6 Apr 1639	Renewal of alliance of 1625 with Denmark	Gluckstat
28 Oct 1641	Capitulation between His Majesty and the Ottoman Empire	Constantinople
29 Jan 1642	Treaty of peace, commerce and amity with Portugal	London
29 Dec 1652	Preliminary articles to treaty of peace with Portugal	Westminster
5 Apr 1654	Treaty of peace and union with the Netherlands (with a secret article, 4 May)	Westminster
11 Apr 1654	Treaty of peace and commerce with Sweden	Upsala
10 July 1654	Treaty of peace, commerce and amity with Portugal (with a secret article)	Westminster
15 Sep 1654	Treaty of peace and alliance with Denmark	Westminster
3 Nov 1655	Treaty of peace with France (accession: the Netherlands, 20 April 1656)	Westminster
23 Mar 1657	Treaty with France	–
9 May 1657	Treaty with France	Paris
28 Mar 1658	Treaty with France	–
3 Feb 1659	Treaty with France for facilitating a peace between Sweden and Denmark	Westminster
21 May 1659	Treaty with France and the Netherlands for obliging the Northern kings to make peace	The Hague
24 July 1659	Treaty with the Netherlands for inducing Sweden and Denmark to make peace	The Hague
4 Aug 1659	Convention with France and the Netherlands for procuring a peace between Sweden and Denmark	The Hague
28 Apr 1660	Treaty of alliance with Portugal	London
13 Feb 1661	Treaty of peace and commerce with Denmark	London
17 May 1661	Agreement with the Elector of	–

Date signed		Place signed
	Brandenburg for guardianship and preservation of the person and estates of the Prince of Orange	
23 June 1661	Treaty with Portugal for marriage of Charles II and Princess Catherine	London
20 July 1661	Treaty of alliance with the Elector of Brandenburg	Westminster
21 Oct 1661	Treaty of peace and commerce with Sweden	London
11 June 1662	Treaty with Algiers	–
4 Sep 1662	Treaty of peace and alliance with the Netherlands	Whitehall
5 Oct 1662	Treaty of peace and commerce with Tunis	Tunis
18 Oct 1662	Treaty of peace with Tripoli	Tripoli
27 Oct 1662	Treaty for sale of Dunkirk to the French	London
10 Nov 1662	Articles of peace with Algiers (separate article, 30 October 1664)	–
1 Mar 1665	Treaty of defensive alliance with Sweden	Stockholm
29 Apr 1665	Treaty of commerce with Denmark	–
3 May 1665	Secret article concluded with the King of Denmark	–
13 June 1665	Treaty of alliance with the Bishop of Munster	London
23 Nov 1665	Articles of peace with Morocco	–
17 Dec 1665	Treaty of peace and commerce with Spain	Madrid
29 Jan 1666	Articles of peace with Morocco	–
16 Feb 1666	Treaty of commerce with Sweden	Stockholm
12 Apr 1666	Treaty of peace with Morocco	Tangier
23 May 1667	Treaty of peace and friendship with Spain	Madrid
31 July 1667	Articles of peace and alliance with the King of Denmark and Norway	Breda
31 July 1667	Treaty of peace with France	Breda
31 July 1667	Treaty of peace and alliance with the Netherlands	Breda
31 July 1667	Articles of navigation and commerce with the Netherlands	Breda
23 Jan 1668	Treaty with the Netherlands (accession: Sweden, 23 January)	–
17 Feb 1668	Treaty of commerce with the Netherlands	The Hague
15 Apr 1668	Treaty with France and the Netherlands for procuring a peace between France and Spain	St Germain-en-Laye
25 Apr 1668	Treaty with the Netherlands and Sweden, amending Triple League of 23 January	Westminster

Date signed		*Place signed*
6 Oct 1668	Confirmation of articles of peace of 3 May 1662 with Algiers	Algiers
7 May 1669	Convention with Sweden and the Netherlands guaranteeing Spanish territory	The Hague
9 Sep 1669	Treaty of friendship and commerce with Savoy	Florence
29 Nov 1669	Treaty concerning commerce with Denmark	Westminster
22 May 1670	Secret treaty with France	Dover
6 July 1670	Treaty of peace and friendship with Spain for settling all disputes in America	Madrid
11 July 1670	Treaty of peace and commerce with Denmark	Copenhagen
21 Dec 1670	Secret treaty with France	Whitehall
29 Nov 1671	Treaty with Algiers	–
12 Feb 1672	Treaty of alliance with France	Whitehall
16 July 1672	Treaty for strict union of interests with France against the Netherlands	The camp of Hesurick
1672	Treaty of peace with Algiers	–
15 Jan 1673	Agreement with Hamburg	Whitehall
19 Feb 1674	Treaty of peace with the Netherlands	Westminster
10 Oct 1674	Treaty with Sweden	Westminster
1 Dec 1674	Treaty with the Netherlands	London
4 Feb 1675	Treaty with Tunis	Tunis
18 Mar 1675	Articles with the Netherlands for preventing disputes between English and Dutch East India Companies	London
Sep 1675	Capitulations and articles of peace with Ottoman Empire	Adrianople
5 Mar 1676	Treaty of peace and commerce with Tripoli	Tripoli
1 May 1676	Treaty of commerce with Tripoli	Tripoli
24 Feb 1677	Treaty of commerce with France	St Germain-en-Laye
10 Jan 1678	Treaty of defensive alliance with Netherlands	The Hague
26 Jan 1678	Treaty with the Netherlands for bringing France and Spain to consent to a peace	The Hague
3 Mar 1678	Treaty of defensive alliance with the Netherlands	Westminster
26 July 1678	Treaty of alliance with the Netherlands	The Hague
10 June 1680	Defensive league with Spain	Windsor
10 Apr 1682	Treaty of peace and commerce with Algiers (separate article, 5 March 1683)	Algiers

Date signed		*Place signed*
15 July 1683	Articles of peace and commerce with Algiers	–
27 July 1683	Treaty of marriage between Prince George of Denmark and Princess Anne	Whitehall
17 Aug 1685	Treaty with the Netherlands for renewing alliance	Windsor
5 Apr 1686	Treaty of peace and commerce with Algiers	Algiers
2 Oct 1686	Treaty of peace and commerce with Tunis	Tunis
16 Nov 1686	Treaty of peace with France, for a neutrality in America	Whitehall
1 Dec 1687	Agreement with France respecting peace in America	Whitehall

9 OVERSEAS TRADE AND THE COLONIES

MAIN TERRITORIES UNDER
BRITISH RULE BY 1688

Territory	Original entry into British rule and status in 1688
Antigua	Colony (1663)
Bahamas	First settled 1646
Barbados	First settled 1627. Colony (1662)
Bermuda	First settled 1609. Colony (1684)
British Honduras	First settled 1638
Cayman, Turks and Caicos Islands	Ceded (1670)
Connecticut	First settlement 1635
Delaware	First settlement 1683
Gambia	Settlement began 1618
India	Settlement began 1601
Jamaica	Colony (seized 1655 and ceded 1670)
Maryland	First settlement 1634
Massachusetts	First settlement 1620
Montserrat	First settled (1642) as colony
Newfoundland	Settlement began 1623
New Hampshire	First settlement 1623
New Jersey	First settlement 1664
New York	First settlement 1614
North Carolina	First settlement 1650
Pennsylvania	First settlement 1682
Rhode Island	First settlement 1636
St Christopher (St Kitts) and Nevis	Colony (1625)
St Helena	Administered by East India Company 1673
South Carolina	First English settlement 1670
Virgin Islands	Colonies (1666)
Virginia	First English settlement 1607

LANDMARKS IN BRITISH COLONIAL POLICY

1601-3   First voyage of Sir James Lancaster to Achin in Sumatra and Bantam in Java for the East India Company.

1604   Voyage of Sir Henry Middleton to the Indies.

1606   Formation of the Royal Council for Virginia and its two bodies of investors, the London Company and the Plymouth Company; John Knight's voyage to discover the North-West Passage.

1607   Foundation of Virginia; site of Jamestown chosen by Christopher Newport; Henry Hudson's first voyage to Greenland and Spitzbergen; William Hawkins obtains from the Great Mogul the right to set up a factory at Surat.

1609   Royal charter granted to the Virginia Company; Robert Harcourt's colony founded on the Wiapoco (failed by 1613); Sir George Somers wrecked on Bermuda; Hudson's third voyage brought discovery of the Hudson River.

1610   Sir Thomas Roe's voyage to Guiana; arrival of Lord Delaware as Governor of Virginia; charter granted to John Guy for colonisation of Newfoundland – first settlement at Cuper's Cove.

1611   Mutiny on Hudson's final voyage to discover the North-West passage; unfortified English factory at Masulipatam started.

1612   Charter granted to the North West Passage Company; Sir Thomas Button discovered the western shore of Hudson's Bay; Bermuda added to the charter of the Virginia Company; victory of Thomas Best over Portuguese fleet at Swally Roads (outside Surat); Thomas Aldworth organised the first English factory in Surat.

1613   First shipment of tobacco from Virginia; first terminable joint-stock venture by the East India Company.

1614   William Gibbon's voyage to Labrador.

1615   Bermuda placed under the Somers Islands Company; first voyage of William Baffin and Robert Bylot; Nicholas Downton defeats the Portuguese at Swally Roads, confirming British fortunes in Surat; Sir Thomas Roe's embassy to the Emperor Jehangir.

1616   Second voyage of Baffin and Bylot reached 78°N in Baffin Bay.

1617   Raleigh's last voyage to the Orinoco; clash with the Spaniards at San Thome.

1619   Foundation of the Amazon Company, chief promoter Captain Roger North; first Virginia Assembly, with two burgesses chosen from each of eleven constituencies; last enterprise of the North West Passage Company under William Hawkridge achieved nothing; Spice Islands Treaty between England and Holland.

1620 Formation of the New England Council (the Plymouth Company resigning its rights in New England); voyage of the *Mayflower* and foundation of Plymouth.

1621 Virginia ordered to ship its tobacco exclusively to England (in order that duties might be collected in English customs houses); William Bradford appointed Governor of Plymouth.

1622 English capture of Portuguese fortress of Ormuz in the Persian Gulf.

1623 Dissolution of the Virginia Company; territory thenceforth a crown colony; Massacre of Amboyna.

1624 St Kitts colonised by Sir Thomas Warner.

1625 Barbados claimed for the British Crown by Captain John Powell.

1627 Formation of the Guiana Company; colonisation of Barbados begun; Earl of Carlisle made Lord Proprietor of the Caribbee Islands by patent.

1628 London made sole port of entry for tobacco; colonisation of Nevis begun; origin of Massachusetts with pioneer party of John Endicott to Salem.

1629 Charter granted to the Massachusetts Bay Company.

1630 Providence Island Company formed; foundation of Massachusetts by John Winthrop.

1632 Colonisation of Antigua and Montserrat; Lord Baltimore created Lord Proprietor of Maryland.

1633 Foundation of Connecticut; English factory at Balasore (in India).

1634 First settlement in Maryland (St Mary's).

1635 Spaniards captured Association (Tortuga); French began to occupy Martinique and Guadeloupe; Convention of Goa, under which the Portuguese conceded to the English the right to trade in ports in Western India; formation of Courten's Association to trade in the Indies.

1636 First of successive bands of settlers colonise Rhode Island (led in 1636 by Roger Williams).

1638 New Haven founded by John Davenport and Theophilus Eaton.

1639 The first Barbados Assembly; acquisition of Madras; creation of Fort St George.

1640 Introduction of sugar-planting to Barbados.

1642 Caribbean colonists cease all payments to the Carlisle proprietorship;

Tasman's voyage discovers Tasmania and New Zealand.

1643   Charter obtained from Parliament by Roger Williams combining the Rhode Island settlements; New England Confederation formed (Massachusetts, Plymouth, Connecticut and New Haven) for joint defence against enemies.

1646   First settlements in the Bahamas (cotton planting in New Providence; salt-making in Eleothera).

1649   The Colonial Rebellion – Barbados, Antigua, Bermuda, Virginia and Maryland repudiate the Commonwealth and proclaim Charles II; Commission for Plantations established.

1650   Foundation of Hughli; Navigation Act – all foreign ships forbidden to trade in any of the colonies.

1651   Commonwealth fleet under Sir George Ayscue reached Barbados; Willoughby surrenders (January 1652); first colonisation of Surinam begun; passage of the Navigation Act prohibiting the import of any goods from Asia, Africa or America save in English, Irish or colonial ships with the majority of the crew of English etc. nationality, and prohibiting the import of European goods save in English etc. ships or ships of the country in which the goods had been produced. A few exceptions were permitted, including the import from Spain and Portugal of goods produced in the colonies of those countries).

1654   Cromwell's 'Western Design' against the Spanish Empire.

1655   Failure of the 'Western Design' at Hispaniola; but subsequent capture and eventual successful plantation of Jamaica.

1657   Reorganisation of the East India Company by Cromwell.

1661   Charles II continues privileges of the East India Company; French settlement at Placentia in Newfoundland; Bombay and Tangier included in the dowry of Catherine of Braganza.

1662   Royal Adventurers to Africa chartered, with a monopoly to sell slaves to the plantations; royal charter granted to Connecticut.

1663   Proprietary grant of Carolina made by Charles II; first settlement of North Carolina; extinction of Carlisle proprietorship; royal charter granted to Rhode Island; passage of the Staple Act.

1664   Hostilities with the Dutch on the West African coast; New Amsterdam (renamed New York) taken by expedition under Colonel Richard Nicholls; first Assembly in Jamaica; New French East India Company established by Colbert.

1666   Surinam falls to the Dutch; St Kitts, Antigua and Montserrat fall to the French.

1667 English recapture of Antigua, Montserrat and Surinam; Treaty of Breda gives England New York, but Surinam reverts to the Dutch.

1668 First trading voyage by Groseilliers to Hudson Bay; Bombay made over to the East India Company.

1670 Settlement of South Carolina; under the Treaty of Madrid, Spain recognised English possession of Jamaica; foundation of the Hudson Bay Company, with Prince Rupert as first Governor.

1671 Sack of Panama by buccaneers under Henry Morgan.

1672 Formation of the Royal African Company, successor to the Royal Adventurers.

1673 New York captured by the Dutch.

1674 Restoration of New York by the Treaty of Westminster; Quaker interest in emigration to New Jersey; establishment of French base at Pondicherry.

1675 Outbreak of Philip's War; major Indian rising in New England.

1676 Rebellion of Nathaniel Bacon in Virginia against the Governor, Sir William Berkeley.

1678 Proprietary rights to Maine bought by Massachusetts.

1679 Regular government for New Hampshire as a crown colony.

1681 William Penn becomes Lord Proprietor of Pennsylvania, under a grant which provided for religious toleration and parliamentary government; beginnings of colonisation of Pennsylvania.

1684 Abolition of the Somers Island Company, bringing Bermuda directly under the Crown; annulment of the Massachusetts charter.

1686 Evacuation of Hughli; first British occupation of Calcutta; annulment of the Rhode Island charter; all captured forts of the Hudson Bay Company (except Fort Charles) restored by the French.

1687 Annulment of the Connecticut charter; formation by James II of the short-lived Dominion of New England under Governor Sir Edmund Andros.

1688 Outbreak of war between the East India Company and the Moguls; William Dampier's visit to the north-western coast of Australia.

TRADING COMPANIES

AFRICAN ASSOCIATION: Founded in London, 1788, by Sir Joseph Banks to explore the African Continent. Agents, especially Mungo Park, were mainly concerned with the Niger. The Association was merged into the Royal Geographical Society in 1881.

AFRICAN COMPANY, ROYAL: Founded by royal charter in 1672 for the slave-trade with the Guinea Coast. In 1821 it was wound up, after the abolition of the slave trade in 1807.

CHARTERED COMPANIES: The earliest English chartered trading companies were the Merchant Staplers and Merchant Adventurers. Developed from medieval trading guilds. The discovery of India and America caused merchants to form monopolistic groups safeguarded by royal charter. The Eastland and Africa Companies were formed. Merchants did not share profits, but did obey the same trading regulations. For business purposes they were independent. The Muscovy and East India Companies were 'joint stock' organisations. Members held shares entitling them to a proportion of profits. Chartered companies prospered in the sixteenth and seventeenth centuries. Their restrictive nature caused their downfall. The British South Africa, Royal Niger and British North Borneo Companies were founded in the nineteenth century, but did not have exclusive trading rights.

COURTEN'S ASSOCIATION, or the ASSADA MERCHANTS: Founded in 1635, by charter from Charles I to Sir William Courten, Sir Paul Pindar and Captain John Weddell, to trade in parts of the East where the East India Company did not. The two united in 1649. Cromwell's 1657 charter formed them into one joint stock company with a total monopoly of Eastern trade.

EAST INDIA COMPANY: The East India Company was founded at the end of the sixteenth century in order to compete with Dutch merchants, who had obtained a practical monopoly of the trade with the Spice Islands and had raised the price of pepper from 3s. to 8s. per lb. Queen Elizabeth incorporated the company by royal charter, dated 31 December 1600, under the title 'The Governor and Company of Merchants of London trading into the East Indies'. This charter conferred upon the company for a term of fifteen years the sole right of trading with the East Indies, i.e. with all countries lying beyond the Cape of Good Hope or the Straits of Magellan. Unauthorised interlopers were liable to forfeiture of ships and cargo. There were 125 shareholders in the original East India Company, with a capital of £72,000; the first governor was Sir Thomas Smythe.

HUDSON'S BAY COMPANY: Was created by royal charter from Charles II to Prince Rupert in 1670, to trade with the lands surrounding Hudson's Bay. Surrendered its exclusive rights to the Canadian government in 1869.

LEVANT COMPANY: Was incorporated as a 'regulated' company in 1592 after the amalgamation of two joint-stock companies (the Turkey Company, founded in 1581, and the Venice Company, founded in 1583 to import fruit and wine from Venice). It confined operations to Europe, Syria and Mesopotamia. Prospered for 200 years, and surrendered its charter in 1821.

MUSCOVY COMPANY: Was formed in 1555, after Richard Chancellor's expedition to Moscow through the White Sea, to secure trade with Tsar Ivan the Terrible. Most of its business was with Russia, but it also traded with Armenia, Media, Persia and the Caspian. It was the first joint-stock company, with £6000 capital and 240 shares of £25. Members included Henry Hudson and Anthony Jenkinson. After Charles I's execution English merchants were expelled from Russia. Charles II had no success in re-establishing business, but the company continued till the end of the eighteenth century.

COLONIAL GOVERNORS

(Lt) Gov. = (Lieutenant) Governor; Pres. = President

ACADIA

GOVERNORS
1654–7	John Leverett
1657–70	Thomas Temple

ANTIGUA

GOVERNORS
1635–9	Edward Warner	1664–6	Robert Carden
1639–40	Rowland Thompson	1666	Daniel Fish
1640–52	Henry Ashton	1666–7	(under France)
1652–60	Christopher Keynell	1667–70	Henry Willoughby
1661–4	John Bunckley	1670–1	Samuel Winthrop

DEPUTY OR LIEUTENANT GOVERNORS
1671–5	Philip Warner	1680–2	Valentine Russell
1675–8	Rowland Williams	1682–3	Paul Lee
1678–80	James Vaughan	1683–8	Edward Powell

BAHAMA ISLANDS

GOVERNORS
1671–6	John Wentworth	1682–4	Richard Lilburne
1676–7	Charles Chillingsworth	1684–7	(abandoned)
1677–82	Robert Clarke	1687–90	Thomas Bridges

BANTAM

CHIEF FACTORS
1613–15	John Jourdain (1)	1615–16	John Jourdain (2)
1615	Thomas Elkington	1616–17	George Berkley

PRESIDENTS

1617–18	George Ball	1625–8	Henry Hawley
1618–19	John Jourdain (3)	1628–9	Richard Bix
1620–3	Richard Fursland	1629–30	George Muschamp (1)
1623–5	Thomas Brockeden		

AGENTS

1630–1	George Willoughby (1)	1632–3	Thomas Woodson
1631–2	William Hoare	1633–4	John Ling

PRESIDENTS

1634–6	George Willoughby (2)	1640–3	Aaron Baker (1)
1636–7	Robert Coulson	1643–5	Ralph Cartwright
1637–8	William Johnson	1645–9	Aaron Baker (2)
1638–9	Gerald Pinson	1649–50	Thomas Peniston
1639–40	George Muschamp (2)	1650–2	Aaron Baker (3)

BARBADOS

GOVERNORS

1628–9	Charles Wolferston	1663–7	Francis Willoughby (2)
1629	John Powell	1667–8	William Willoughby (1)
1629	Robert Wheatley	1668–9	Christopher Codrington (1)
1629–30	William Tufton	1669–70	William Willoughby (2)
1630–9	Henry Hawley	1670–2	Christopher Codrington (2)
1639–41	Henry Huncks		
1641–50	Philip Bell (Lt Gov.)	1672–3	William Willoughby (3)
1650–1	Francis Willoughby (1)	1673–4	Peter Colleton (Pres.)
1651–2	George Ayscue	1674–80	Jonathan Atkins
1652–60	Daniel Searle (Lt Gov.)	1680–5	Richard Dutton
1660	Thomas Modyford	1685–90	Edwin Stede (Lt Gov.)
1660–3	Humphrey Walrond (Pres.)		

BENCOOLEN

DEPUTY GOVERNORS

1685	Ralph Ord
1685–90	Benjamin Bloome

BERMUDA

GOVERNORS

1609–10	George Somers	1611–12	Richard Walters
1610–11	Matthew Somers	1612–16	Richard Moore

1616–19	Daniel Tucker	1627–9	Philip Bell
1619–22	Nathaniel Butler	1629–37	Roger Wood
1622	John Harrison (1)	1637–41	Thomas Chaddock
1622–3	John Bernard	1641–2	William Sayle
1623	John Harrison (2)	1642–3	Josias Forster (1)
1623–7	Henry Woodhouse		
(Collegial rule)			
1643–5	William Sayle (1)	1644–5	William Wilkinson (1)
1644–5	Samuel Paynter (1)		
		1645–6	Josias Forster (2)
(Collegial rule)			
1646–7	William Sayle (2)	1659–62	William Sayle (3)
1646–7	Samuel Paynter (2)	1662–8	Florentia Seymour (1)
1646–7	William Wilkinson (2)	1668–9	Samuel Whatley
		1669–81	John Heydon
1647–9	Thomas Turnor	1681–2	Florentia Seymour (2)
1649–50	John Trimingham	1682–3	Henry Durham
1650	James Jennings	1683–7	Richard Cony
1650–9	Josias Forster (3)	1687–91	Robert Robinson

BOMBAY

GOVERNORS

1664–6	Humphrey Cooke	1675–6	Philip Gifford (2)
1666–7	Gervase Lucas	1676–7	John Petit
1667–8	Henry Gary	1677–9	Henry Oxinden
1668	George Oxinden	1679–81	John Child (1)
1668–9	Henry Young	1681–2	Mansell Smith
1669–70	James Adams	1682–4	Charles Ward
1670	Matthew Gray	1684–5	Charles Zinzan
1670–2	Philip Gifford (1)	1685–7	John Wyborne
1672–4	John Shaxton	1687–90	John Child (2)

CONNECTICUT

GOVERNORS

1639	John Haynes (1)	1651	John Haynes (7)
1640	Edward Hopkins (1)	1652	Edward Hopkins (6)
1641	John Haynes (2)	1653	John Haynes (8)
1642	George Wyllys	1654	Edward Hopkins (7)
1643	John Haynes (3)	1655–6	Thomas Welles (1)
1644	Edward Hopkins (2)	1656–7	John Webster
1645	John Haynes (4)	1657–8	John Winthrop (1)
1646	Edward Hopkins (3)	1658–9	Thomas Welles (2)
1647	John Haynes (5)	1659–76	John Winthrop (2)
1648	Edward Hopkins (4)	1676–83	William Leete
1649	John Haynes (6)	1683–98	Robert Treat
1650	Edward Hopkins (5)		

THE GAMBIA (JAMES FORT)

AGENTS

1661	Francis Kerby	1677–80	Thomas Thurloe
1661–2	Morgan Facey	1680–1	Thomas Forde
1662–4	Stephen Ustick	1681–4	John Kastell
1664–6	John Ladd	1684–8	Alexander Cleeve
1672–4	Rice Wight	1688–93	John Booker

GOLD COAST

1632–51	Company of Merchants trading to Guinea
1651–8	Company of London Merchants
1658–63	East India Company
1663–72	Company of Royal Adventurers
1672–1751	Royal African Company

HUDSON'S BAY COMPANY

GOVERNORS

1670–83	Prince Rupert	1685–91	John Churchill
1683–5	James Stuart		

JAMAICA

GOVERNORS

1655–6	Edward D'Oyley (1)	1675–8	John Vaughan
1656–7	William Brayne	1678–80	Charles Howard, Earl of Carlisle
1657–62	Edward D'Oyley (2)		
1662–3	Thomas Hickman Windsor	1680–2	Henry Morgan (Lt Gov.)
1663	Charles Lyttleton (Lt Gov.)	1682–4	Thomas Lynch (3)
		1684–7	Hender Molesworth
1663–4	Thomas Lynch (Lt Gov.) (1)	1687–8	Christopher Monck, Duke of Albemarle
1664–71	Thomas Modyford	1688–90	Francis Watson (Pres.)
1671–5	Thomas Lynch (Lt Gov.) (2)		

LEEWARD ISLANDS

GOVERNORS

1671–2	Charles Wheler	1685–9	Nathaniel Johnson
1672–85	William Stapleton		

MADRAS

GOVERNORS

1641–3	Andrew Cogan		1665	George Foxcroft (1)
1643–4	Francis Day		1665–8	Edward Winter (2)
1644–8	Thomas Ivie		1668–70	George Foxcroft (2)
1648–52	Henry Greenhill (1)		1670–8	William Langhorne
1652–5	Aaron Baker		1678–81	Streynsham Master
1655–8	Henry Greenhill (2)		1681–7	William Gyfford
1659–61	Thomas Chamber		1687–92	Elihu Yale
1661–5	Edward Winter (1)			

MARYLAND

GOVERNORS

1634–47	Leonard Calvert		1660–1	Philip Calvert
1647–8	Thomas Green		1661–76	Charles Calvert (1)
1648–54	William Stone		1676–81	Thomas Noltey
1654–7	Richard Bennett		1681–4	Charles Calvert (2)
1657–60	Josias Fendall		1684–8	William Joseph

MASSACHUSETTS BAY

GOVERNORS

1629	Matthew Cradock		1646–9	John Winthrop (4)
1629–34	John Winthrop (1)		1649–50	John Endecott (2)
1634–5	Thomas Dudley (1)		1650–1	Thomas Dudley (4)
1635–6	John Haynes		1651–4	John Endecott (3)
1636–7	Henry Vane		1654–5	Richard Bellingham (2)
1637–40	John Winthrop (2)		1655–65	John Endecott (4)
1640–1	Thomas Dudley (2)		1665–72	Richard Bellingham (3)
1641–2	Richard Bellingham (1)		1672–9	John Leverett
1642–4	John Winthrop (3)		1679–86	Simon Bradstreet
1644–5	John Endecott (1)		1686	Joseph Dudley
1645–6	Thomas Dudley (3)		1686–9	Edmund Andros

MONTSERRAT

DEPUTY OR LIEUTENANT GOVERNORS

1632–54	Anthony Brisket		1672–8	Edmond Stapleton
1654–63	Roger Osborne		1680–2	James Cottar
1665	Moyer Byde		1685–7	Redmond Stapleton
1668–72	William Stapleton		1687–95	Nathaniel Blackistone

NEWFOUNDLAND

Cuper's Cove
1611–14   John Guy
1615–21   John Mason

Bristol's Hope
1618–28   Robert Hayman

Trepassey
1618–20   Richard Whitbourne

South Falkland
1623–5   Francis Tanfield

Avalon
1621–5   Edward Wynne   1629–34   (unknown)
1626–7   Arthur Aston   1634–8   William Hill
1627–9   George Calvert, Baron
          Baltimore

All settlements
1638–51   David Kirke
1652–60   John Treworgie

NEW HAMPSHIRE

PRESIDENTS OF THE COUNCIL
1680–1   John Cutt   1685–6   Walter Barefoot
1681–2   Richard Waldron   1686   Joseph Dudley
1682–5   Edward Cranfield

NEW HAVEN

GOVERNORS
1643–58   Theophilus Eaton   1660–4   William Leete
1658–60   Francis Newman

NEW JERSEY

GOVERNORS
East Jersey
1667–82   Philip Carteret   1686–7   Neil Campbell
1682–4   Thomas Rudyard   1687–97   Andrew Hamilton (1)
1684–6   Gawen Lawrie

West Jersey

1680–4	Samuel Jennings	1684–92	John Skene
1684	Thomas Ollive		

NEW PLYMOUTH

GOVERNORS

1620–1	John Carver	1639–44	William Bradford (4)
1621–33	William Bradford (1)	1644–5	Edward Winslow (3)
1633–4	Edward Winslow (1)	1645–57	William Bradford (5)
1634–5	Thomas Prence (1)	1657–72	Thomas Prence (3)
1635–6	William Bradford (2)	1673–80	Josias Winslow
1636–7	Edward Winslow (2)	1680–6	Thomas Hinckley (1)
1637–8	William Bradford (3)	1686–9	Edmond Andros
1638–9	Thomas Prence (2)		

NEW YORK

GOVERNORS

1664–8	Richard Nichols	1678–81	Edmund Andros (2)
1668–73	Francis Lovelace	1681–3	Anthony Brockholls (2)
1673–4	(under the Netherlands)	1683–8	Thomas Dongan
1674–7	Edmund Andros (1)	1688	Edmund Andros (3)
1677–8	Anthony Brockholls (1)	1688–9	Francis Nicholson

NORTH CAROLINA

GOVERNORS

1664–7	William Drummond	1678	Seth Sothel (1)
1667–70	Samuel Stephens	1678–9	John Harvey
1670–2	Peter Carteret	1680–1	John Jenkins (2)
1672–7	John Jenkins (1)	1682–9	Seth Sothel (2)
1677	Thomas Miller		

PENNSYLVANIA

GOVERNORS

1681–2	William Markham	1684–8	Thomas Lloyd
1682–4	William Penn	1688–90	John Blackwell

RHODE ISLAND

GOVERNORS

Portsmouth

1638–9	William Coddington
1639–40	William Hutchinson

Newport
1639–40   William Coddington

Newport and Portsmouth
1640–7   William Coddington (1)

Newport, Portsmouth, Providence, Warwick

1647–8	John Coggeshall	1649–50	John Smith
1648–9	Jeremy Clarke	1650–1	Nicholas Easton (1)

Newport and Portsmouth
1651–3   William Coddington (2)
1653–4   John Sanford

Providence

1630–6	Philip Bell	1638–40	Nathaniel Butler
1636–8	Robert Hunt	1640–1	Andrew Carter

Providence and Warwick

1651–2	Samuel Gorton	1653–4	Gregory Dexter
1652–3	John Smith		

Newport, Portsmouth, Providence, Warwick

1654	Nicholas Easton (2)	1660–2	William Brenton
1654–7	Roger Williams	1662–3	Benedict Arnold (2)
1657–60	Benedict Arnold (1)		

All settlements

1663–6	Benedict Arnold	1678	William Coddington (2)
1666–9	William Brenton	1678–80	John Cranston
1669–72	Benedict Arnold	1680–3	Peleg Sanford
1672–4	Nicholas Easton	1683–5	William Coddington, Jr
1674–6	William Coddington (1)	1685–6	Henry Bull
1676–7	Walter Clarke (1)	1686	Walter Clarke (2)
1677–8	Benedict Arnold (2)	1686–9	Edmond Andros

RUPERT'S LAND

York Fort (Fort Nelson)
CHIEFS

1672–4	Charles Bayly (1)	1682–3	John Bridgar
1674–5	William Lydall	1683–6	Thomas Phipps
1675–9	Charles Bayly (2)	1686–93	George Geyer
1679–82	John Nixon		

Albany

1679–81	John Bridgar	1683–6	Henry Sergeant
1681–3	James Knight	1686–93	(under France)

SAINT HELENA

GOVERNORS

1659-61	John Dutton	1673	Richard Munden
1661-71	Robert Stringer	1673-4	Richard Kedgwin
1671-2	Richard Coney	1674-8	Gregory Field
1672-3	Anthony Beale	1678-90	John Blackmore

SAINT KITTS

GOVERNORS

1623-49	Thomas Warner	1660-6	William Watts
1649-51	Rowland Rich (Redge)	1666-71	(under France)
1651-60	Clement Everard		

DEPUTY OF LIEUTENANT GOVERNORS
1671-81	Abednego Mathew
1682-97	Thomas Hill

SOUTH CAROLINA
GOVERNORS

1670-1	William Sayle	1684	Richard Kyrle
1671-2	Joseph West (1)	1684-5	Joseph West (3)
1672-4	John Yeamans	1685	Robert Quary
1674-82	Joseph West (2)	1685-6	Joseph Morton (2)
1682-4	Joseph Morton (1)	1686-90	James Colleton

SURAT
GOVERNORS

1616-21	Thomas Kerridge (1)	1652-4	Jeremy Blackman
1621-5	Thomas Rastell (1)	1654-5	John Spiller (1)
1625-8	Thomas Kerridge (2)	1655-6	Edward Pearce
1628-30	Richard Wylde	1656-7	John Spiller (2)
1630	John Skibbow	1657-8	Thomas Revington
1630-1	Thomas Rastell (2)	1659-62	Matthew Andrews
1631-3	John Hopkinson	1662- 9	George Oxinden
1633-8	William Methwold	1669-77	Gerald Aungier
1638-44	William Fremlen	1677-82	Thomas Rolt
1644- 9	Francis Breton	1682-7	John Child
1649-52	Thomas Merry		

TANGIER
GOVERNORS

1661-3	Henry Mordaunt, Earl of Peterborough
1663-4	Andrew Rutherford, Earl of Teviot

1664–5	John Fitzgerald
1665–6	John, Baron Belasyse
1666–9	Henry Norwood
1669–74	John Middleton, Earl of Middleton
1675–80	William O'Brien, Earl of Inchiquin
1680	Palmes Fairbourne
1680–1	Edward Sackville
1681–3	Piercy Kirke
1683–4	George Legge, Baron Dartmouth

VIRGINIA

GOVERNORS

1607	Edward Maria Wingfield (Pres. of Council)
1607–8	John Ratcliffe (Pres. of Council)
1608– 9	John Smith (Pres. of Council)
1609–10	George Percy (Pres. of Council)
1610	Thomas Gates (Deputy Gov.) (1)
1610–11	Thomas West, Lord de la Warr
1611	Thomas Dale (1)
1611–14	Thomas Gates (2)
1614–16	Thomas Dale (2)
1616–17	George Yeardley (Lt Gov.) (1)
1617–19	Samuel Argall (Lt Gov.)
1619–21	George Yeardley (2)
1621–6	Francis Wyatt (1)
1626–7	George Yeardley (3)
1627–9	Francis West (Pres. of Council)
1629–30	John Pott (Pres. of Council)
1630–5	John Harvey (1)
1635–6	John West (Deputy Gov.)
1636–9	John Harvey (2)
1639–42	Francis Wyatt (2)
1642–52	William Berkeley (1)
1652– 5	Richard Bennett
1655–8	Edward Digges (Pres. of Council)
1658–60	Samuel Mathews (Pres. of Council)
1660–77	William Berkeley (2)
1677–8	Herbert Jeffries (Lt Gov.)
1678–80	Henry Chichele (Deputy Gov.) (1)
1680	Thomas Culpeper, Baron Thorsway (1)
1680–2	Henry Chichele (Deputy Gov.) (2)
1682–3	Thomas Culpeper, Baron Thorsway (2)
1683– 4	Nicholas Spencer (Pres. of Council)
1684– 8	Francis Howard, Baron Effingham (Lt Gov.)
1688–90	Nathaniel Bacon (Pres. of Council)

WILLOUGHBY

GOVERNORS

| 1651–2 | Anthony Rowse | 1654–7 | (none) |
| 1652–4 | Richard Holdip | 1657–67 | William Byam |

10 EDUCATION
AND LEARNING

EDUCATION

At the beginning of the seventeenth century, the majority of boys would, if lucky, receive their rudimentary education in elementary or dame schools. Run often by a poor woman from the village, these schools offered, in return for a small weekly charge, no more than reading, some writing and the learning of Scripture. There was clearly no obligation to attend and certainly no opportunity for pauper children whose parents could not afford the fee.

Sons of the middle classes were normally sent on to the local grammar school (see list of schools below). These endowed schools were usually subject to ecclesiastical control, according to the terms of their charters. The emphasis in the curriculum was strictly on Latin, with some Greek and a little Hebrew; the emphasis in teaching method was on learning by rote. Some of the schools (such as St Paul's and Merchant Taylors') refused admission to pupils who could not already read or write, whilst others were prepared to give elementary instruction as a preliminary to the main grammar course. No place, however, was found either for English or for the increasing range of 'new subjects' – science, mathematics, geography, history and modern languages.

This is perhaps one explanation of the rapid growth of private schools of a specialist nature. Humphrey Baker's Private School, (established 1562), for 'arithmetic and other similars', had already set the pattern. To 'cyphering schools' (for arithmetic) and 'writing schools', which were increasing in demand, now were added schools of modern languages (inspired partly by the recent publication of books of French, Italian, Spanish and Dutch grammar). By the end of the century, some of these private schools were beginning to offer a more complete curriculum of English, Latin, mathematics, modern languages and book-keeping.

Girls of better families were educated either at home by their mothers or at boarding school. On the whole it was not thought fitting for a girl to pursue highly academic studies. It was sufficient to prepare her to manage the household and to take part in intelligent conversation. Defoe commented, 'Their youth is spent to teach them to stitch and sew, or make baubles; they are taught to read indeed, and perhaps to write their names or so; and that is the height of a woman's education.' Some girls, nevertheless, were sent away to boarding schools such as Mrs Perwick's School at Hackney (1643) or Mrs Bathsua Makin's

School at Tottenham High Cross (1673). There the pupils would learn 'dancing, music, singing, writing, keeping accounts', together with Latin, French and other languages. Cooking, astronomy, geography, arithmetic and history were listed as optional extras.

Boys from the wealthier established families were sent to the public schools, which, like the grammar schools, remained firmly committed to traditional studies of Latin and Greek. Grammar composition and rhetoric took up much of the time in the course. There was little opportunity for writing, arithmetic, English or modern languages – and none at all for science. Life at public school was notoriously rough and discipline severe. By 1700 the public schools were beginning to decline in popularity and numbers, although Eton, Westminster and Winchester still commanded a favourable reputation (see list of schools below). Growing discontent with the type of education offered at school in the seventeenth century caused many wealthy families to opt out of the traditional system by employing a private tutor, who first taught the boy at home and then accompanied him to university.

By the middle of the century many thinkers and writers were also beginning to express serious concern about the failure of English education to adapt to the changing circumstances of the times. Reforms were strongly advocated. John Brinsley urged the need for the teaching of English; John Comenius, with eager support from Francis Bacon, stressed the claims of the 'new subjects', improved teaching methods and 'real studies' (i.e. natural phenomena); Charles Hoole wanted a school in every town and village; Samuel Hartlib and his friends (Woodward, Dury and Petty) worked for a state system of schools and studies of a 'useful' type. Demand for reform of the curriculum inevitably developed into a heated controversy between the supporters of the ancient learning (led by Sir William Temple and Charles Boyle) and the supporters of modern learning (led by William Wotton and Richard Bentley). But at least some progress could be witnessed in schools: boys at Westminster School were taught geography from Honter's *Cosmographic* in the 1620s, whilst Christ's Hospital established a mathematical school in 1673.

The Act of Uniformity of 1662 brought about the dismissal of a large number of clergy and other graduates involved in teaching who were unwilling to take the oath. Some of these set up small schools of their own, which became known as dissenting academies (see list below). Here boys were prepared for careers in medicine, the church, the law and other professions, often preferring to complete their studies at the academy rather than to proceed to university. The earlier academies closely followed the curriculum of the grammar schools, but those founded later in the century began to offer a wider education, including modern subjects. Always subject to closure under the Conformity Laws, most survived at least until the renewed wave of persecution during the reign of Queen Anne, culminating in the Schism Act of 1714.

The universities themselves had not been exempt from the critical eye of the reformers. Content of curriculum and method of teaching at both Oxford and Cambridge remained essentially mediaeval, with philosophical disputations as the main exercise in preparation for the degree.

This, to some, seemed totally irrelevant to the demands of seventeenth century life. Milton, amongst others, was in favour of replacing the universities with academies in every English city, which would combine the functions of school and university. An unsuccessful attempt to abolish universities was, in fact, made by the Barebones Parliament in 1653, whilst several abortive schemes were put forward to end the monopoly of Oxford and Cambridge by opening a new university at Manchester (1642), London (1647), York (1652) and Durham (1657). Changes in curriculum were inevitably canvassed by Milton, who wanted the concrete study of nature and modern languages to replace the abstract philosophy of Latin and Greek. Although the intellectual life of the universities stagnated after the Restoration, drawing increasingly the charge of idleness and lethargy, the system was nevertheless defended with great passion. Seth Ward in 1654 pointed out that the deficiencies of university teaching were more than compensated for by the enlightened approach of individual college tutors, who inspired their pupils to investigate the new sciences, languages and English literature. Nor was opportunity entirely lacking: for example, from 1659 Peter Stael taught science at Oxford.

EDUCATION AND THE LAW

1603   Act forbidding any person to keep a school or to become a schoolmaster except in a public or free grammar school, or in the house of a non-recusant, and unless he had been licensed by the archbishop or bishop. Penalty: a fine of 40s. per day.

1604   The English Church Canons stated, 'No man shall teach either in public school or private house, but such as shall be allowed by the Bishop of the diocese or Ordinary of the place under his hand and seal, being found meet as well as for his learning and dexterity in teaching as for sober and honest conversation, and also for right understanding of God's true religion.' He was also to subscribe to the Article of the King's Supremacy and accept the Church of England as a true and apostolic Church.

1641   The Commons ordered (16 April) 'that it be referred to the Committee for Scandalous Ministers to consider of the state of all the Hospitals and Free-schools within the Kingdom of England and Wales, and to consider of the Misemployment and Abuses of the Revenues and Government of them; and of some way of redress'.
(15 June) The Commons resolved 'That all the Lands, taken by this Bill from Deans and Chapters, shall be employed to the Advancement of Learning and Piety.'
(16 November) The Commons declared 'That this House intends to vindicate themselves from the Imputation laid upon them of Discouraging of Learning; and that they will advance Learning and the Maintenance of preaching Ministers.'

1643   An ordinance for sequestering the estates of delinquents (27 March) stipulated that money which had previously been paid 'for maintaining of any College or Hospital . . . Grammar School or Schollers . . . shall continue to be paid and disposed and allowed by the Sequestrators as they were heretofore.'
(21 September) An ordinance confirmed that Crown revenues, which previously had been used for the maintenance of any college, grammar school, scholars or school house, were to be employed as before.

(18 October) The Commons ordered 'that the Committee for Plundered Ministers, shall have power to enquire after malignant school-masters'.

1646   An ordinance to abolish the government of the Church by archbishops and bishops (effectively ended the need for a bishop's licence by teachers).

1647   An ordinance to impose the monthly rate for the maintenance of Fairfax's army stipulated that 'nothing in this Ordinance contained shall be extended to charge any of the colleges of Winchester, Eton or Westminster, or any Hospital or Alms House or any free school, or any of the rents and revenues due and payable to them'.

1649   Act for the Maintenance of Preaching Ministers, and Other Pious uses (8 June); an annual sum of £20,000 was vested in trustees for educational purposes, including the payment of schoolmasters.
(12 October) The Commons resolved 'that all and every the Masters, Fellows, Schoolmasters and Scholars, in all and every the Colleges of Eton, Winchester and Westminster, do take the said Engagement – I do declare and promise, that I will be true and faithful to the Commonwealth of England, as the same is now established, without a King or House of Lords'.

1650   (22 February) Act for the Propagation of the Gospel in Wales: Commissioners were appointed with powers to eject schoolmasters on proof of delinquency, scandal etc.; to grant certificates to fit schoolmasters 'of approved piety and learning'; and to establish new schools. Over sixty new schools were established (e.g. at Neath, Newport, Carew).
Act for the Better Propagating and Preaching of the Gospel of Jesus Christ in the Four Northern Counties, and for the Maintenance of Godly and Able Ministers and Schoolmasters there (1 March). The commissioners established new schools at Sunderland, Ferry Hill, Stanhope, Brancepeth, Easington, Shincliffe, Lanchester, etc.

1651   The Commons ordered 'that all Primers, formerly used in the Time of Kingship in this Nation, be suppressed; and shall from henceforth be no further used in any school, either public or private, within this Commonwealth'.

1652   The Commissioners of Charitable Uses appropriated unattached charities to found schools at Halesowen and Llan Egryn.

1654   (28 August) An ordinance to appoint commissioners to examine school-masters who were ignorant, scandalous, insufficient or negligent and to eject them. Scandalous behaviour included blasphemy, swearing, holding 'Popish opinions', adultery, the haunting of taverns, the frequent playing of cards or dice, the frequent use of the Book of Common Prayer, and the countenancing of wakes, morris dancing and stage plays.
(2 September) An ordinance to appoint commissioners to visit Oxford, Cambridge, Westminster, Winchester, Merchant Taylors' and Eton to consider any statute needed 'for the well ordering and governing of the said Colleges and Schools respectively, for the better advancement of Piety, Learning and good Nurture'.

1655   An order of Council stipulated that 'none who have been, or shall be ejected from any benefice, college or school, for delinquency or scandal are after 1st November 1655 to keep any school'. Penalty: first offence – three months' imprisonment; second offence – six months' imprisonment; third offence – banishment.

1662   The Act of Uniformity ordered that 'every schoolmaster keeping any public or private school, and every person instructing or teaching any youth in any house or private family as a tutor or a schoolmaster' on 1 May 1662 should subscribe a declaration expressing abhorrence at armed resistance to the King and readiness to conform to the Book of Common Prayer, and renouncing the Solemn League and Covenant as unlawful. Schoolmasters who refused were to be deprived. A licence, costing 12d., from the archbishop or bishop was needed by all teachers. Penalty: first offence – three months' imprisonment; second offence – three months plus £5 fine.

1665   The Act for Restraining Non-Conformists from Inhabiting Corporations (the 'Five Mile Act') stipulated that Dissenters were not to teach in any public or private school. Penalty: a fine of £40.
Archibishop Sheldon issued a letter to bishops 'concerning schoolmasters and instructors of youth'. They were to supply details of all free schools in their diocese with all their masters and ushers, plus a list of all teachers in public and private schools. This information was to show whether the teachers 'do themselves frequent the public prayers of the church, and cause their scholars to do the same; and whether they appear well affected to the government of his Majesty and the doctrine and discipline of the Church of England.'

1670   Bates's Case: judgement was given in favour of William Bates that a schoolmaster might teach without a licence, if he was appointed by the founder or lay patron of a school. This encouraged non-conformists to found schools (the dissenting academies).

LEADING PUBLIC SCHOOLS ESTABLISHED BEFORE 1650

Charterhouse

Christ's Hospital

Eton

Harrow

Merchant Taylors'

Repton

Rugby

Sedbergh

Shrewsbury

St Paul's

Westminster

Winchester

GRAMMAR SCHOOLS IN ENGLAND, 1600–60

BEDFORDSHIRE
Bedford, Biggleswade, Clapham, Clifton, Eaton Socon, Egginton, Felmersham, Hexton, Holme, Houghton, Leighton, Luton, Ockley, Potton, Ravensden, Sandy, Shefford, Shillington, Southill, Stotford, Sutton, Toddington, Woburn, Wymington.

BERKSHIRE
Abingdon, Childrey, Hungerford, Newbury, Reading, Wallingford, Wantage, Windsor.

BUCKINGHAMSHIRE
Amersham, Aylesbury, Beachampton, Buckingham, Chenies, Denham, Eton, High Wycombe, Marlow, Pitston, Stony Stratford.

CAMBRIDGESHIRE
Bassingbourn, Brinkley, Burwell, Cambridge (King's College School and Perse School), Castle Camps, Chesterton, Cheveley, Ditton, Dullingham, Elsworth, Ely, Fulbourne, Great Shelford, Harston, Hauxton, Hinxton, Linton, Newton, Oakington, Orwell, Sutton, Swaffham, Swavesey, West Wratting, Wilbraham, Wimpole, Wisbech, Wood Ditton.

CHESHIRE
Anderton, Audlem, Bunbury, Chester, Congleton, Daresbury, Frodsham, Goostrey, Halton, Hargrave, Holms Chapel, Knutsford, Lymm, Macclesfield, Marple, Middlewich, Morton Green, Mottram-in-Longendale, Nantwich, Northwich, Stockport, Tarvin (and Hargrave School), Wallasey, West Kirby, Witton, Wybunbury.

CORNWALL
Bodmin, Launceston, Liskeard, Penryn, St Ives, Saltash, Stratton, Truro.

CUMBERLAND
Addingham, Blencow, Bridekirk, Bromfield, Carlisle, Cockermouth, Dacre, Dalston, Dean, Harrington, Keswick, Maughanby, Ortwaite, Penrith, St Bees, Whicham and Millom, Wreay.

DERBYSHIRE

Ashbourne, Ashover, Aston, Bakewell, Buxton, Caldwell, Chesterfield, Dawbery, Denby, Derby, Dronfield, Duffield, Glossop, Hartshorn, Hayfield, Little Chester, Mackworth, Mellor, Norton, Repton, Risley, Rowsley, Staveley, Tideswell, Wirksworth.

DEVONSHIRE

Ashburton, Atherington, Barnstaple, Brauton, Broad Clyst, Chulmleigh, Clanaborough, Colebrook, Colyton, Combe Martin, Crediton, Dartmouth, Exbourne, Exeter (Free Grammar School and High School), Fremington, Honiton, Ilfracombe, Knowstone, Landkey, Modbury, Ottery St Mary, Plymouth, Plymton, Tavistock, Tawstock, Tiverton, Topsham, Torrington, Totnes.

DORSET

Blandford, Bridport, Cranborne, Dorchester, Evershot, Frampton, Gillingham, Lyle, Milton Abbas, Netherbury, Rampisham, Shaftesbury, Sherborne, Wimborne.

DURHAM

Barnard Castle, Barton, Bishop Auckland, Brancepeth, Croxdale, Darlington, Durham, Farington, Gainford, Hartlepool, Houghton le Spring, Heighington, Houghton, Newbiggen, Norton, Ryton, Wearmouth, Wolsingham.

ESSEX

Ashdon, Bardfield, Barking, Billericay, Bocking, Braintree, Brentwood, Bumpstead, Bures, Chelmsford, Chesterford, Chigwell, Chishall, Clavering, Coggeshall, Colchester, Crossing, Debden, Dedham, Earls Colne, Elmdon, Epping, Felsted, Fordham, Foxearth, Gosfield, Halstead, Harwich, Hatfield, Havering, Hutton, Kelvedon, Langham, Little Birch, Little Warley, Loughton, Maldon, Markshall, Moreton, Newport, Orsett, Pebmarsh, Ramsey, Rayleigh, Romford, Saffron Walden, Springfield, Standon, Stansted Mountfitchet, Waltham, Walthamstow, Wethersfield, Yeldham.

GLOUCESTERSHIRE

Bristol, Cheltenham, Chipping Camden, Chipping Sodbury, Cirencester, Gloucester (Cathedral School and Crypt School), Henbury, Newland, Northleach, Stow-on-the-Wold, Tetbury, Tewkesbury, Thornbury, Westbury, Winchcombe (The King's School and Lady Frances Chandos' Free School), Wotton-under-Edge.

HAMPSHIRE

Alton, Andover, Basingstoke, Godshill, Newport, Ringwood, Ropley, Southampton, Twyford, Winchester (Winchester College and Peter Symonds' School), Wolverton.

HEREFORDSHIRE

Bosbury, Bromiard, Colwall, Eardisland, Hereford, Kington, Ledbury, Leominster, Ross.

HERTFORDSHIRE

Aldenham, Aston, Baldock, Barnet, Bennington, Berkhampstead, Bishop's Stortford, Blewhouse, Bramfield, Buntingford, Bygrave, Chipping Barnet, Elstree, Hertford, Hitchin, Hoddesdon, Letchworth, Northaw, Rickmansworth, Rushden, Sacomb, St Albans, St Ippolitts, St Johns, Sarratt, Sawbridgeworth, Shenley, Shephall, Stanstead Abbots, Stevenage, Tring, Walkern, Ware, Watford, Watton, Wormley.

HUNTINGDONSHIRE

Botolph Bridge, Catworth, Godmanchester, Holywell, Huntingdon, Kimbolton, Little Gidding, Orton, Ramsey, St Ives, St Neots, Thurning, Upwood, Warboys.

KENT

Ashford, Biddenden, Bromley, Canterbury, Charlton, Chatham, Cranbrook, Dartford, Deal, East Malling, East Sutton, Faversham, Folkestone, Gravesend, Greenwich, Hadlow, Hawkhurst, Hollingbourne, Horton, Leeds, Lewisham, Maidstone, New Romney, Rochester, Sandwich, Selling, Sevenoaks, Sheldwich, Sundridge, Sutton Valence, Tenterden, Tonbridge, Westerham, Wingham, Wye.

LANCASHIRE

Anderton, Ashley, Ashton-in-Makerfield, Bispham with Norbreck, Blackburn, Blackrod, Bolton-le-Moors, Bolton-le-Sands, Bretherton, Broughton, Burnley, Burtonwood, Bury, Cartmel, Catterall, Chorley, Colne, Dalton, Darwen, Denton, Eccles, Ellell, Farnworth, Garstang, Great Crosby, Halsall, Haslingden, Hawkshead, Heskin, Holton, Kirby Ireleth, Kirkham, Lancaster, Leigh, Leyland, Littleborough, Little Urswick, Liverpool, Manchester, Middleton, Much Woolton, Newton, Oldham, Ormskirk, Penwortham, Prescott, Preston, Rivington, Rochdale, Standish, Tarleton, Urswick, Walton, Warrington, Warton, Whalley, Whitworth, Widnes, Wigan, Winwick.

LEICESTERSHIRE

Ashby-de-la-Zouch, Barrow, Belgrave, Billesdon, Bosworth, Bottesford, Bottlebridge, Bowden, Buckminster, Church Langton, Cossington, Glooston, Hinckley, Kegworth, Kibworth, Kirby Bellars, Leicester, Long Clawson, Loughborough, Lutterworth, Market Harborough, Markfield, Melton Mowbray, Mesam, Milton, Normanton, Norton, Osgathorpe, Scalford, Scraptoft, Seagrave, Shawell, Sileby, Skeffington, Slawston, Stockerston, Thurnby, Tugby, Wymondham.

LINCOLNSHIRE

Alford, Althorpe, Anderby, Asterby, Blankney, Bolingbroke, Boothby, Boston, Bourne, Brant Broughton, Broughton, Burgh, Caistor, Carrington, Digby, Donington, East Rasen, Falkingham, Gainsborough, Grantham, Grimsby, Heighington, Horncastle, Kettlethorpe, Kirton-in-Holland, Kirton-in-Lindsey, Laughton, Lincoln, Linwood, Lobthorpe, Louth, Market Rasen, Middle Rasen,

Moulton, Navenby, Orby, Partney, Pinchbeck, Rosby, Saltfleetby, Sedgebrook, Sleaford, Somerby, Spalding, Spilsby, Stamford, Stroxton, Swineshead, Tattershall, Wainfleet, Well, Welton, Whaplode, Witham, Withern, Wold Newton, Wragby.

LONDON

Aldermanbury, Aldersgate, Blackfriars, Charterhouse, Christ's Hospital, College Hill, Grey Friars, Mercers', Merchant Taylors', St Anthony's, St Clement's, St Dunstan in the West, St Lawrence, St Mary Axe, St Paul's, Westminster, St Margaret's, St Peter's, Whitefriars.

MIDDLESEX

Edmonton, Enfield, Fulham, Greenford, Gunnersbury, Hackney, Hadley, Hampton, Harlington, Harrow-on-the-Hill, Highgate, Hoxton, Isleworth, Islington, Limehouse, Staines, Stepney, Stratford-le-Bow, Tottenham High Cross, Willesden.

MONMOUTHSHIRE

Abergavenny, Llan Egryn, Llantilio Crossenny, Monmouth, Newport, Usk.

NORFOLK

Acle, Alborough, Aldeby, Ameringhall, Ashmanhaugh, Attleborough, Aylsham, Baconsthorpe, Bale, Banham, Barnham Broom, Bassingham, Bawburgh, Beechamwell, Beetley, Bexwell, Bircham, Blofield, Blo Norton, Booton, Bramerton, Breckles, Brockdish, Brooke, Brumstead, Buckenham Ferry, Bunwell, Burgh, Burnham Ulph, Burnham Westgate, Cantley, Castle Acre, Claxton, Collishall and Oxnead, Colton, Corpusty, Cossey, Coston, Cranwich, Cromer, Dalling, Deopham, Diss, Downham, Dunham, East Bilney, East Dereham, East Lexham, East Tuddenham, East Winch, Eaton, Edgefield, Ellingham, Elsing, Erpingham, Fakenham, Feltwell, Foulden, Framingham, Fransham, Frenze, Garboldisham, Garveston, Great Bircham, Great Melton, Gressenhall, Grimston, Griston, Gunthorpe, Gunton, Hardingham, Harleston, Harling, Harpley, Hassingham, Heacham, Hedenham, Hellington, Heydon, Hillington, Hingham, Holt, Honingham, Hoveton St John, Hunworth, Ingworth, Itteringham, Kenninghall, Kimberley, King's Lynn, Little Fransham, Little Massingham, Little Walsingham, Loddon, Low Shottesham, Mattishall Burgh, Methwold, Mileham, Moulton, Mulbarton, Narford, North Elmham, North Walsham, Norwich, St Peter's, Oby, Old Buckenham, Outwell, Pickenham, Plumstead, Poringland, Pulham Market, Pulham St Mary, Rainham, Raveningham, Reepham, Reymerstone, Ringstead, Roughton, Roydon, Rudham, Ryburgh, Saham Tony, Salthouse, Sandringham, Santon, Saxthorpe, Scarning, Sco Ruston, Scottow, Scoulton, Sculthorpe, Sedgeford, Sharrington, Shelfanger, Shipdham, Shottesham, Snettisham, Southacre, South Creake, South Lynn, Southolt, South Pickenham, South Repps, Stow Bedon, Strumpshaw, Suffield, Surlingham, Swaffham, Swannington, Swanton Morley, Syderstone, Tacleston, Tharston, Thetford, Thompson, Tibenham, Tittleshall, Tivetshall, Tottenhill, Tunstead, Walsingham, Walsoken, Warham, Weeting,

Westfield, West Lynn, West Newton, Weston, Wiggenhall, Wilton, Winfarthing, Witchingham, Wiveton, Wolterton, Wymondham, Yarmouth, Yelverton.

NORTHAMPTONSHIRE
Abthorpe, Adstone, Ashley, Aynhoe, Barnack, Blisworth, Brackley, Burton Latimer, Carlton, Collyweston, Cottesbrook, Courteenhall, Daventry, Everton, Findon, Fotheringhay, Geddington, Glinton, Grendon, Gretton, Harrington, Higham Ferrers, Kelmarsh, Kettering, Kingsthorpe, Northampton, Oundle, Peterborough, Plumpton, Preston, Preston Capes, Rothwell, Strixton, Sywell, Tichmarsh, Towcester, Wellingborough, Wildon.

NORTHUMBERLAND
Alnwick, Barwick, Berwick-on-Tweed, Cheeseburn Grange, Greenhead, Hexham, Kirkley, Morpeth, Newcastle-on-Tyne, Warkworth.

NOTTINGHAMSHIRE
Averham, Basford, Bilsthorpe, Bingham, Carcolston, Carlton, Caunton, Clifton, Cossall, East Retford, Elston, Hickling, Kelham, Kneesal, Laneham, Laxton, Mansfield, Misterton, Newark, Nottingham, Scrooby, Southwell, Sutton Bonnington, Tuxford, Watnall, Worksop.

OXFORDSHIRE
Bampton, Banbury, Burford, Chipping Norton, Cropredy, Dorchester, East Adderbury, Ewelme, Henley, Oxford (Christ Church Cathedral School, Magdalen College School, and Nixon's Free Grammar School), Steeple Aston, Thame, Williamscot, Woodstock.

RUTLAND
Ketton, Luffenham, Oakham, Ridlington, Uppingham.

SHROPSHIRE
Addley, Bridgnorth, Donnington, Great Ercol, Kinnerley, Ludlow, Market Drayton, Newport, Oswestry, Shiffnal, Shrewsbury, Wellington, Wem, Whitchurch, Worfield.

SOMERSET
Bath, Bridgwater, Bruton, Crewkerne, Frome, Ilminster, Martock, Pitminster, Selworthy, Shepton Mallet, Taunton, Wells, Yeovil.

STAFFORDSHIRE
Abbot's Bromley, Audley, Barton-under-Needwood, Bramley, Brewood, Burton-upon-Trent, Chell, Colwich, Dilhorne, Gnosall, Grindon, Haughton, Kinver, Leek, Lichfield, Madeley, Newcastle-under-Lyme, Rolleston, Rugeley, Stafford, Stoke, Stone, Tamworth, Uttoxeter, Walsall, Whitmore, Wolverhampton.

SUFFOLK
Ashfield, Barsham, Beccles, Benacre, Benhall, Botesdale, Boxford, Bradwell, Brandeston, Brandon, Bungay, Bures, Bury St Edmunds, Cavendish,

Chedburgh, Clare, Cotton, Cove, Cransford, Cuckfield, Dalham, Debenham, Denston, Depden, Earl Soham, Earl Stonham, East Bergholt, Elmdon, Exning, Eye, Framlingham, Fressingfield, Frostenden, Gazeley, Gislingham, Glemham, Glemsford, Great Brisett, Great Wratting, Groton, Hadleigh, Halesworth, Haverhill, Hawstead, Hickling, Honnington, Hopton, Hoxne, Ipswich, Kelsale, Kenton, Lavenham, Lowestoft, Melford, Mendlesham, Mildenhall, Monewdon, Monk Soham, Moulton, Mutford, Necton, Needham Market, Newton, Norton, Onehouse, Otley, Pakenham, Palgrave, Rede, Redgrave, Saxham, Shadingfield, Shelley, 'Skylson', Sotherton, Southolt, Southwold, Stanton, Sternfield, Stoke, Stonham Aspall, Stowmarket, Stradbroke, Stuston, Sudbury, Sutton, Theberton, Thornham Parva, Thorpe Market, Thurlow, Thurston, Tuddenham, Wenhaston, Westhorpe, Westleton, Wingfield, Winston, Wissett, Withersfield, Woodbridge, Wordwell, Worlingworth, Wrentham, Wyverston, Yoxford.

SURREY
Borough Street, Banstead, Battersea, Betchworth, Bletchingley, Camberwell, Charlwood, Cheam, Clapham, Cobham, Croydon, Dulwich, Farnham, Godalming, Guildford, Kingston-on-Thames, Mickleham, Ockham, Richmond, Southwark, St Saviour's, Streatham, Waddon.

SUSSEX
Albourne, Battle, Buxted, Chichester, Cuckfield, East Grinstead, Hartfield, Hastings, Horsham, Lamberhurst, Lewes, Mayfield, Oving, Pulborough, Rye, Stanmer, Steyning, Wadhurst, Whatlington.

WARWICKSHIRE
Alveston, Aston, Atherstone, Attleborough, Birmingham, Coleshill, Coventry, Great Harborough, Grendon, Hampton Lucy, Monk's Kirby, Nuneaton, Priors Salford, Rugby, Solihull, Stratford-upon-Avon, Sutton Coldfield, Warwick, Wolverton.

WESTMORLAND
Appleby, Bampton, Barton, Beetham, Brough, Burton-in-Kendal, Crosby Ravensworth, Heversham, Hugill, Kendal, Kirkby Lonsdale, Kirkby Stephen, Lowther, Middleton, Old Button, Skelsmergh, Stainmore, Troutbeck, Warcop, Winton.

WILTSHIRE
Devizes, Downton, Heddington, Marlborough, Salisbury (Cathedral School and Grammar School), West Lavington, Whiteparish.

WORCESTERSHIRE
Bewdley, Bromsgrove, Droitwich, Dudley, Evesham, Feckenham, Halesowen, Hanley Castle, Hartlebury, Kidderminster, King's Norton, Leigh, Martley, Rock, Stourbridge, Wolverley, Worcester.

YORKSHIRE

Aberford, Acaster, Adlingfleet, Aldbrough, Almondbury, Arkengarthdale, Arncliffe, Askrigg, Aughton, Barkisland, Barwick-in-Elmet, Batley, Bedale, Bentham, Beswick, Beverley, Bingley, Birstal, Bolton, Bolton Percy, Bradford, Brandsburton, Brandsby, Bridlington, Brignall, Bromley, Burnsall, Burton-in-Bishopdale, Butter Crammbe, Calverley, Carleton, Catterick, Cawthorne, Colthorpe, Conisborough, Coniston, Copmanthorpe, Coxwold, Craven, Criggleston, Danby, Danby Wiske, Dent, Doncaster, Earby, Easington, Edlington, Fishlake, Giggleswick, Gilling, Gisburn, Guisborough, Halifax, Halton-in-Craven, Harpham, Harthill, Hatfield, Haworth, Helmsley, Hemsworth, Heptonstall, Hetton, Hipperholme, Hollym, Howden, Hutton, Ilkley, Kildwick, Kilham, Kilsden, Kingston-upon-Hull, Kippax, Kirby Fleetham, Kirby-on-the-Hill, Kirby Underdale, Kirkby-Malham, Kirkby Ravensworth, Kirkheaton, Kirkley, Kirk Sandall, Knaresborough, Lartington, Laughton, Leake, Leeds, Levisham-in-Pickering, Linton, Long Preston, Market Weighton, Masham, Melton, Middleton, Naburn, Netherton (near Dewsbury), Newburgh, Newforest, Newton, Normanton, Northallerton, North Cave, Northowram, Old Malton, Otley, Oughton (near Howden), Peniston, Pickering, Pocklington, Pontefract, Rastrick, Rawcliffe, Rawmarsh, Richmond, Ripon, Roecliffe, Romaldkirk, Rossington, Rotherham, Royston, Saltmarsh, Sancton, Scarborough, Sedbergh, Sheffield, Sherburn, Shipton, Skipton, Sledmere, Snaith, Sneaton, South Cave, South Dalton, Sowerby, Stainton, Swallington, Tadcaster, Tanfield, Tankersley, Thirsk, Thornhill, Thornton, Thribergh, Tickhill, Topcliffe, Ulleskelf, Wakefield, Well, Whitby, Whitgift, Woolley, Worsborough, Wragby, Yarm, Yoresbridge, York (Holgate's Free School, and St Peter's).

GRAMMAR SCHOOLS IN WALES, 1600–60

ANGLESEY

Amlwch, Beaumaris.

BRECKNOCK

Brecon.

CARDIGANSHIRE

Cardigan.

CARMARTHENSHIRE

Carmarthen.

CARNARVONSHIRE

Bangor, Bottwnog, Conway.

DENBIGHSHIRE

Llanelian, Llanrwst, Ruabon, Ruthin, Wrexham.

FLINTSHIRE
Hawarden, Northop, Overton, St Asaph.

MONTGOMERYSHIRE
Aberhafesp.

PEMBROKESHIRE
Haverfordwest, St David's.

RADNOR
Presteigne.

SOURCE: W. A. L. Vincent, *The State and School Education, 1640–1660, in England and Wales* (1950).

SCHOOLS ESTABLISHED BY THE COMMITTEE FOR THE PROPAGATION OF THE GOSPEL IN WALES, 1650–3

* denotes probable grammar school. 'Wales' here includes Monmouthshire.

ANGLESEY
Amlwch.

BRECKNOCK
Brecon*, Builth, Llanbedr, Llanbister, Llangorse*, Llanigon, Llanthetty, Talgarth, Talybont, Tretower.

CARDIGANSHIRE
Cardigan*, Lampeter.

CARNARVONSHIRE
Carnarvon*.

DENBIGHSHIRE
Abergele, Denbigh, Glynceiriog, Holt, Llandegla, Llanfair DC, Llangollen, Llanrwst, Llansilin, Ruthin, Wrexham*.

FLINTSHIRE
Hanmer.

GLAMORGAN
Cardiff, Cowbridge, Llantwit Major, Merthyr, Neath*, Penmark, St Mary Hill, Swansea*.

MERIONETHSHIRE
Bala, Corwen, Dolgelly*, Ffestiniog, Llanfair.

MONMOUTHSHIRE
Abergavenny*, Chepstow, Magor, Newport*, Usk.

MONTGOMERYSHIRE
Llanfyllin, Llanidloes, Llansantffraid, Machynlleth, Montgomery*, Newtown*, Welshpool*.

PEMBROKESHIRE
Carew, Tenby.

RADNOR
Bleddfa, Clyro, Llangunllo, Nantmel, New Radnor, Rhayader.

SOURCE: Vincent, *The State and School Education in England and Wales.*

DISSENTING ACADEMIES FOUNDED 1663–88

Bethnal Green (1680–96)
Bromsgrove (1665–92)
Brynllwarch, Glam. (1668–97)
Coventry (1663–1700)
Dartmouth (1668–91)
Islington (1) (1672–80)
Islington (2) (1672–1707)
Knell, Radnor (1675–?)
Lincoln (1668–80)
Nettlebed, Oxon (1666–97)
Newington Green (1) (1665–1706)
Newington Green (2) (1667–1706)

Nottingham (1680–?)
Rathmell, Yorks (1669–98)
Saffron Walden (1680–?)
Sheriffhales (1663–97)
Shrewsbury (1663–1730)
Sulby, Northants (1680–8)
Taunton (1672–1759)
Tewkesbury (1680–1719)
Tubney, Berks (1668–99)
Wapping (1675–80)
Whitchurch (1668–80)
Wickhambrook, Suffolk (1670–96)

SOURCE: I. Parker, *Dissenting Academies in England* (1914).

CONTEMPORARY WRITINGS ON EDUCATION

Brinsley, J., *Ludus Literarius, or The Grammar Schoole* (1612).
Brokesby, F., *Of Education with Respect to Grammar Schools and the Universities* (1612).
Comenius, J. A., *Opera Didactica Omnia* (1657).
Cowley, A., *A Proposition for the Advancement of Experimental Philosophy* (1660).
Dell, W., *The Right Reformation of Learning, Schools and Universities, According to the State of the Gospel* (1653).
Dury, J., *The Reformed School* (1650).
——, *The Reformed Librarie-Keeper with a Supplement to the Reformed School* (1650).
Hall, J., *An Humble Motion to the Parliament of England Concerning the Advancement of Learning: And Reformation of the Universities* (1641).
Hall, T., *Vindiciae Literarum, the Schools Guarded* (1654).
Harmer, S., *Vox Populi, or Glostersheres Desire* (1642).
Hartlib, S., *A Description of the Famous Kingdom of Macaria* (1641).
——, *A Reformation of Schooles* (1642).
——, *Considerations Tending to the Happy Accomplishment of England's Reformation in Church and State* (1647).

——, *London's Charity Inlarged, Stilling the Orphan's Cry* (1650).

——, *The True and Readie Way to Learne the Latine Tongue* (1654).

Hoole, C., *A New Discovery of the Old Art of Teaching Schoole, in Four Small Treatises* (1660).

Makin, B., *An Essay to Revive the Antient Education of Gentlewomen in Religion, Manners, Arts and Tongues* (1673).

Milton, J., *Of Education. To Master Samuel Hartlib* (1644).

Morrice, T., *An Apology for Schoole-Masters* (1619).

Needham, M., *A Discourse Concerning Schools and Schoolmasters* (1663).

Petty, W., *Advice of W. P. to Mr. S. Hartlib for the Advancement of Some Particular Parts of Learning* (1648).

Walker, O., *Of Education especially of Young Gentlemen* (1678).

Ward, S., *Vindiciae Academiarum* (1654).

Wase, C., *Considerations Concerning Free Schools, as Settled in England* (1678).

Webbe, J., *An Appeale to Truth, in the Controversie between Art and Use* (1622).

Webster, J., *Academiarum Examen* (1654).

Woodward, H., *A Light to Grammar* (1641).

Wotton, H., *An Essay on the Education of Children in the First Rudiments of Learning* (1672).

CENSORSHIP

1553 The licensing of printing first introduced.

1557 The Stationers' Company chartered; made responsible for the control of printing and the discovery of seditious libel.

1559 Royal injunctions forbade the printing of any book without a licence from a bishop or a university chancellor.

1566 Star Chamber ordinances gave the Master and Wardens of the Stationers' Company the right to search workshops for seditious material.

1586 Star Chamber ordinances restricted all printing activity to London, Oxford and Cambridge; set a limit on the number of authorised printers; banned the printing of unlicensed books.

1607 John Cowell's dictionary *The Interpreter* suppressed by proclamation of James I because some of its definitions concerned the royal prerogative.

1613 James I instructed the Court of High Commission to enforce the 1586 ordinances; George Withers imprisoned for his satire *Abuses Stript and Whipt*.

1614 Suppression of Sir Walter Raleigh's *History of the World* 'for being too saucy in censuring Princes'.

1622 Thomas Archer and Nicholas Bourne authorised to print weekly periodicals dealing exclusively with foreign news.

1624 The Privy Council banned further performances of Thomas Middleton's play *A Game at Chesse*, which dealt with the failure of Prince Charles to secure a wife in Spain. A royal proclamation forbade the printing or import of any book on the subjects of religion or state affairs without prior approval.

1626 A royal proclamation forbade all writing on controversial matters in religion as a further measure to control Puritan opinion.

1632 The Star Chamber banned the printing of all newsbooks.

1634 William Prynne tried before the Star Chamber for writing *Histriomastix* (1633), in which he had attacked the theatre (and, indirectly, the Queen's participation in drama); fined £5000, pilloried, ordered to lose both ears and imprisoned for life.

1637 Trial by the Star Chamber of William Prynne (for his attack on Bishop Wren in *News from Ipswich*), Dr Henry Burton (for his attack on Laud in *For God and King* (1636) and John Bastwick (for his attack on the archbishops in *The Litany of John Bastwick*); each sentenced to a £5000 fine and imprisonment for life. Prynne, in addition, branded with the letters 'SL' ('Seditious Libeller').

Star Chamber ordinances, instigated by Archbishop Laud, increased penalties for breaking the ordinances of 1586; the Lord Chief Justice to license law books, the Secretaries of State books on history and politics, the Earl Marshal books on heraldry, the Archbishop of Canterbury and Bishop of London all other books; no foreign books to be sold unless sanctioned by representatives of the Church; no English books to be printed abroad.
Trial by the Star Chamber of John Lilburne for printing English books at Rotterdam for importation; he was pilloried and whipped.

1638 Nicholas Bourne and Nathaniel Butter granted by the Star Chamber sole right to print foreign news.

1641 The Star Chamber abolished by Act of Parliament; its licensing ordinances were no longer valid. This temporary and unintentional lapse in censorship produced a flood of political pamphlets and a growth of newsbooks dealing with domestic affairs.

1642 The Long Parliament ordered the closing of all theatres.

1643 Censorship renewed by the Long Parliament; Henry Walley, Clerk to the Stationers' Company, appointed Licenser; the Old Bailey succeeded the Star Chamber as the court to try offenders; royalist pamphlets suppressed in London.

1644 John Milton protested against censorship in *Areopagitica*; John Rushworth appointed Licenser.

1645   Parliamentary ordinance confirmed the monopoly of the Stationers' Company in controlling the press; John Lilburne imprisoned for evading censorship.

1647   Parliamentary ordinance branded all actors as rogues, to be punished as such; raids on theatres commenced, seats destroyed, spectators fined 5s. for attendance.

1649   Bradshaw's Press Act during the Rump Parliament imposed penalties on those who wrote, printed, published or bought unauthorised books; many newsbooks suppressed. Richard Hatter appointed Licenser.

1653   Gilbert Mabbott appointed Licenser.

1655   Cromwell's Printing and Printers' Ordinance of the first Protectorate parliament: further suppression of newsbooks, which left only the 'official' publications (e.g. *Mercurius Politicus, The Publicke Intelligencer*) written by Marchamont Nedham.

1659   The restored Rump permitted (April) a revival of licensed newsbooks; but these were again suppressed (December) by the Council of State, leaving four 'official' publications written by Marchamont Nedham and Oliver Williams.

1660   The restored Long Parliament attempted to check the growth of unlicensed pamphlets by the issue of general search warrants; its messengers were permitted to assist the Master and Wardens of the Stationers' Company in performing their duties. After the Restoration, Clarendon appointed Sir John Berkenhead (former editor of the royalist newsbook *Mercurius Aulicus*) as Licenser; an order-in-council commanded the Stationers' Company to seize various anti-monarchical publications. Theatres reopened in London (The King's, The Duke's and the Theatre Royal).

1662   The Licensing Act restricted the number of master printers in the Stationers' Company to twenty and prevented new appointments without the prior authority of the Archbishop of Canterbury and Bishop of London; books were not to be published without a licence granted by an authorised censor (as outlined in the 1637 ordinances); printing presses were restricted to the cities of London, Oxford and Cambridge; searches for illegal presses and libellous material were authorised.

1663   Sir Roger L'Estrange appointed Surveyor of the Imprimery and Printing Presses and Licenser for all books not covered by the 1662 Act; retained office until 1688.

1664   John Twyn hung, drawn and quartered for printing a seditious pamphlet, *Mene Tekel, or The Downfall of Tyranny*. Brewster, Dover and Brookes (booksellers) prosecuted as common law criminals for the sale of seditious books.

1666   *The London Gazette*, edited by Henry Muddiman, gained an almost complete monopoly of news.

1679   Lapse of the Licensing Act produced a spate of political pamphlets.

1680   Ben Harris found guilty of selling a pernicious pamphlet; Henry Carr found guilty of publishing a newsbook without authority. Lord Chief Justice Scroggs based his judgments on common law, ruling that even inoffensive newsbooks were illegal if printed without authority.

1685   Revival of the Licensing Act.

NEWSPAPERS AND JOURNALS

1603–42

By the start of the seventeenth century there had been a noticeable growth of public interest in foreign wars and current affairs. The wealthy employed their own professional writers (such as John Chamberlain and Henry Muddiman) to send them personal newsletters regularly from court. Many of the intelligent middle classes, however, were obliged to rely on the casual gossip of travellers or the occasional instruction of sermons for their information. The publication of journals on domestic matters was thwarted by three factors (at least until 1641): the licensing laws, the ordinances of the Star Chamber and the attitude of the monarchy, which regarded circulation of all news as a royal prerogative and its discussion by the general public as a dangerous precedent. There was, however, some relaxation over the publication of news from abroad, stimulated by the marriage of Princess Elizabeth to Frederick of the Palatinate in 1613 and by their subsequent involvement in the Thirty Years' War. At first English newsbooks were printed in the Netherlands (from 1620), carrying reports of battles on the continent. Then, in 1622, two stationers, Nicholas Bourne and Thomas Archer, were authorised by the Star Chamber to publish weekly journals containing foreign news. They were quickly joined by others, including Nathaniel Butter. These early newsbooks were usually called 'corantos' (i.e. 'currents' of news) or 'novellas'. On 17 October 1632, however, the Star Chamber imposed a total ban on the printing of all corantos. This was not relaxed until 20 December 1638, when Bourne and Butter were given the sole right to print foreign news. Examples of the corantos of this period are as follows.

> *The Relation of All the Last Passages of the Warres in the Palatinate* (18 July 1622).
> *A Relation of Many Memorable Passages from Rome* (14 Sep 1622).
> *Weekly News. A Coranto. Relating Divers Particulars Concerning the Newes* (7 Nov 1622).
> *The Continuation of Our Weekly Newes* (22 Nov 1624, *et seq*).
> *The Continuation of Our Forraine Occurences* (20 Aug 1631, *et seq*).

The Continuation of Our Late Avisoes (20 Oct 1631, *et seq).*

An Abstract of Some Speciall Forreigne Occurences Brought down to the Weekly News (20 Dec 1638).

The News this Week from Norimberg, Frankford and Holland (23 Apr 1640).

An Exact Coranto from Most Parts of Christendom (20 July 1642).

For a list of corantos see F. Dahl, *A Bibliography of English Corantos and Periodical Newsbooks, 1620–1642* (1952).

1642–60

The abolition of the Star Chamber on 5 July 1641 brought about a temporary halt to effective censorship, which was not restored until the appointment of an official Licenser by the Long Parliament in June 1643. Encouraged by this lull, printers produced a mass of pamphlets on those burning issues which finally resulted in civil war. Once hostilities had started, weekly 'diurnals' or newsbooks began to appear, reporting on events, though often in a partisan and inaccurate manner. Nevertheless, they satisfied a real need for information on the domestic front and continued to flourish after the war – at least until the new licensing restrictions of the Rump drove the more critical newsbooks out of business (20 Sep 1649). This left a number of 'official' organs of government such as *Mercurius Politicus* and *Severall Proceedings.* After Cromwell's death and the recall of the Rump, licensed newsbooks were again permitted on a wider scale (April 1659) only to be suppressed once more by the Council of State in December 1659. Four 'official' publications survived. These early diurnals quickly developed some of the features of the modern newspaper, with regular 'catchwords' as titles, reports from local correspondents and editorial comment. The most notable newsbook of this period were the following.

A Brief Relation (1649–50), ed. Walter Frost: official.

A Perfect Diurnall (1643–9), ed. Samuel Pecke: the first newsbook exclusively to report domestic news; impartial and reliable.

Mercurius Aulicus (1643–5), ed. John Berkenhead in Oxford: royalist, but reliable and superior in quality.

Mercurius Britanicus (1643–6), ed. Thomas Audley (who became Deputy Licenser in September 1644) and later by Marchamont Nedham: Parliamentarian and scurrilous.

Mercurius Civicus (1643–6), ed. Richard Collings: the first illustrated journal (with woodcuts); Presbyterian; finally suppressed for being too sympathetic to the King.

Mercurius Politicus (1650–60), ed. Marchamont Nedham and later by John Canne: official.

Mercurius Pragmaticus (1647–50), ed. Samuel Sheppard, John Cleveland and Marchamont Nedham: royalist.

Perfect Occurences (1645–9) ed. Henry Walker: impartial.

Several (or Perfect) Proceedings (1649–55), ed. Henry Walker: official.

The Kingdomes Weekly Intelligencer (1643–9), ed. Richard Collings: Presbyterian.

The Moderate (1648–9), ed. Gilbert Mabbot: Leveller.

The Moderate Intelligencer (1645–9), ed. John Dillingham: Presbyterian and royalist.

The Parliament Scout (1643–5), ed. John Dillingham: Presbyterian and royalist.

The Publicke Intelligencer (1655–60), ed. Marchamont Nedham and later by John Canne: official.

The Weekly Account (1643–7), ed. Daniel Border.

For a list of the newsbooks available in the British Museum collection known as The Thomason Tracts, see I. W. Fortescue: *Catalogue of the Pamphlets, Books, Newspapers and Manuscripts Relating to the Civil War, the Commonwealth and Restoration, Collected by George Thomason, 1640–61*, 2 vols (1908).

1660–88

The Licensing Law of 1662 prevented any rapid growth of newsbooks. Indeed, the official organ of the government (first *The Intelligencer* and then, from 1666, *The London Gazette*) maintained an almost complete monopoly of news. Their editors, Sir Roger L'Estrange and Henry Muddiman, were virtually the only journalists who were permitted to write. With the lapse of censorship in 1679, however, there was a spate of short-lived political journals, mostly relating to the case of Titus Oates (e.g. *The True Protestant Mercury*, 1680–2, and *The Loyal Protestant*, 1681–3). Censorship returned in 1685, only to be removed again ten years later.

PROSE: GENERAL, RELIGIOUS, PHILOSOPHICAL, POLITICAL

At the beginning of the century poetry dominated the scene of English literature. Even prose tended to be poetic prose, based on the models of Sir Philip Sidney and John Lyly. Most scholars, however, still favoured Latin as the most suitable language for prose. When English was used, it was frequently written in a Latinised form, with long, artificial phrases. Nevertheless, with the rapid growth of trade and commerce, the ever-expanding ranks of the intelligent middle class felt an increasing need for books written in English. At first this demand was satisfied by the translation of such classics as Don Quixote and the Decameron.

During the course of the century several influences helped to shape the development of a purely English prose. The pattern was undoubtedly set by James I's *Authorised Version of the Bible* in 1611, which used words of English origin in a simple and dignified style. Later religious writings owed much to this monumental work. The sermons of Wilkins and Tillotson had a directness which was far removed from the involved style and classical quotations of Andrewes and Donne. Similarly, the books of William Penn and John Bunyan made great use of clear, popular language, which heightened their appeal.

Nor was the need to convey religious truth the only influence which demanded clarity of expression in English prose. The world of business and the rapidly growing world of scientific experiment both required precise and economic use of words. French influences, too, were important: Francis Bacon to a large extent modelled his *Essays* on the work of Montaigne. French prose placed great stress on simplicity of form and succinctness of exposition. The writers of the Restoration, of whom the foremost was Dryden, wrote, therefore, in colloquial English using brief sentences and arguments which flowed with smooth progression.

Among the most important prose writings of the period 1603–88 are the following.

WRITERS OF GENERAL PROSE

Robert Burton (1576–1640)
The Anatomy of Melancholy (1621).

Thomas Coryate (1577?–1627)
Coryat's Crudities (1611).

Thomas Dekker (1570?–1641)
Wonderful Yeare (1603).
Legende of Goode Women.
Seaven Deadly Sinnes of London (1606).
News from Hell Brought by the Divells Carrier (1606).
Belman of London (1608).
Guls Horn-Book (1609).

John Dryden (1631–1700)
Essay of Dramatic Poesy (1668).
Notes and Observations on the Empress of Morocco (1674).

Thomas Fuller (1608–1661)
The Holy State and the Profane State (1642).
Good Thoughts in Bad Times (1645).
Church History of Britain (1655).
The History of the Worthies of England (1661).

John Milton (1608–74) [NB. The following works are listed here as they are not histories in the strict sense.]
History of Britain (1670).
Brief History of Moscovia (1682).

William Penn (1644–1718)
Travels in Holland and Germany (1677).

A General Description of the Province of Pennsylvania (1683).

George Savile, Viscount Halifax (1633–95)
Character of King Charles the Second (1685).
Character of a Trimmer (1685).
A Letter to a Dissenter (1687).
Advice to a Daughter (1688).

John Stephens.
Satirical Essays, Characters and Others (1615).

Izaak Walton (1593–1683)
The Compleat Angler (1653).
The Lives of Dorre, Wotton, Hooker, George Herbert (1670).

WRITERS OF RELIGIOUS PROSE

Bishop Lancelot Andrewes (1555–1626)
Sermons (1629).
The Moral Law Expounded (1642).

Isaac Barrow (1630–77)
Commentary on Dominical Prayer.
Commentary on the Decalogue.
On Papal Supremacy (1680).

Richard Baxter (1615–91)
Saints' Everlasting Rest (1650).
Holy Commonwealth (1659).

Sir Thomas Browne (1605–82)
Religio Medici (1642).
Pseudodoxia Epidemica (1647).
The Garden of Cyrus (1658).
Hydriotaphia, or Urn Burial (1658).

John Bunyan (1628–88)
Some Gospel Truths Opened (1656).
The Holy City, or The New Jerusalem (1665).
Grace Abounding to the Chief of Sinners (1666).
The Strait Gate (1676).
The Pilgrim's Progress (1678).
The Life and Death of Mr Badman (1680).
The Holy War (1682).

John Donne (1573–1631)
Pseudo-Martyr (1610).
Devotions upon Emergent Occasions (1624).
Eighty Sermons (1640).
Essays in Divinity (1651).

George Herbert (1593–1633)
A Priest to the Temple (1652).

Henry More (1614–1687)
Grand Mystery of Godliness (1660).
Divine Dialogues (1668).

William Penn (1644–1718)
The Sandy Foundation Shaken (1668).
No Cross, no Crown (1670).
The People's Ancient and Just Liberties Asserted (1670).

William Prynne (1600–69)
Histriomastix (1633).
The Antipathy of English Lordly Prelacy (1641).
A Breviate of the Life of William Laud (1644).
Hidden Works of Darkness Brought to Public Light (1645).
Canterbury's Doom (1646).

Jeremy Taylor (1613–67)
A Discourse of the Liberty of Prophesying (1646).
Holy Living (1650).
Holy Dying (1651).

John Tillotson (1630–94)
The Works . . . Containing Two Hundred Sermons (1717).

WRITERS OF PHILOSOPHICAL PROSE AND POLITICAL THEORY

Antony Ascham.
A Discourse: Showing what is particularly Lawful (1648).

Francis Bacon (1561–1626)
The Advancement of Learning (1605).
Novum Organum (1620).
Essays: Counsels Civil and Moral (1597, 1612, 1625).
Apophthegms New and Old (1624).

Richard Burthogge.
Organum Vetus et Novum, or a Discourse of Reason and Truth (1678).

Abraham Cowley (1618–1667)
A Proposition for the Advancement of Experimental Philosophy (1661).
Several Discourses, by Way of Essays, in Verse and Prose (1668).

Ralph Cudworth (1617–88)
True Intellectual System of the Universe (1678).

Edward Forsett.
A Comparative Discourse of the Bodies Natural and Politique (1606).

Edward Gee.
The Divine Right and Originall of the Civill Magistrate from God (1658).

James Harrington (1611–77)
Commonwealth of Oceana (1656).
The Prerogative of Popular Government (1658).

Thomas Hobbes (1588–1678)
Elements of Law, Natural and Politic (1640).
Philosophical Rudiments Concerning Government and Society – De Cive (1651).
Leviathan, or the Matter, Forme and Power of a Commonwealth Ecclesiastical and Civil (1651).
De Corpore (1655).
De Homine (1658).

John Lilburne (1614?–1657)
Jonah's Cry out of the Whale's Belly (1647).
The Legall Fundamental Liberties of the People of England Revived, Asserted, and Vindicated (1649).
England's New Chains Discovered (1649).

Andrew Marvell (1621–78)
The Rehearsall Transposed (1672).
Account of the Growth of Popery, and Arbitary Government (1677).
A Seasonal Argument for a New Parliament (1677).

John Milton (1608–74)
Areopagitica, a Speech for the Liberty of Unlicensed Printing (1644).
Treatise on Education (1644).
Eikonoklastes (1649).
Tenure of Kings and Magistrates (1649).
Readie and Easie Way to Establish a Free Commonwealth (1660).

Henry More (1614–87)
Collection of Several Philosophical Writings (1662).

Marchamont Nedham.
The Excellence of a Free State (1656).

Sir William Temple (1628–99)
Observations upon the United Provinces of the Netherlands (1673).
Essay upon the Origin and Nature of Government (written about 1671).

HISTORICAL WRITING

The seventeenth century witnessed a growing interest in historical writing, which was partly brought about by the desire of Parliamentary lawyers to find precedents from the past to employ against the monarchy. This interest helped to produce a gradual improvement in the quality of the history being written. Old chronicles and annals slowly gave way to histories which took account of political thought and literary style, instead of merely providing a comprehensive list of events. There was, however, as yet no philosophy of history as a subject, no concept of progress. The aim, as G. N. Clark has pointed out, was 'to narrate or explain some self-contained story with a beginning and an end'.

Nevertheless, there was a growing feeling that lessons could be learnt from the past. Sir Walter Raleigh, for instance, wrote his *History of the World* 'to teach by example of times past such wisdom as may guide our desires and actions'. The Earl of Clarendon, too, wrote his *History of the Rebellion and Civil Wars in England* partly as a guide to enable future statesmen to learn from the errors made by royalist politicians during the conflict. History was also used increasingly to add political weight to one side or another in party controversies. What Clarendon had done for the royalists, John Vicars, John Rushworth and Bulstrode Whitelocke attempted to do for the Parliamentarians (though less effectively).

Progress in the art of writing history was noticed at first in Bacon's *Historie of the Reigne of King Henry the Seventh*, which provided a personal assessment of character; in Lord Herbert's *Life and Reign of King Henry the Eighth*, which made full use of original documents; in Peter Heylyn's *History of the Reformation*, which attempted an impartial survey. The climax, however, was reached with Clarendon, who produced a blend of succinct narrative and delightful character study based on both personal experience and documentary material. Writing in a clear and unpretentious style, he managed to attain reasonable perspective and a surprising objectivity. Historical biography seldom lived up to these high standards. Often frank and usually prejudiced, it was frequently no more than a mere narrative of the man and his times, with little attempt at character analysis. The period did, however, witness an increased concern for the collection and publication of state documents (e.g. Rushworth's *Collections*), family papers (e.g. Howell's *Epistolae Ho-Elianae*, Loveday's *Letters Domestick and Forrein*) and memoirs (e.g. those of Ludlow, Digby and Hutchinson).

The most important publications are as follows.

HISTORIES AND ANNALS

Bacon, Francis, *The Historie of the Reigne of King Henry the Seventh* (1622).
Baker, Sir Richard, *A Chronicle of the Kings of England* (1641).
Buck, Sir George, *The History of the Life and Reigne of Richard the Third* (1646).
Burnet, Gilbert, *History of My Own Times, 1660–1702* (1724).

Clarendon, Earl of, *The History of the Rebellion and Civil Wars in England* (1702–4).

Daniel, Samuel, *The Collection of the History of England* (1612).

Fuller, Thomas, *The Church History of Britain* (1655).

Godwin, Francis, *Annals of the Reign of Queen Mary* (1616).

Habington, Thomas, *Historie of Edward IV of England* (1640).

Herbert, Lord, *The Life and Reign of King Henry the Eighth* (1649).

Heylyn, Peter, *Ecclesia Restaurata, or the History of the Reformation* (1661).

——, *Aerius Redivivus, or the History of Presbyterianism* (1670).

Hobbes, Thomas, *Behemoth: The History of the Causes of the Civil Wars of England* (1679).

L'Estrange, Hamon, *Annals of the Reign of King Charles I* (1655).

Luttrell, Narcissus, *A Brief Historical Relation of State Affairs, 1678–1714* (1857).

May, Thomas, *The Reigne of King Henry the Second* (1633).

——, *The Victorious Reigne of King Edward the Third* (1635).

Nalson, John, *An Impartial Collection of the Great Affairs of State, 1639–1649* (1682).

Prynne, William, *The First Part of an Historical Collection of the Ancient Parliaments of England* (1649).

Raleigh, Sir Walter, *History of the World* (1614).

Rushworth, John, *Historical Collections of Private Passages of State, 1618–1649* (1659–1701).

Stow, John, and Howes, Edmund, *Annals or a General Chronicle of England* (1631).

Vicars, John, *Jehovah Jireh, or England's Parliamentarie Chronicle* (1643–6).

Whitelocke, Bulstrode, *Memorials of the English Affairs* (1682).

Wilson, Arthur, *The History of Great Britain, being the Life and Reign of King James the First* (1653).

BIOGRAPHIES

Arnway, John, *The Tablet, or Moderation of Charles the First, Martyr* (1649).

Aubrey, John, *Brief Lives, Chiefly of Contemporaries, Set down by John Aubrey, between the Years 1669 and 1696* (1813).

Clarendon, Earl of, *The Life of Edward, Earl of Clarendon, 1660–1667* (1759).

Forde, Thomas, *Virtus Rediviva; or a Panegyrick on the Late K. Charles the I* (1660).

Fletcher, Henry, *The Perfect Politician, or a Full View of the Life and Actions, Military and Civil, of O. Cromwell* (1660).

Fuller, Thomas, *The History of the Worthies of England* (1662).

Gerard, John, *During the Persecution. Autobiography of Father John Gerard* (1886).

Gerbier, Balthazar, *The Non-such Charles and His Character* (1651).

Heath, James, *Flagellum; or The Life and Death, Birth and Burial of Oliver Cromwell, the Late Usurper* (1663).

Herbert, Lord Edward, *The Life of . . . Written by Himself* (1764).

Howell, James, *Lustra Ludovici, or the Life of the late Victorious King of France, Louis the XIII* (1646).

Jones, Wharton, *A True Relation, of the Life and Death of William Bedell, Lord Bishop of Kilmore in Ireland* (1872).

Lilly, William, *Several Observations on the Life and Death of Charles, late King of England* (1651).

Sanderson, Sir William, *A Complete History of the Life and Reign of Charles I; from His Cradle to His Grave* (1658).

——, *A Compleat History of the Lives and Reigns of Mary, Queen of Scotland and Her Son James* (1656).

Sikes, George, *The Life and Death of Sir Henry Vane* (1662).

Walton, Izaak, *The Lives of Dr John Donne, Sir Henry Wotton, Mr Richard Hooker, Mr George Herbert, Dr Sanderson* (1670).

DIARIES, JOURNALS AND MEMOIRS

Ailesbury, Earl of (Thomas Bruce), *Memoires*, ed. W. E. Buckley (1890).

Anglesey, Earl of (Arthur Annesley), *Memoirs*, ed. Sir P. Pett (1693).

Baxter, Richard, *Reliquiae Baxterianae*, ed. M. Sylvester, (1696).

Berkeley, Sir John, *Memoirs* (1699).

Buckingham, Duke of (John Sheffield), *Memoirs* (1723).

Bulstrode, Sir Richard, *Memoirs and Reflections upon the Reign and Government of King Charles I and King Charles II* (1721).

Carey, Robert (Earl of Monmouth): *Memoirs, Written by Himself* (1759).

D'Ewes, Sir Simonds, *Journal*, ed. W. Notestein (1923).

Digby, Sir Kenelm, *Private Memoirs*, ed. Sir N. H. Nicholas (1827).

Evelyn, John, *Memoirs Illustrative of the Life and Writings of* (1818).

Fairfax, Lord Thomas, *Short Memorials of the Northern Action in which I Was Engaged, 1642–4* (1699).

Halkett, Lady, *Autobiography*, ed. J. G. Nichols (1875).

Herbert, Sir Thomas, *Memoirs of the Last Two Years of the Reign of King Charles I* (1815).

Holles, Lord Denzil, *Memoirs from 1641 to 1648* (1699).

Hopton, Sir Ralph, *Bellum Civile*, ed. C. E. H. Chadwyck-Healey (1902).

Hutchinson, Lucy, *Memoirs of the Life of Colonel Hutchinson* (1806).

Laud, William, *The History of the Troubles and Tryal of . . . wrote by himself* (1695).

Ludlow, Edmund, *Memoirs*, ed. C. H. Firth (1894).

Naunton, Sir Robert, *Fragmenta Regalia, or Observations on the Late Queen Elizabeth Her Times and Favorites* (1641).

Newcastle, Duchess of (Margaret Cavendish), *The Life of William Cavendish, Duke of Newcastle*, ed. C. H. Firth (1906).

Pepys, Samuel, *Diary of, 1660–1669*, ed. H. B. Wheatley (1893).

Poyntz, Sydnam, *A True Relation of These German Warres 1624–6*, ed. A. T. S. Goodrick (1908).

Reresby, Sir John, *Memoirs* (1739).

Rous, John, *Diary, 1625–1642*, ed. M. A. Everett Green (1856).

Slingsby, Sir Henry, *Original Memoirs, Written during the Great Civil War*, ed. Sir W. Scott (1806).

Turner, Sir James, *Memoirs of His Own Life and Times, 1632–70*, ed. T. Thomson (1879).

Wallington, Nehemiah, *Historical Notices of Events Occurring Chiefly in the Reign of Charles I*, ed. R. Webb (1869).

Warwick, Sir Philip, *Memoirs of the Reigne of King Charles I* (1701).

Welldon, Sir Anthony, *The Court and Character of King James. Written and Taken by Sir A. W. Being an Eye, and Eare Witnesse* (1650).

Whitelocke, Bulstrode, *Annales of His life, 1653–6*.

——, *Memoirs, Biographical and Historical (1860)*.

Wilbraham, Sir Roger, *Journal, 1593–1616* (1642).

Wilson, Arthur, *Observations of God's Providence in the Tract of My Life*, ed. F. Peck (1735).

Wynne, Sir Richard, *A Brief Relation of What Was Observed by the Prince's Servants in Their Journey into Spain*, 1623, ed. T. Mearne (1729).

Yonge, Walter, *Diary, 1604–1628*, ed. G. Roberts (1848).

DRAMA

What is generally called 'Elizabethan drama' continued until 1642, with themes centred increasingly on noble characters at court. During this period Shakespeare wrote his tragedies, regarded by many as his best. The reign of James I saw, in particular, the continuation of romantic drama, illustrated especially in the joint works of Fletcher and Beaumont. This form gradually gave way to the realistic drama of Ben Johnson, based on the classical style. Chronicle plays went out of fashion, but the spectacular masque, devised by writers such as Jonson, Shirley and Davenant, began to make its appearance. Towards the end of the period, a decline was noticeable in both standard and content. Writers pandered to the increased depravity and immorality of court life, as witnessed by some of the plays of John Ford and Philip Massinger. Characters became types rather than individuals; the plot was based unceasingly on the witty and debauched life of high society. Bawdy satire of the middle class in general and Puritan principles in particular easily gained the approval of courtly patrons.

The outbreak of civil war, with the closing of the theatres in 1642, brought a temporary halt to dramatic activity. Restoration drama, however, saw a return of satirical comedies in the works of Etherege, Wycherley and Dryden, who poured scorn on middle-class virtues and the traditions of marriage. Their plays were often witty, usually immoral and mostly intended to shock. Their characters were still artificial types in the main. By 1680, however, there were clear signs of change. Heroic tragedy was in rapid decline; blank verse was staging a revival. A reaction was setting in against corruption and against French influence, which had become so strong at the Restoration. There was an awakening desire to restore a type of drama which was English in its style and national in its appeal. This led, after the end of our period, to the work of William Congreve, with whom, probably, Restoration comedy reached its climax in terms of quality.

There follows a catalogue of the principal plays of the period 1603–88. Dates given are those of first performance, as nearly as can be known.

JACOBEAN DRAMATISTS, 1603–25

George Chapman (1559?–1634)
  All Fools (1605).
  Monsieur d'Olive (1606).
  Gentleman Usher (1606).
  Bussy d'Ambois (1607).
  The Conspiracy (1608).
  Tragedy of Charles, Duke of Biron (1608).
  May Day (1611).
  The Widdow's Tears (1612).
  The Revenge of Bussy d'Ambois (1613).
  The Wars of Pompey and Caesar (1631).

John Day (1574–?)
  The Isle of Gulls (1606).
  Law Trickes (1608).
  Humour out of Breath (1608).
  Parliament of Bees (1641).

Thomas Dekker (1570?–1641)
  The Shoemaker's Holiday (1599).
  Old Fortunatus (1600).
  Satiro-mastix (1602).
  The Honest Whore (1604).
  The Whore of Babylon (1607).
  Match Me in London (1631).
  The Wonder of a Kingdom (1636).

Nathaniel Field (1587–1633)
  A Woman is a Weathercock (1610).
  Amends for Ladies (1618).

John Fletcher (1579–1625)
  Wit Without Money (1614).
  Valentinian (1614).

Bonduca (1614).
The Loyal Subject (1618).
The Humorous Lieutenant (1619).
Women Pleas'd (1619).
Monsieur Thomas (1621).
The Pilgrim (1621).
The Wild-Goose Chase (1621).
The Island Princess (1621).
A Wife for a Month (1624).
Rule a Wife and have a Wife (1624).

John Fletcher and Francis Beaumont (1584–1616)
Philaster (1609).
The Scornful Lady (1610).
The Knight of the Burning Pestle (1610).
The Coxcomb (1610).
The Maid's Tragedy (1611).
A King and No King (1611).
Cupid's Revenge (1612).

Thomas Heywood (1575?–1650)
Warning for Fair Women (1599).
A Woman Killed with Kindness (1603).
Yorkshire Tragedy (1608).
The Rape of Lucrece (1609).
English Traveller (1633).
A Challenge for Beauty (1636).
The Royal King and the Loyal Subject (1637).

Ben Jonson (1572–1637)
The Case Is Altered (1597).
Every Man in His Humour (1598).
Cynthia's Revels (1601).
The Poetaster (1602).
Sejanus (1603).
Volpone, or the Fox (1605).
Epicoene, or the Silent Woman (1609).
The Alchemist (1610).
Catiline (1611).
Bartholomew Fair (1614).
The Devil Is an Asse (1616).
The Staple of News (1625).
The New Inn (1629).
The Magnetic Lady (1632).
A Tale of a Tub (1633).

John Marston (1575?–1634)

The History of Antonio and Mellida (1602).
Antonio's Revenge (1602).
The Malcontent (1604).
The Dutch Courtesan (1605).
Parasitaster, or the Fawn (1606).
What You Will (1607).
The Insatiate Countess (1613).

Thomas Middleton (1570?–1627)

Michaelmas Term (1604).
A Trick to Catch the Old One (1606).
A Mad World, My Masters (1606).
Your Five Gallants (1606).
A Chaste Maid in Cheapside (1612).
Women Beware Women (1612).
A Game at Chess (1624).

Thomas Middleton and William Rowley (1585?–1642)

A Fair Quarrel (1616).
The Changeling (1621).
Spanish Gipsy (1623).

William Shakespeare (1564–1616)

Measure for Measure (1603).
Othello (1604).
Lear (1605).
Macbeth (1607).
Timon of Athens (1607).
Coriolanus (1608).
Pericles (1608).
Cymbeline (1610).
The Winter's Tale (1611).
The Tempest (1611).

Cyril Tourneur (1575?–1626)

The Revenger's Tragedy (1607).
The Atheist's Tragedy (1611).

John Webster (1575?–1624)

The White Devil, or Vittoria Corombona (1612).
The Duchess of Malfi (1623).
The Devil's Law Case (1623).
Appius and Virginia (published 1654; joint work with Thomas Heywood?)

CAROLINE DRAMATISTS, 1625–42

Sir William Davenant (1606–68)
The Platonic Lovers (1636).
Love and Honour (1642).
The Siege of Rhodes (1656).

John Ford (1586–1639?)
The Lover's Melancholy (1629).
The Broken Heart (1629).
'Tis Pity She's a Whore (1633).
Love's Sacrifice (1633).
Perkin Warbeck (1634).
The Ladies' Trial (1639).

Philip Massinger (1584–1639)
The City Madam (1619).
The Fatal Dowry (1619).
The Duke of Milan (1620).
The Unnatural Combat (1621).
The Maid of Honour (1622).
The Bondman (1623).
The Renegado (1624).
A New Way to Pay Old Debts (1625).
The Roman Actor (1626).
The Picture (1629).
The Emperor of the East (1631).
The Guardian (1633).

Thomas Randolph (1605–35)
Aristippus (1629).
The Conceited Pedlar (1630).
The Jealous Lovers (1632).
The Muses' Looking-Glass (1638).
Amyntas, or the Fatal Dowry (1638).

William Rowley (1585?–1642?)
A Search for Honey (1609).
A New Wonder (1632).
All's Lost by Lust (1633).
A Match at Midnight (1633).
A Shoemaker a Gentleman (1638).

James Shirley (1596–1666)
The Maid's Revenge (1626).
The Wedding (1626).
The Grateful Servant (1629).

The Traitor (1631).
The Changes (1632).
Hyde Park (1632).
The Gamester (1633).
The Lady of Pleasure (1635).
The Cardinal (1641).

Sir John Suckling (1609–42)
Aglaura (1638).
The Goblins (1646).

RESTORATION DRAMATISTS, 1660–88

John Crowne (1640–1712)
The Country Wit (1676).
The Destruction of Jerusalem (1677).
Sir Courtly Nice (1685).

John Dryden (1631–1700)
The Wild Gallant (1663).
The Rival Ladies (1664).
The Maiden Queen (1667).
The Indian Empress (1667).
Almanzor and Almahide, or the Conquest of Granada (1669–70).
The Assignation (1672).
Marriage-à-la-Mode (1672).
Aureng-Zebe (1675).
Limberham (1678).
Troilus and Cressida (1679).
The Spanish Friar (1681).

Sir George Etherege (1634?–90)
The Comical Revenue, or Love in a Tub (1664).
She Would if She Could (1668).
The Man of Mode, or Sir Fopling Flutter (1676).

Nathaniel Lee (1653?–92)
Nero (1675).
Sophonisba (1676).
The Rival Queens (1677).
Mithridates (1678).
Theodosius (1680).
Caesar Borgia (1680).
Lucius Junius Brutus (1681).
The Princess of Cleves (1681).
Constantine the Great (1682).

Thomas Otway (1652–85)
 Alcibiades (1675).
 Don Carlos (1676).
 The Orphan (1680).
 The Soldier's Fortune (1681).
 Venice Preserved (1682).

Thomas Shadwell (1642–92)
 Epsom Wells (1672).
 The Squire of Alsatia (1688).

William Wycherley (1640–1716)
 Love in a Wood (1671).
 The Gentleman Dancing-Master (1671).
 The Country Wife (1673).
 The Plain Dealer (1674).

POETRY (EXCLUDING POETIC DRAMA)

The Spenserian tradition of poetry, descriptive and sensuous with its emphasis on pictorial beauty and chivalry, continued for a while, at the start of the seventeenth century, in the patriotic and spirited works of Michael Drayton, George Chapman and Samuel Daniel. Their poems were a mixture of the pastoral, the historical and the satirical. With the growing popularity of music, however, the Shakespearean sonnet quickly gave way to the lyric, a form already popular in France and Italy. Ben Jonson's influence in this field was soon visible in the writings of such men as Robert Herrick, Thomas Carew and Sir John Suckling. The epigram, too, became increasingly fashionable, thanks to the efforts of Sir John Harrington, Sir John Davies and many others. At the same time a more philosophical approach was taken by a group of 'Metaphysical' poets, led by John Donne and George Herbert, who took their imagery from outside the physical world. This deep concern for truth was also reflected in the sacred poetry of Richard Crashaw, Henry Vaughan, Francis Quarles and, the greatest of the Puritan poets, John Milton. His *Paradise Lost* was a heartfelt lament at the overthrow of the Puritan revolution. Later in the century, however, such burning issues found less scope in the poetry of the period. French ideas, sponsored at court by M. de Saint-Evremond, demanded a greater concern for style, taste and form based on the classical model. Political satire now became the vogue, with John Dryden, Samuel Butler and John Oldham as its chief advocates.

The most important poets of the period are as follows.

THE DISCIPLES OF SPENSER

William Brown (1591–1643)
Britannia's Pastorals (1613).
The Shepherd's Pipe (1614).

Samuel Daniel (1562–1619)
The Vision of the Twelve Goddesses (1604).
The Queen's Arcadia (1606).

Michael Drayton (1563–1631)
The Barons' Wars (1603).
The Owl (satire, 1604).
The Man in the Moon (satire, 1605).
Poems Lyrick and Pastorall (c. 1605).
Poly-Olbion (patriotic, 1612, 1622).
Nymphidia (fantasy, 1627).
Muses Elizium (1630).

Giles Fletcher (1588–1623)
Christ's Victory and Triumph (allegorical, 1610).

Phineas Fletcher (1582–1650)
The Purple Island (allegorical, 1633).

THE CAVALIER LYRISTS

Thomas Carew (1594–1640)
Coelum Britannicum (court masque, 1634).
Poems (1640)

Abraham Cowley (1618–67)
Poeticall Blossomes (1633).
Sylva (odes, 1636).
The Puritan and the Papist (satire, 1643).
The Mistress (1647).
Pindarique Odes (1656).
Davideis (1656).
Verses on Several Occasions (odes, 1643).
A Poem on the Late Civil War (1679).

Sir William Davenant (1606–68)
Madagascar, with Other Poems (1638).
London, King Charles his Augusta . . . (historical, heroic, 1648).
Gondibert; an Heroick Poem (1651)
Poem upon his Sacred Majesties Most Happy Return to His Dominions (1660)
The Works of Sr William Davenant Kt (1673)

Robert Herrick (1591–1674)
  Hesperides (1648).

Ben Johnson (1573–1637)
  Epigrammes (1616).
  The Forrest (1616).
  Underwoods (1641).

Richard Lovelace (1618–58)
  Lucasta: Epodes, Odes, Sonnets, Songs etc. to which is added Amarantha, a Pastorall (1649).

Sir John Suckling (1609–42)
  Fragmenta Aurea (1658).

Edmund Waller (1606–87)
  Poems (1645).
  A Panegyrick to my Lord Protector (1653).
  Upon the Late Storme, and of the Death of His Highnesse Ensuing the Same (1658).
  To the King, upon His Majesty's Happy Return (1660).
  Instructions to a Painter (1665).
  Divine Poems (1685).

George Wither (1588–1667)
  Abuses Stript and Whipt (satire, 1613).
  Juvenilia (collection, 1622).

METAPHYSICAL AND SACRED POETS

Joseph Beaumont (1616–99)
  Psyche, or Love's Mystery . . . displaying the Intercourse betwixt Christ and the Soul (1648).

Richard Crashaw (1612–49)
  Epigrammatum Sacrorum Liber (1634).
  Steps to the Temple (1646).
  Carmen Deo Nostro, Te Decet Hymnus, Sacred Poems (1652).

John Donne (1573–1631)
  An Anatomy of the World (1611).
  Poems (1633).

George Herbert (1593–1633).
  The Temple, Sacred Poems and Private Ejaculations (1633).

Henry King (1592–1669)
  The Legacy.
  The Exequy.

Silence.
The Dirge.

Henry More (1614–87)
  Psychozoia Platonica (1642).

Francis Quarles (1592–1644)
  A Feast of Wormes (1620).
  Hadassa; or the History of Queene Ester (1621).
  Sions Elegies Wept by Jeremie the Prophet (1624).
  Sions Sonnets. Sung by Solomon the King (1625).
  Divine Poems (1630).
  Divine Fancies (1632).
  Emblemes (1635).
  Hieroglyphikes of the Life of Man (1638).
  Solomon's Recantation (1645).

Thomas Traherne (1634–74)
  Roman Forgeries. By a Faithful Son of the Church of England (1673).
  Christian Ethicks (1675).
  A Serious and Patheticall Contemplation of the Mercies of God (1699).

Henry Vaughan (1622–95)
  Poems, with the Tenth Satyre of Juvenal Englished (1646).
  Silex Scintillans; or Sacred Poems and Private Ejaculations (1650).
  Olor Iscanus. A Collection of Some Select Poems (1651).
  The Mount of Olives: or Solitary Devotions (1652).

JOHN MILTON (1608–74)

  A Maske Presented at Ludlow Castle (Comus) (*1637*).
  Lycidas (1638).
  Poems of Mr John Milton, both English and Latin, Compos'd at Several Times
    (1645).
  Paradise Lost (1667, 1674).
  Paradise Regain'd (1671)
  Samson Agonistes (1671).

ANDREW MARVELL (1621–78)

  The First Anniversary of the Government under His Highness the Lord Protector
    (1655).
  Miscellaneous Poems (1681).
  A Collection of Poems on Affairs of State (1689).
  The Character of Holland (1665).

JOHN DRYDEN (1631–1700)

A Poem upon the Death of His Late Highness Oliver Lord Protector of England, Scotland and Ireland (1659).
Astraea Redux. A Poem on the Happy Restoration and Return of His Sacred Majesty Charles the Second (1660).
To his Sacred Majesty, a Panegyrick on His Coronation (1661).
Annus Mirabilis: The Year of Wonders, 1666 (1667).
Absalom and Achitopel (satire on the Duke of Monmouth, 1681).
The Medall: A Satyre against Sedition (1682).
Religio Laici, or a Layman's Faith (1682).
Threnodia Augustalis; a Funeral-Pindarique Poem sacred to the Happy Memory of King Charles II (1685).
The Hind and the Panther (1687).
Britannia Rediviva: a Poem of the Birth of the Prince (1688).

OTHER SATIRISTS

Samuel Butler (1612–80)
Hudibras (satire on fanatical Puritanism, 1663).

Thomas Creech (1659–1701)
The Odes, Satires and Epistles of Horace Translated (1684).

John Oldham (1653–1683)
A Satyr upon a Woman (1678)
A Satyr against Vertue (1679)
Satyrs upon the Jesuits (1681, 1682, 1685).
A Satyr concerning Poetry.
A Satyr address'd to a Friend.

Thomas Otway (1642–85)
The Poet's Complaint of his Muse, or a Satire against Libels (1680).

Samuel Pordage (1633–91)
Azaria and Hushai (1682).
The Medal Revers'd. A Satyre against Persecution (1682).

Thomas Shadwell (1642–92)
The Medal of John Bayes: A Satyr against Folly and Knavery (1682).
A Choice Collection of 120 Loyal Songs (1684).
Loyal Poems and Satyrs upon the Times (1685).

THE COURT POETS

Charles Sackville, Earl of Dorset (1638–1706)
A New Miscellany of Original Poems on Several Occasions (1701).

Sir Charles Sedley (1639–1701)
The Poetical Works of the Honorable Sir Charles Sedley (1707).

John Sheffield, Earl of Mulgrave (1642–1721)
Ode on Love.
The Vision.
Essay on Satire (1679).
An Essay on Poetry (1691).

Wentworth Dillon, Earl of Roscommon (1633–85)
Horace's Art of Poetry (1680).
A Prospect of Death (1704).
A Collection of Divine Hymns and Poems (1709).
Poems by the Earl of Roscommon (1717).

John Wilmot, Earl of Rochester (1648–80)
A Satyr against Mankind (1675).
The Enjoyment (1679).
A Pastoral Dialogue (1682).
Upon Nothing (1711).

ART, MUSIC AND ARCHITECTURE

1604   Orlando Gibbons (1583–1625) is appointed organist of the Chapel Royal.

1610   Inigo Jones (1573–1652) is appointed Surveyor of the Works to Henry, Prince of Wales.

1612   Orlando Gibbons publishes his *Madrigals and Motets of Five Parts.*

1615   Inigo Jones is appointed Surveyor of the King's Works.

1616   Inigo Jones begins work on the Queen's House at Greenwich (completed in 1635).

1618   Inigo Jones helps to design Lincoln's Inn Fields.

1619   Inigo Jones designs a new Banqueting House in Whitehall (completed in 1622) to replace that destroyed by fire.

1621   Anthony van Dyck (1599–1641) pays his first visit to England.

1622   Orlando Gibbons writes his anthem *O Clap Your Hands.*

1623   Inigo Jones begins work on the Queen's Chapel in St James's Palace (completed in 1627).

1632   Cornelius Johnson (1593–1661) is appointed 'His Majesty's servant in Ye quality of Picture Maker' to Charles I.

1632 Van Dyck, a pupil of Rubens, becomes Court Painter to Charles I and settles in England.

1633 Henry Lawes (1596–1662) is appointed musician in ordinary to Charles I.

1634 Henry Lawes writes the music for Milton's masque *Comus*, which is performed at Ludlow Castle.

1641 William Dobson (1610–46) is appointed Court Painter to Charles I.

1644 Parliament orders the removal from churches and destruction of all organs.

1648 Henry and William Lawes publish their *Choice Psalms Put into Musick for Three Voices*.

1649 Parliament orders the sale of Charles I's magnificent collection of paintings, which are dispersed throughout the world.

1650 John Playford, England's first full-time music publisher, publishes *The English Dancing Master*. Samuel Cooper (1609–72) begins an active period of painting miniatures.

1653 Peter Lely (1618–80) paints the portrait of Oliver Cromwell.

1654 John Playford publishes *A Brief Introduction to the Skill of Musick*.

1656 The first English opera, *Siege of Rhodes* by William Davenant (1606–68), is performed at the Cockpit Theatre, Drury Lane, with music by Henry Lawes.

1658 Sir William Davenant's opera *The Cruelty of the Spaniards in Peru* is performed.

1661 Henry Lawes composes a setting of *Zadok the Priest* for the coronation of Charles II.

Peter Lely is appointed Court Painter to Charles II.

1663 Samuel Cooper is appointed His Majesty's Lymner to Charles II.

1664 Christopher Wren (1632–1723) designs the Sheldonian Theatre, Oxford.

1666 Christopher Wren produces a plan for rebuilding the City after the Great Fire of London.
Robert Hooke is appointed City Surveyor after the Fire of London and designs the new Bethlehem Hospital (Moorfields), Montague House and the College of Physicians.

1668 Christopher Wren is appointed Surveyor General for the rebuilding of the City of London; he personally designs fifty-one churches and thirty-six companies' halls.

1669 John Blow (1649–1708) is appointed Musician of the Virginals to Charles II.

1672   John Banister, formerly Master of the King's Band for Charles II, begins the first series of daily public concerts in his home in Whitefriars.

1673   Christopher Wren begins work on rebuilding St Paul's Cathedral in London.

1674   John Blow is appointed Gentleman of the Chapel Royal and Master of the Children, thereby becoming the teacher of Henry Purcell.

1677   Henry Purcell (1659–95) is appointed Composer in Ordinary to Charles II.

1678   Thomas Britton, a coal merchant, begins a series of weekly concerts in his warehouse loft in Clerkenwell.

1680   Henry Purcell composes the first of his celebration odes for State occasions, *A Song to Welcome Home the King from Windsor.*
Geoffrey Kneller (1646–1723) becomes Court Painter to Charles II on the death of Lely.

1682   Henry Purcell is appointed organist in the Chapel Royal.
Michael Dahl (1659–1743) pays his first visit to England, associating with Geoffrey Kneller.
Sir Christopher Wren begins work on Chelsea Hospital.

1683   Henry Purcell is appointed Keeper of the King's Instruments and composes his first chamber music, *Sonatas of III Parts.*

1685   John Blow writes his anthem *God Spake Sometime in Visions* for the coronation of James II, and his only masque, *Venus and Adonis.*
Henry Purcell writes the anthem *My Heart is Inditing* for the coronation of James II.

1688   Lord Thomas Wharton (1648–1715) composes *Lilliburlero*, an anti-Jacobite song set to the music of Purcell.

SOURCES: G. P. Gooch, *Annals of Politics and Culture, 1492–1899* (1905); Edwin Riddell (ed.), *Lives of the Stuart Age, 1603–1714* (1976); etc.

SCIENCE

1614   John Napier (1550–1617) invents logarithms and publishes his *Mirifici Logarithmorum Canoris Descriptio.*

1617   John Napier publishes his *Rabdologia*, outlining the use of 'Napier's bones' in multiplication and division. Henry Briggs (1561–1630) constructs new logarithm tables calculated to a base of 10.
The Society of Apothecaries receives its own charter and is charged with the examination of apprentices, the supervision of apothecaries in London and the control of medicines.

1618   The College of Physicians celebrates its centenary and publishes its
        Pharmacopœia Londinensis.

1619   Henry Briggs becomes Savilian Professor of Astronomy at Oxford.
        Sir William Harvey (1578–1657), in lectures at St Bartholomew's
        Hospital, outlines his discovery of the circulation of the blood.
        Henry Briggs and John Napier use the decimal notation for fractions.

1620   Francis Bacon (1561–1626) suggests that heat may be a movement.

1624   Henry Briggs publishes his *Arithmetica Logarithmica*, thereby extending
        the work of John Napier.

1628   Sir William Harvey publishes his *De Motu Cordis et Sanguinis*, based on
        years of work in dissecting animals.

1631   William Oughtred publishes his *Clavis Mathematicae Denuo Limata*, a
        textbook of arithmetic and algebra.

1632   William Harvey is appointed physician to Charles I (until 1646).

1633   Henry Briggs's *Trigonometria Britannica* is published, containing his
        tables of the logarithms of sines, tangents and secants.

1638   Jeremiah Horrocks applies the elliptical theory to the moon.

1639   Jeremiah Horrocks first observes the transit of Venus.

1645   Robert Boyle, John Wallis, John Wilkins, Seth Ward, Robert Hooke,
        William Petty and others begin to meet weekly at Gresham College,
        London to discuss 'Physick, Anatomy, Geometry, Astronomy, Nav-
        igation, Staticks, Magnetics, Chymicks, Mechanicks, and Natural Ex-
        periments'.

1648   John Wilkins (1614–72) is appointed Warden of Wadham College and
        attracts to Oxford many of the scientists from Gresham College to form
        the 'Invisible College'.

1651   Sir William Harvey publishes his *De Generatione Animalium*, thus
        establishing embryology.

1652   Nicholas Culpeper publishes *The English Physician*.

1654   Robert Boyle (1627–91) copies Guericke's vacuum pump to demonstrate
        that air pressure is equal in all directions.

1657   Christopher Wren (1632–1723) is appointed Professor of Astronomy at
        Gresham College, London.

1660   John Wilkins and other scientists again begin to meet at Gresham
        College, London and decide to found a 'colledge for the promoting of
        Physico-Mathematicall Experimentall Learning'. Charles II joins.
        Robert Boyle publishes *The Spring and Weight of the Air*.

Robert Hooke (1635–1703) produces Hooke's Law on springs.
John Ray (1627–1705) publishes his catalogue *Flora of Cambridge*.

1661   Christopher Wren is appointed Savilian Professor of Astronomy of Oxford.
Robert Boyle discovers his Law of Compressibility ('Boyle's Law') and publishes *The Sceptical Chymist* on the composition of matter and the characteristics of chemical compounds.

1662   Robert Boyle, John Wilkins, John Wallis, Christopher Wren and others are incorporated as the Royal Society of London for Improving Natural Knowledge. They meet weekly to hear lectures by members.
Robert Hooke is appointed Curator of Experiments to the Royal Society.

1663   Isaac Newton (1642–1727) discovers the Binomial Theorem.

1664   Thomas Willis (1621–75) publishes his *Anatome Cerebri*, an investigation of the brain, and is elected an honorary Fellow of the Royal College of Physicians.

1665   The Royal Society publishes its first *Philosophical Transactions*.
Robert Boyle proves that a candle cannot burn nor an animal breathe without air.
Robert Hooke publishes his *Micrographia*, a study of observations made through the microscope, and is appointed Professor of Geometry at Gresham College, London.

1666   The Royal Society establishes a museum.
Isaac Newton uses the notation of fluxions, measures the moon's orbit, discovers gravitation, explains the rainbow and discovers the dispersion of light.
Robert Boyle publishes his *Origin of Forms and Qualities*.

1668   Isaac Newton makes the first successful reflecting telescope.

1669   Richard Lower publishes his *Tractatus de Corde*.
Isaac Newton is appointed Lucasian Professor of Mathematics at Cambridge (until 1701).

1670   The Royal Society hears the papers of Malpighi and Grew on vegetable anatomy.
John Ray publishes his *Catalogue of Plants*.

1672   Isaac Newton is elected to the Royal Society at the age of twenty-nine and reports to them on the laws of refraction.

1675   The Royal Observatory is established at Greenwich; John Flamsteed (1646–1719) is appointed the first Astronomer Royal.

1676   John Ray edits Francis Willoughby's *Ornithology*.
Wiseman publishes his *Seven Chirurgical Treatises*.

1677   Robert Hooke is elected Secretary of the Royal Society (until 1683).

1678   Robert Hooke's *Lectures de Potentia Restitutive* (containing Hooke's Law) is published.

1679   Edmund Halley (1656–1742) publishes his *Catalogus Stellarum Australium* and is elected a Fellow of the Royal Society.

1681   Sir Christopher Wren is appointed President of the Royal Society (until 1683).
        The Royal Society hears Papin describe his steam engine.

1682   John Ray publishes his *Methodus Plantarum Nova*, suggesting a system for the classification of plants.
        Nehemiah Grew's *The Anatomy of Plants* is published, demonstrating the use of the microscope in the study of plants.

1686   Francis Willoughby and John Ray publish their *Historia Piscium*. John Ray also publishes the first volume of his *Historia Plantarum Generalia*, a study of theoretical botany.

1687   Isaac Newton, in *Principia* (his great work of mechanics and dynamics), shows that all the important characteristics of the motions of the solar system are explicable by three fundamental laws of motion and by the law of gravitation.

SOURCES: G. P. Gooch, *Annals of Politics and Culture, 1492–1899* (1905); Edwin Riddell (ed.), *Lives of the Stuart Age, 1603–1714* (1976).

11 POPULATION AND THE TOWNS

THE LARGER ENGLISH TOWNS c.1688

Over 10,000 inhabitants
Bristol
Colchester
Exeter
Great Yarmouth

London
Newcastle
Norwich
York

c.5000–10,000 inhabitants
Birmingham
Bury St Edmunds
Cambridge
Canterbury
Chatham
Coventry
Hull
Ipswich
Kings Lynn
Leeds
Leicester

Liverpool
Manchester
Nottingham
Oxford
Plymouth
Portsmouth
Salisbury
Shrewsbury
Sunderland
Tiverton
Worcester

URBANISATION IN ENGLAND, 1603–95

Increase in population in selected towns

Town	1603	1695	% increase
London	c. 200,000	c. 575,000	287
Norwich	15,000	29,332	95
Bristol	12,000	19,043	62
York	11,000	12,000[a]	9
Exeter	9,000	12,500[a]	39
Salisbury	7,000	6,976	–
Coventry	6,500	6,710	3
Bury St Edmunds	4,500	6,200	14
Leicester	3,500	5,000	43
Warwick	3,000	3,300	10

[a] Figures are for c.1670.
SOURCE: Peter Clark and Paul Slack, *English Towns in Transition 1500–1700* (1971).

COMPARATIVE DEGREES OF URBANISATION
IN EUROPEAN COUNTRIES c. 1660

	%
France	16
Lower Austria	17
England	20
Dutch Republic	59

PROVINCIAL TOWNS: RANK ORDER OF SIZE, 1662

Rank	Town	No. of hearths taxed
1	Norwich	7302
2	York	7294
3	Bristol	6925
4	Newcastle	5967
5	Exeter	5294
6	Ipswich	5020
7	Great Yarmouth	4750
8	Oxford	4205[a]
9	Cambridge	4133[a]
10	Canterbury	3940
11	Worcester	3619
12	Deptford	3554
13	Shrewsbury	3527
14	Salisbury	3498
15	Colchester	3414
16	East Greenwich	3390
17	Hull	3390
18	Coventry	3301
19	Chester	3004
20	Plymouth	2600 (est.)
21	Portsmouth	2600 (est.)
22	Vings Lynn	2572
23	Rochester	2271
24	Lincoln	2211
25	Dover	2208
26	Nottingham	2190
27	Gloucester	2174
28	Bury St. Edmunds	2109
29	Winchester	2069
30	Sandwich	2033
31	Maidstone	1900

32	Leeds	1798
33	Leicester	1773
34	Northampton	1610
35	Chatham	1588
36	Ely	1554
37	Chichester	1550 (est.)
38	Gateshead	1532
39	Southampton	1500
40	Derby	1479
41	Ludlow	1467
42	Warwick	1467

[a] Excluding the colleges. 1664 Derby Day Assessment.

INCORPORATION OF BOROUGHS, 1603–88

1604	Berwick		Salisbury
	Bradninch		Wokingham
	Dartmouth	1615	Tiverton
	Evesham		Welshpool
	Godmanchester	1617	Oswestry
	Harwich	1618	Berkhampstead
	Lancaster	1619	Bridport
	Ripon	1621	Penryn
	Shaftesbury	1622	Southwell
1605	Blandford	1623	Newport (Mon.)
	Cambridge		Okehampton
	Chipping Campden	1626	Leeds
	Devizes		Liverpool
	Oxford		Queenborough
1606	Bury St Edmunds	1627	Taunton
	Chipping Norton		Walsall
1607	Newport (Isle of Wight)	1633	Whitehaven
	Retford	1634	Sunderland
1608	Cardiff	1635	Halifax
	Hadleigh		Malmesbury
	London	1636	Kidderminster
	Lostwithiel	1637	Carlisle
	Great Yarmouth	1655	Swansea
1609	Yarmouth (Isle of Wight)	1661	Falmouth
1610	Dorchester	1662	Denbigh
	Haverfordwest		Morpeth
1612	Derby		Wigan

1664	Albrighton	1684	Bedford
1665	Chard		Sandwich
1673	Llanfyllin	1685	Tintagel
1679	Garstang	1687	Calne
1681	Chipping Sodbury	1688	Grimsby
1682	Cowbridge		
	Tavistock		

SELECT BIBLIOGRAPHY

(Appropriate biographical works are cited in the biography section.)

Ashley, M. P., *Financial and Commercial Policy under the Cromwellian Protectorate* (London, 1962 edn).

Aylmer, G. E., *The King's Servants: the Civil Service of Charles I, 1625–1642* (London, 1974 edn).

——, *The State's Servants: the Civil Service of the English Republic, 1649–1660* (London, 1973).

——, *The Struggle for the Constitution, 1603–1689* (London, 1963).

Baxter, S. B., *The Development of the Treasury, 1660–1714* (London, 1957).

Brunton, D. and Pennington, D. H., *Members of the Long Parliament* (Cambridge, 1954).

Burne, A. H. and Young, P., *The Great Civil War* (London, 1959).

Bush, D., *English Literature in the Early Seventeenth Century* (Oxford, 1962 edn).

Cheney, C. R. (ed.), *Handbook of Dates for Students of English History* (1945).

Clarendon, Edward Hyde, Earl of, *History of the Rebellion and Civil Wars in England*, ed. W. D. Macray, 6 vols (Oxford, 1888).

Clark, G. N., *The Later Stuarts, 1660–1714* (Oxford, 1955 edn).

Davies, G., *The Early Stuarts, 1603–60* (Oxford, 1959 edn).

——, *The Restoration of Charles II* (London, 1955).

Davies, G. and Keeler, M. F., *Bibliography of British History: Stuart Period, 1603–1714* (Oxford, 1970 edn).

Dietz, F. C., *English Public Finance, 1558–1641* (London, 1932).

Firth, C. H., *Cromwell's Army* (London, 1962 ed.).

——, *The Last Years' of the Protectorate*, 2 vols (London, 1909).

Ford, B. (ed.), *From Donne to Marvell* (1956).

Frank, J., *The Beginnings of the English Newspaper, 1620–1660* (Oxford, 1961).

Gardiner, S. R., *History of England from the Accession of James I to the Outbreak of Civil War, 1603–1642*, 10 vols (London, 1883–4).

——, *History of the Great Civil War*, 4 vols (London, 1893).

——, *History of the Commonwealth and Protectorate*, 3 vols (London, 1894–1901).

Haller, W., *The Rise of Puritanism* (London, 1938).

Haydn, J., *The Book of Dignities* (1890).

Hexter, J. H., *The Reign of King Pym* (Oxford, 1941).

Hill, C., *Puritanism and Revolution* (London, 1958).
——, *The Century of Revolution, 1603–1714* (London, 1961).
——, *The World Turned Upside Down* (1972).
Kearney, H. F., *Origins of Scientific Revolution* (London, 1964).
Keeler, M. F., *The Long Parliament, 1640–1641* (Philadelphia, 1954).
Kennedy, W., *English Taxation, 1640–1799* (London, 1964 ed.).
Kenyon, J. P., *The Stuarts* (London, 1966 edn).
——, *The Stuart Constitution 1603–88* (Cambridge, 1966).
Lamont, W. M., *Godly Rule; Politics and Religion, 1603–60* (London, 1969).
Matthew, D., *The Jacobean Age* (London, 1938).
Ogg, D., *England in the Reign of Charles II*, 2 vols (Oxford, 1955 edn).
——, *England in the Reigns of James II and William III* (Oxford, 1955).
Parker, I., *Dissenting Academies in England* (Cambridge, 1914).
Powicke, F. M. and Fryde, E. B. (eds), *Handbook of British Chronology* (London, 1961).
Richardson, R. C., *The Debate on the English Revolution* (London, 1977).
Riddell, E. (ed.), *Lives of the Stuart Age, 1603–1714* (London, 1976).
Roots, I. A., *The Great Rebellion, 1642–60* (London, 1966).
Stone, L., *The Crisis of the Aristocracy, 1559–1641* (Oxford, 1965).
Summerson, J., *Architecture in Britain, 1530–1830* (Harmondsworth, 1953).
Thirsk, J., *The Restoration* (1976).
Trevelyan, G. M., *England under the Stuarts* (London, 1966 edn).
Turner, E. R., *The Privy Council of England in the Seventeenth and Eighteenth Centuries, 1603–1784*, 2 vols (Oxford, 1927–8).
Vincent, W. A. L., *The State and School Education, 1640–1660* (1950).
Waterhouse, E. K., *Painting in Britain, 1530–1790* (London, 1953).
Webb, S. and Webb, B., *English Local Government from the Revolution to the Municipal Reform Act*: vol. 1, *The Parish and the County*; vols II–III, *The Manor and the Borough* (1924).
Wedgwood, C. V., *The Great Rebellion: the King's Peace, 1637–1641* (London, 1955)
——,*The Great Rebellion: the King's War, 1641–1647* (London, 1958).
——, *The Trial of Charles I* (London, 1964).
——, *Poetry and Politics under the Stuarts* (Cambridge, 1960).
Whinney, M. and Millar, O., *English Art, 1625–1714* (Oxford, 1957).
Wilson, C., *England's Apprenticeship, 1603–1763* (London, 1965).
Woolrych, A. H., *Battles of the English Civil War* (London, 1961).
Young, P. and Holmes, R., *The English Civil War: A Military History of Three Civil Wars, 1645–51* (London, 1974).
Yule, G., *The Independents in the English Civil War* (Cambridge, 1958).